**Computer Science Series**
*Consulting Editor:*
Professor F.H. Sumner, University of Manchester

F.D. Rolland, *Programming with VDM*

A.G. Sutcliffe, *Human-Computer Interface Design, second edition*

C.J. Theaker and G.R. Brookes, *Concepts of Operating Systems*

M. Thorin, *Real-time Transaction Processing*

M.R. Tolhurst *et al.*, *Open Systems Interconnection*

A.J. Tyrrell, *Eiffel Object-Oriented Programming*

I.R. Wilson and A.M. Addyman, *A Practical Introduction to Pascal, second edition*

*Other titles*

Ian O. Angell and Dimitrios Tsoubelis, *Advanced Graphics on VGA and XGA Cards Using Borland C++*

N. Frude, *A Guide to SPSS/PC+, second edition*

Peter Grossman, *Discrete Mathematics for Computing*

Percy Mett, *Introduction to Computing*

Tony Royce, *COBOL - An Introduction*

Tony Royce, *Structured COBOL - An Introduction*

# Eiffel
# Object-Oriented
# Programming

**A.J. Tyrrell**
*Manchester Metropolitan University*

First published 1995 by
MACMILLAN PRESS LTD
Houndmills, Basingstoke, Hampshire RG21 6XS
and London
Companies and representatives
throughout the world

ISBN 0-333-64554-5

A catalogue record for this book is available
from the British Library.

10   9   8   7   6   5   4   3   2   1
04   03   02   01   00   99   98   97   96   95

Printed in Great Britain by
Antony Rowe Ltd, Chippenham, Wiltshire

Eiffel™ is a trademark of the Non-profit International Consortium for Eiffel.

Eiffel/S™ is a trademark of SiG Computer GmbH.

# Contents

v

# Preface

This year Eiffel celebrates its tenth anniversary, and it is also some seven years since the publication of Bertrand Meyer's now classic study, *Object-Oriented Software Construction*. In the last two years it has begun to achieve wider recognition both for teaching and for the production of quality software. There are now at least four vendors supplying a range of Eiffel compilers, and a number of student texts have recently appeared. In the author's view there is currently no better language for learning about object-oriented programming.

This text aims to provide an accessible introduction to programming with Eiffel. It is intended principally for those who have at least some basic knowledge of programming in an imperative language such as Pascal or C. It is also suitable for those who have some knowledge of object-orientation, and wish to find out about the Eiffel language. The emphasis of the text is very much on practical examples, which the reader is encouraged to try out.

Chapter 1 provides a general introduction to object-oriented principles. It also includes an overview of the Eiffel language.

Chapters 2, 3, 4 and 5 take a more bottom up approach, and cover the essentials of Eiffel as a programming language; in these chapters, ideas of object-orientation have a secondary role; advanced readers should be able to use these chapters largely for reference purposes.

Chapter 6 returns to object orientation, and deals with instantiation of objects from classes, and issues of object comparison and assignment. Chapter 7 provides an introduction to library support for strings and arrays, which in Eiffel are not part of the language. Chapters 8 to 13 cover advanced features, and the material in these chapters is more challenging: chapter 8 deals with assertions and design by contract; chapters 9, 11 and 13 cover inheritance; chapter 10 deals with generic classes; chapter 12 deals with abstract classes.

The final chapter consists of two case studies, which are intended to show how bigger problems may be solved using object-oriented design. The first, which builds on classes developed in earlier chapters, provides a solution to the eight queens problem; the second designs and implements a back propagating neural network.

The text takes an informal approach to design. No particular methodology or notation is pushed. The author broadly shares Bertrand Meyer's scepticism about language independent design methodologies: ultimately somebody has to write some code which runs on a real machine. If a language is sufficiently high-level to allow us to use it to design and to reason about design, as is Eiffel, then the design and implementation process may be seamless: design in Eiffel and let the compiler write the C code!

The text does emphasise that design for reuse is difficult, and that object-oriented designers should not expect to get the best solution first time. An object-oriented approach encourages us to model an application; model-building is itself a learning process which helps us to understand the application better, and hence to build a better model. The author never tires of telling his students about the experiences of the creators of Smalltalk, who, having completed the project, were told to throw it away and do it again, a luxury which, unfortunately, is experienced by few software developers. More experienced readers can probably think of many current software products which could have benefitted from such a practice. The examples in the text are, therefore, not presented as final solutions. If they stimulate thought, and provoke readers to produce better designs, this will be regarded as a sign of success. It is to be hoped that many readers will come to share the view of the author, and of others in the growing Eiffel community, that programming with Eiffel is challenging, but also very satisfying.

Some of the longer examples and other supporting material may be accessed via the internet: http://www.doc.mmu.ac.uk/STAFF/J.Tyrrell

My thanks to numerous students taught using early drafts of this text, whose comments were usually honest, and always useful. I must also thank the following: Michael O'Docherty of the PEVE unit at the Victoria University of Manchester, an indefatigable Eiffel enthusiast, for giving both encouragement and criticism; Roger Browne of Everything Eiffel, for his readiness to share his encyclopaedic knowledge of the Eiffel language; my colleague, Pamela Quick, for comments on some of the introductory material; my colleague Zuhair Bandar, without whom the neural networks case study would never have been written; Stuart Kent at Brighton University, for many constructive comments on the draft of the text; Malcolm Stewart of Macmillan Press, for his encouragement, patience and good humour. Finally, my special thanks to Inger Marie, for her unfailing support throughout the period when this was being written.

A.J. Tyrrell

# 1 Introduction to Object Orientation

There is little that is new in object-oriented software development. Its main ideas have been known for over two decades since the development of the programming languages Simula and Smalltalk. It is now a well-established technology, and its advantages are well understood. If only we could learn to use it well, we should be able to build high quality software systems which

are modularised and decentralised;

are factored around data rather than processes;

are built using existing well-tested components;

promote the development of new components;

are easy to understand and maintain;

are better able to withstand change;

allow a relatively seamless transition from analysis through to design and implementation.

Older approaches are however, still very much in evidence, and most readers of this text are likely to have had some exposure to more traditional approaches to software development. This chapter begins therefore by comparing the process-oriented and object-oriented approaches to software development. It also provides an introduction to the main concepts of object-orientation, and concludes with an introduction to the Eiffel programming language.

## 1.1 Process-oriented software development: a text formatter

Process or functional approaches have dominated software design since the beginning of computing. Systems developed in this way are conventionally subdivided into relatively abstract sub-functions, which may be further subdivided into sub-functions recursively until, at the bottom of the hierarchy, there are the primitive operations which perform the actual computation. Such an approach was particularly well suited to designing systems for the commercial batch applications for which the COBOL language has been primarily used. It was also well suited to the design of text processing systems such as compilers and formatters. As an example we may take a text processor which has a file of text with embedded print directives as its input, and a print file with appropriate paragraphing and indentation as output, as shown in figure 1.1.

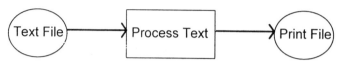

**Figure 1.1**

The process involves transforming the information read from the input file into that suitable for the output file. Such systems are typically decomposed as shown in figure 1.2.

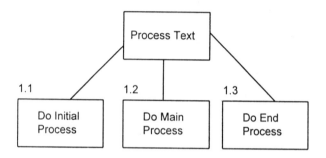

**Figure 1.2**

The above abstract solution indicates the sequence of operations: sub-processes are executed from left to right. The sub-processes could be sub-routines, or in larger systems they could be separately compiled programs.

Initial processing conventionally includes the initialisation of data items and the opening of files. End processing consists mainly of closing the files, and possibly the output of summary totals if required, e.g. number of words, number of lines, number of pages and so on.

The main process requires an iteration or loop which indicates that each line of the source text must be processed until the end of the source file is reached:

```
    1.2 Main_Process
       do until End_Text_file
          1.2.1 Read Line of Text
          1.2.2 Process Line of Text
       end -- Do Until
    end Main Process
```

The above algorithm also indicates that the sub-processes *Read Line of Text* and *Process Line of Text* must at some stage be refined. A possible solution for the second is shown below:

> 1.2.2 *Process Line of Text*
>     **if** *first char is a format character*
>         **then** *Process Format String*
>     **end - -** if
>     *write text to file*
>   **end** *Process Line of Text*

This would then require further refinement of *Process Format String*: e.g. /P/ might indicate a new page, /8/ might indicate indent 8 spaces and so on.

As already indicated this problem is a relatively simple one, which is easily solved using a process-oriented approach. In order to illustrate the difference between the two approaches, the next section solves the same problem using an object-oriented approach.

## 1.2 An object-oriented approach to developing a text formatter

An OO developer would take a totally different approach, and would seek to identify objects or classes of object in the system. (For the moment no distinction will be made between a class and an object - see section 1.4.) Obvious candidates in this case would be

> text file *or* print file

Less obvious might be

> line of text   *or* format string

In addition a controller, called TEXT_FORMATTER, might be specified. While not essential, it is frequently useful to have such an object. The application, consisting of five objects, could be described as follows:

TEXT_FORMATTER sends a message to TEXT_FILE asking it for a line of characters. TEXT_FILE reads a line of characters from disk, and passes a line of characters back to TEXT_FORMATTER; TEXT_FORMATTER creates a LINE_OF_TEXT from the line of characters, and asks the LINE_OF_TEXT to send itself to PRINT_FILE; the LINE_OF_TEXT checks whether it contains format characters, and if it does then creates a FORMAT_STRING and asks it to send itself to PRINT_FILE; it then sends its character string to PRINT_FILE, and returns control to

TEXT_FORMATTER. TEXT-FORMATTER repeats the process until TEXT-FILE can provide no more lines of text.

The result of approaching development in this way is to decompose a system into units based not on function, but on data. The text file and the print file are obviously data structures, the line of text is likewise a sequence of characters, which may be simply a string of printable characters such as

This is a line of text

or may include a format string

/8/

which is a sequence of characters enclosed by "/", which have a particular meaning within the context of our system.

The only object which is not a data structure is the controller, TEXT_FORMATTER. It could of course be eliminated, in which case TEXT_FILE or PRINT_FILE would become the controller.

Some designers might argue about the need for FORMAT_STRING, which is also not essential. Clearly there are losses in efficiency in having such an object, but there are also potential maintenance gains. If, for example, an additional set of allowable embedded commands was introduced, the only component which would need to be amended would be FORMAT_STRING. The ability to isolate the effects of change is one of the essentials of developing maintainable software.

The relationships between the objects may be analysed as follows:

| Object | Collaborators | |
|---|---|---|
| TEXT_FORMATTER | SOURCE-FILE LINE_OF_TEXT | PRINT-FILE |
| SOURCE_FILE | | |
| PRINT_FILE | | |
| LINE_OF_TEXT | FORMAT_STRING | |
| FORMAT_STRING | PRINT_FILE | |

It can be seen that the two file handling objects are purely passive: they respond only to calls, and need no knowledge of any other objects within the system. If TEXT_FORMATTER were eliminated, and SOURCE_FILE or PRINT_FILE to be made the controller, then the one selected would need to collaborate with other objects.

One advantage of this approach is that each object could be implemented, compiled and tested separately, even by different programmers, although for such a small system this would be most unlikely.

The tasks required to produce a formatted print file would be distributed in the object-oriented system as indicated below:

| Object | Task |
|---|---|
| TEXT_FILE | *opens file*<br>*closes file*<br>*reads a line of characters from disk*<br>*passes string of characters back to caller* |
| PRINT_FILE | *opens file*<br>*closes file*<br>*writes to disk a character string passed in by caller* |
| LINE_OF_TEXT | *separates into format string and character string*<br>*creates FORMAT_STRING*<br>*asks FORMAT_STRING to write itself to*<br>*PRINT_FILE*<br>*sends its own character string to PRINT_FILE* |
| FORMAT_STRING | *sends appropriate characters (spaces, control*<br>*characters) to PRINT_FILE* |
| TEXT_FORMATTER | *asks files to open themselves*<br>*asks files to close themselves*<br>*controls process* |

The development of the last object would be done later than in the process-oriented approach illustrated earlier. TEXT_FORMATTER might however, be used as a harness to test each object in turn as it was completed. Once testing of separate objects was finished, the code required to control the system could then be inserted in TEXT_FORMATTER:

> *ask files to open themselves*
> **do until** *no more lines of text to process*
>     *get string of characters from SOURCE-FILE*
>     *ask LINE_OF_TEXT to print itself on PRINT_FILE*
> **end** -- do until
> *ask files to close themselves*

Should it be required, it would be relatively simple to dispense with TEXT_FORMATTER, and to transfer this small amount of code to one or the other of the file objects as previously suggested.

## 1.3 Object-oriented and process-oriented approaches compared

The difference between an object-oriented and a more conventional top down approach may be summarised as follows:

1. A conventional developer divides a system into program units corresponding to the operations or processes which it must perform; an OO developer decomposes, or modularises, systems around objects, which are a combination of data and functionality;

2. A conventional developer views a system as a sequence of operations; an OO developer views a system primarily as a collection of objects which collaborate with each other to perform a set of tasks;

3. In a conventional top-down system a sub-process should be called only by a single higher level process; within an OO system an object may respond to requests for services from any other object;

4. Whilst sequence is not important to an OO developer, the state of an object at the point when it is requested to perform some action is a concern. It may be necessary to stipulate what conditions must hold at the time when an object is asked to perform an action. For example, going back to the text formatter, it might be agreed that TEXT_FILE should not be asked to produce a line of text if it is empty - the caller would be required to check that TEXT_FILE could supply a LINE_OF_TEXT before asking it to do so. This is known as a precondition, and is fundamental to Eiffel programming as will be shown later.

Finally, it should be emphasised that object-oriented techniques are particularly suited to modern interactive systems, as will be illustrated by the introduction of a second example, a word processor. The process-oriented approach is less satisfactory for designing event-driven interactive systems which have no real top function, and no clearly defined sequence of operations. It would be difficult to define the top function of a word processor, which must simply wait for a user to press a key or to click a pointing device.

A developer who wished to design a word processor would again begin by identifying the objects or classes in the system. Candidates for initial consideration would include

> menu            text pane
> block of text   text buffer
> file

as shown in figure 1.3.

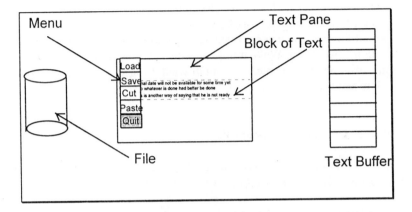

**Figure 1.3 Components of a word processor**

Further investigation might eliminate some of the above, and might include one or two that have been overlooked. The application would for example need a mechanism to handle events - inputs from the keyboard and a mouse. This is system dependent however, and will not be discussed in the abstract.

Once a preliminary list of objects has been defined, the designer must then try to work out the role of each in the system. This process should expose redundancies and also gaps in the set of objects proposed. This involves questions such as

What actions must this object be able to perform?
What does it know? What data must it store?
Which other objects does it collaborate with?

In practice some of the objects mentioned, such as MENU, would probably be available in the class library.

The benefits of an OO approach in designing systems which involve graphical user interfaces ought to be fairly readily apparent:

the kinds of object defined above are likely to be common to many GUI applications;

it is possible to build systems by reusing existing components, or to produce as a by-product well-tested components which may be reused in other applications;

it is easier to make changes to a system designed around objects, such as pane, and menu - which are relatively stable - rather than functions such as 'cut and paste' , 'load file' and 'save as' which are less stable.

Finally, as will be explained in the following section, in practice the OO developer would design **classes** of object rather than single objects. Rather than individual objects, classes such as TEXT_WINDOW and MENU would be used. This would for example make it relatively easy to have more than one window, each with its own menu. Without this capacity to create more than one object of the same class, the development of a multi-windowing word processor would be difficult to achieve.

## 1.4 Objects, Classes and Message Passing

The basic ideas of an OO approach are deceptively simple. The fundamental concepts are those of objects, classes and message passing:

An **object** is:

(i)  an entity in the real world application being modelled or in the computer environment in which the application is being implemented;
(ii) an instance of a class created at run-time; it has state and behaviour.

Objects interact by sending **messages** or requests to each other and sometimes to themselves.

A **class** is a template from which objects may be created at run-time.

In most languages we design classes not objects. This allows us to instantiate more than one object of the same class when a system is executing.

A conventional notation for describing classes of object is shown in figure 1.4. In the top sector the name of the class is given. In the middle sector the data variables that are used to store the state of an object of that class are listed, and in the bottom sector the services which an object of that class offers to a client are listed. The terminology for the last sector varies - there is no standard terminology throughout the OO community - sometimes it may be referred to as the methods of a class, or as the messages to which an object of a class will respond. In Eiffel the services are known as **routines**, and the messages are known as **calls**.

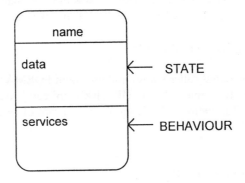

**Figure 1.4**

The notation is used in figure 1.5 to model LINE_OF_TEXT, which was described in the first example above. Each object of this class would contain a single data item, a string of characters, such as

"Do not go gently into that good night"

or

"/8/ Come into the garden Maud"

and would need to respond to one message only, to print itself on a file:

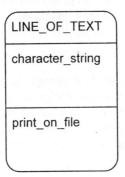

**Figure 1.5**

The tasks which an object of this class is required to perform:

separation into format string and character string
creation of FORMAT_STRING
asking FORMAT_STRING to write itself to PRINT_FILE
sending of its own character string to PRINT_FILE

are not services offered to other objects in the system; they are auxiliary actions necessary to enable a LINE_OF_TEXT to carry out the request:

print yourself on file.

An external caller knows nothing about FORMAT_STRING, and would not be able to request LINE_OF_TEXT to carry out any of the first three actions.This logically leads on to the concept of **information hiding** which is covered in the next section.

### 1.5 Information hiding

A key idea of object-oriented development is that of abstraction: hiding implementation details from the clients of a class. It is useful to distinguish between the interface to a class, and its internal mechanisms, between the **public part** of a class, and its hidden or **private part**. This distinction is important, because it allows the internal mechanisms of a class to be protected from outside interference, and at the same time allows us to provide a more abstract, simpler view of a class.

To return once more to class LINE_OF_TEXT: externally it may be viewed as consisting of simply one service, and one data item; this is all that the caller needs to know. The implementor, however, will need a different, less abstract view: to know about FORMAT_STRING and PRINT_FILE, about which the caller of LINE_OF_TEXT need have no knowledge.

A real world analogy may be used to illustrate this: a car There are at least two views of a car:

1. that of the driver who controls it through the interface supplied: control panel, steering wheel, brakes, accelerator pedal;
2. that of the mechanic (who may also be the owner and sometimes driver of the car) who monitors the collection of components hidden under the bonnet whose proper functioning are necessary to provide the services required by the driver.

It is not necessary for a driver to have much knowledge of what exists under the bonnet, and it is thankfully not necessary to directly manipulate the axles, brake pads, carburettor, gear box and other components in order to drive a car. A simpler interface is provided. So it is with software components. All object-oriented languages should provide mechanisms which may be used to restrict access to data and behaviour and to provide an abstract external view of the facilities which a class makes available.

The concepts of class, object, message passing and information hiding, which have now been introduced are fundamental to an understanding of object-orientation. The concept of **inheritance** must now be introduced.

## 1.6 Inheritance

Inheritance is an important facility provided by all class based object-oriented languages. It is a mechanism which allows classes to be designed so that common behaviour and data may be factored out and implemented at a high level in a class hierarchy. The most general classes in the hierarchy are at and towards the top, and the most specialised classes are at the bottom.

This is illustrated in in figure 1.6. The root of the hierarchy is class VEHICLE, an abstract class. LIGHT_VEHICLE and HEAVY_VEHICLE are also abstract: the reader would not normally say "I am going out to buy a light vehicle", but "I am going to buy a car" or "I am going to buy a van". There might be more than four actual classes, but classes such as HONDA, ROVER, MERCEDES, CHEVROLET would not be allowable. Like engine size, model, and year, these are attributes of a VEHICLE, not specialisations of CAR.

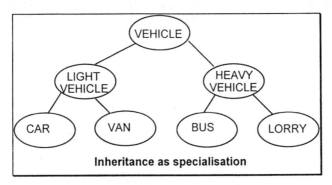

Inheritance as specialisation

**Figure 1.6**

It should be noted that the relationship between a descendant class and an ancestor class is often described as an **is-a** or a **is_a_kind_of** relationship. In the above example we could say that a car is a light_vehicle, and a light_vehicle is a vehicle, but in each case the reverse is clearly not true: a light_vehicle is not a car. These ideas are explored further in chapter 9.

As well as allowing the design of hierarchies of classes from scratch, an inheritance mechanism is frequently used to create a new class out of an existing class. This allows data and behaviour to be reused, as well as the addition and redefinition of data and behaviour in the new class.

The basic idea of inheriting behaviour can be illustrated by going back to the word-processor example. We might decide that a TEXT_PANE should be able to perform the following services for clients:

| | |
|---|---|
| *open* | *close* |
| *scroll up* | *scroll down* |
| *insert n lines at relative position x,y* | *delete n lines at position x,y* |
| *save contents to file* | *load contents from file* |

*copy from buffer*                           *copy to buffer*
*move cursor to relative position x,y*       *move cursor up/down*
*move*

We might find that in our class library we have a class PANE, which fulfils most of the required functionality, but does not have facilities for the following:

*scroll up*                                  *scroll down*
*move cursor up/down/*                       *save to buffer*
*copy from buffer*                           *copy to buffer*
*save contents to file*                      *load contents from file*

In this situation class TEXT_PANE could inherit from PANE, and the additional facilities required could be developed in the new class. The new class would probably require data to keep track of the associated file and text buffer, and some new services. For the following services the code provided in PANE could be reused:

*open*                                       *close*
*move cursor to relative position x,y*       *move*
*insert n lines at relative position x,y*    *delete n lines at position x,y*

The location of the services in the hierarchy is shown in figure 1.7.

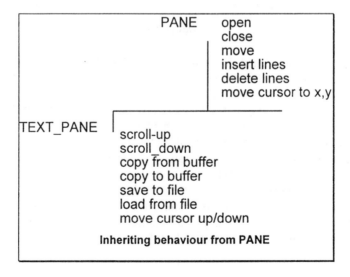

**Figure 1.7**

The inheritance mechanism would allow any instance of class TEXT_PANE to provide the full list of services required, without rewriting or copying any code, and without making any alteration to PANE itself.

If the class library did not provide a MENU, it would be possible to develop this also as a descendant of pane, as shown in figure 1.8.

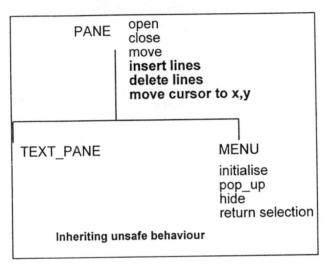

**Figure 1.8**

In this case however, inheritance presents potential dangers; a user of MENU should be prevented from accessing the services displayed in bold face. In this situation the use of inheritance might not be the best solution, and the client relationship might be better.

## 1.7 The concept of client

The concept of a **client** is rarely highlighted in texts on object-oriented programming. It is, however, an important part of object-oriented software development, and merits an early, albeit brief, introduction.

A class may be said to be a client of another if it uses that class. The most common case is known as the **has_a** relationship: a VEHICLE has an engine, has a colour and has a manufacturer or make. It would be wrong to say that a VEHICLE is a kind of ENGINE, is a kind of COLOUR or is a kind of MAKE. *Engine, wheel, colour* and *make* are attributes of a VEHICLE, and VEHICLE is therefore a client of ENGINE, COLOUR and MAKE. Often the choice between an inheritance relationship and a client relationship is not as clear cut as this, as will be found in later chapters.

This concludes the discussion of object-oriented concepts. The rest of this chapter gives a brief overview of the Eiffel language.

## 1.8 An overview of the Eiffel language

This section is aimed largely at those with prior knowledge of object-orientation. The brevity of treatment means that those with less experience will find that much that follows will prove difficult on a first reading. It should, however, serve as a useful reference as the topics are covered in later chapters.

### Classes

The modular unit is the **class**: we write classes and only classes. An Eiffel application is characterised by a structured collection of classes, one of which must be specified at compile-time as the **root** class.

Objects are not recognised as part of the syntax of Eiffel. An object is an instance of a class, created at run-time.

Eiffel allows only two relationships between classes: the **inheritance** relationship and the **client** relationship.
The syntax of the root class does not differ from that of any other class. It must have a **creation routine**, which contains the code which executes immediately a system is activated.

Other classes may also have creation routines, which must be invoked when an instance of the class is created.

### Abstraction

There is no separation between a class interface and a class implementation in Eiffel. An Eiffel environment should provide a tool to generate an interface (a **short** form), from an Eiffel source file.

Eiffel supports information-hiding. All attributes are read-only. Both routines and attributes may be made private, or be made available to specific named client classes.

Descendants may alter the external visibility of inherited features.

### Class features

An instance of a class has data, known as **attributes**, and behaviour, known as **routines**. Both attributes and routines are known as the **features** of a class.

Each attribute has a defined class type. The Eiffel type system is based on the notion of class.

Routines may return a result; the result-type is declared at compile-time.

Routines may have parameters; these are known as **arguments** in Eiffel. Eiffel supports only call by value, so that arguments may not be used to pass back a result. Each formal argument must be declared with a class type.

Eiffel allows the declaration of local variables within a routine; it does not support the nesting of routines.

Eiffel supports recursion.

### Inheritance

Inheritance in Eiffel is open: a class may not limit the facilities available to descendants, nor can it restrict certain facilities to specified descendant classes; such a facility would run counter to the emphasis on reusability and to Meyer's 'open and closed' philosophy.

Facilities are provided for adapting inherited features: these include renaming, redefinition, changing visibility (re-export) and undefinition (making a feature deferred).

Eiffel provides for multiple and repeated inheritance, for deferred (or abstract) classes and for generic classes.

### Instructions

In Eiffel statements are known as **instructions**.

Eiffel enforces the message-passing metaphor: it is not possible to include a file of arbitrary functions or procedures, and every **call** to a routine must have a **target**. When the current object is the target, the target may be implicit, but it can be made explicit by using the identifier *Current*.

Except in the case of the basic types, **assignment** is pointer asignment, and a test for comparison of two objects yields true only when an object is compared with itself.

Eiffel provides a small set of control instructions:

> Loop
> Conditional
> Multi-branch

Control instructions may be nested.

### Library facilities

Eiffel is a small language, and many facilities, including input-output, arithmetic operators and relational operators (except for the '=' operator) are provided in the class libraries rather than as part of the language.

All classes in Eiffel inherit from class ANY which inherits from GENERAL. This class includes a number of standard routines including those used for copying and comparing objects which may be used by instances of any class.

Standard classes in Eiffel (INTEGER, REAL, CHARACTER, DOUBLE) are implemented as **expanded** (non-reference) types.

The language itself has no data structuring facilities other than the class itself. Standard data structures (ARRAY, LIST), and STRING, are supplied in class libraries.

### Memory management

By default Eiffel classes are implemented as references. Instances must therefore be explicitly allocated memory by the programmer using a creation instruction.

No deallocation of memory is required. All Eiffel systems include a garbage collector which keeps track of the memory allocated to a system during its execution, and reclaims memory no longer required. This is consistent with the desire to build a high level abstract language: in such an environment it is inappropriate to require programmers to manage memory.

### Design by contract

The use of **assertions** is central to Eiffel programming. Assertions allow system builders and programmers to reason about the behaviour of instances of classes; they serve as an important tool in specifying classes, documenting classes, and, because of the run-time support provided by all Eiffel systems, in testing and debugging classes.

**Preconditions** define what must be true on entry to a routine.
**Postconditions** define what is guaranteed to be true on exit from a routine.

There are also class and loop **invariants**, loop **variants,** and facilities to aid debugging and to handle exceptions.

## Exercises

1. Make notes on each of the following: attribute, service, object, class, message-passing, information hiding.

2. Identify the main uses of inheritance covered in the chapter. Why might it be unsafe to make MENU inherit from PANE?

3. An information system is being developed to store course results for a university department. The department has a number of courses. Each student is on a single course. Each course has a full-time and part-time variant, and is composed of a collection of modules. Each student takes a collection of modules each semester. A module is taught by a lecturer and is taken by a collection of students. Each student has a mark for each module taken. The following classes have been identified:

DEPARTMENT COURSE    MODULE    STUDENT
LECTURER      MARK    COLLECTION
FULL-TIME      PART_TIME

a) A model is being constructed from the above description. Which of the following seem correct?
   i) course: has a collection of students;   has a lecturer;
          has a collection of modules   is a collection of modules;
   ii)   part-time course has a course;
   iii)  full-time course is a course;
   iv)  a student has a collection of modules;
   v)   student is a collection of marks;
   vi)  department :
          is a collection of lecturers;   has a collection of courses
          has a collection of lecturers   is a collection of courses

b) class MODULE is required to fulfil the following services:
          display the lecturer name
          is lecturer Y responsible for this module?
          display the collection of students and their marks
          is student X taking this module?
          what is the mark for student X on this module?
          what is the average mark of this module?

DEPARTMENT has a collection of COURSES. To answer a request such as *print out the results for student Y*, might require the following scenario:
    "For each course in the collection, DEPARTMENT asks the COURSE whether student X is on the course; if the answer is yes then DEPARTMENT asks the COURSE to display X's marks. For each module in the collection, COURSE asks the MODULE if X is taking the module; if the answer is yes then COURSE asks the MODULE for the mark, and when it receives it, displays it on the screen."

i)    Work out a suitable list of services for class COURSE

ii)   Write scenarios showing how class DEPARTMENT could use the services provided by COURSE and MODULE to achieve the following

> what is the average mark for module X?
>
> what is the average mark for student Y?
>
> display the list of marks for module Z.
>
> display the average marks for the modules taught by
> lecturer XYZ.

# 2  Writing a Simple Class in Eiffel

The reader should already have gathered the following from chapter 1:

a class may be defined as a template from which objects may be created;

in Eiffel a class is also the basic program unit: we write classes, and only classes;

every Eiffel application must have a single root class; conceptually the application may be thought of as an object of this class

the root class must include a creation routine which is executed when a system is loaded;

other classes may or may not have creation routines.

This chapter begins with a simple root class, which the reader is encouraged to enter and compile, and continues with exploration of input-output in Eiffel. The example root class is used to introduce a number of basic concepts, including attributes, call instructions, assignment instructions, and type. The most difficult material covered is likely to be that on reference types in section 2.8, to which a less experienced reader may wish to return at a later stage.

## 2.1  The syntax of an Eiffel class

The syntax of an Eiffel class is shown in very simplified form below.

```
class <class_name>
        [ creation
               <routine_name> ]
        feature
               {routines | attributes }
  end
```

In our notation the special symbols used, known as meta-symbols, have the following meaning:

        <      >     contains a user-defined name

|  |  |  |
|---|---|---|
| { | } | an iteration indicates that the constructs within the brackets occur 0 or more times |
|  | \| | indicates an alternative, either the construct to the left or the right must be selected |
| [ | ] | indicates an option |

All keywords are in bold type, and user-defined names are in italics.

The definition above indicates that a class begins with the keyword, **class,** and is terminated by **end**. The class name is a user-defined name. After the class heading there is an optional creation-part, in which the name of the creation routine is specified. In some cases more than one creation routine may be specified, but this is relatively unusual. A class feature may be either an attribute or a routine. Class features are introduced by the keyword **feature** which may appear more than once in a class.

As a first example we shall look at an Eiffel root class which produces output on the screen. This class, which is called SIMPLE, is extended in the early chapters of the book to illustrate the various Eiffel constructs.

---

```
class SIMPLE
    creation
        test
    feature
      . test is
            -- outputs a string to the screen
        do
            io.putstring("This is my first Eiffel class");
            io.new_line
        end -- test
end -- SIMPLE
```

*Example 2.1 An Eiffel root class*

---

A few additional points may be made about the above class:

1. Class names are by convention written in uppercase. The compiler, however, is not case sensitive, and so makes no distinction between "Simple", "SIMPLE", "simple" or even "siMPle. Both "SIMPLE" and "test" are user-defined names. Keywords may not be chosen as user-defined names.
2. The above class contains three comments. Comments in Eiffel are preceded by a double hyphen :

```
-- This is a comment
```

Comments are intended to make the class text more readable; they are ignored by the compiler. It is a sensible idea to use comments to write the name of a class or a routine at the end, as shown in the example above.

3. The above class has a single feature, a routine, *test*. Usually a class will have several features.

4. The routine *test* is specified as the creation routine. When the class is executed, the body of *test* - the instructions written between the keywords **do** and **end** - are executed. In this case there are two instructions only, and both are calls to *io*. When SIMPLE is compiled, linked and executed, the message

This is my first Eiffel class

should duly appear.


## 2.2 The Eiffel environment

In order to execute class SIMPLE, the reader needs to know how to enter text using the editor provided in the environment being used, and how to invoke the compiler. It is also necessary to know a little about ACE files.

As already indicated, class SIMPLE is intended to be a root class, that is to say that it may be compiled, linked and executed on its own, with support from the kernel library. In order to try the above example, the source code should be entered using an appropriate text editor, and should be saved in a file with a *.e* suffix, which is used for all Eiffel source files.

Prior to compilation the user will need to copy over the default ACE file into the directory in which *simple.e* is stored, and will need to make a few alterations. ACE stands for Assembly of Classes in Eiffel, and is simply a file which contains information that the compiler needs to know. The file includes information about the application's directories, its root class, and any compilation options that are required. The ACE file used by the author to compile the first example is given below:

```
system
        example1
root
        simple(ROOT_CLUSTER): "test"
```

```
default
     precompiled
          ("$EIFFEL3\precompiled\spec\$PLATFORM\base")
cluster
     ROOT_CLUSTER: "$EIFFEL3\ajt\ch1";
end
```

The entry after **system** gives the name of the executable file to be created. The entry after **root** indicates the name of the root class, and the creation routine, *test*. The other entries indicate the location of the precompiled kernel, and the location of the root cluster: "$EIFFEL3\examples\\*ajt\ch1*". The words in italics were the only alterations the author had to make to the default ACE file, which should indicate that it is comparatively easy to get started. The reader should note that not all Eiffel implementors use ACE files, and Eiffel/S uses RCL files instead. Users of Eiffel/S should read appendix 4 before compiling example 1.

Once the ACE has been specified, the programmer may invoke the compiler. This checks class SIMPLE against the rules of Eiffel. Provided that no errors have been made, the compiler generates C code; it then calls the C compiler to create object code, and finally calls the linker to create an executable file. The application may then be run, either by clicking on the appropriate icon, if using a graphic environment, or by entering the name of the executable, which was defined in the ACE as *example1*.

The reader will notice that when SIMPLE is compiled, a number of other classes from the Eiffel library are required, and the executable file produced by the linker is rather large for a system that does so little. This is because any Eiffel application, however small, requires a minimum of support from the kernel classes. The size of an executable does not therefore increase significantly for larger systems.


## 2.3  Call instructions

The call instruction is a fundamental of object-oriented programming and of Eiffel. It is a request by one object for action from another. In Eiffel it takes the form of a call to a routine defined in a client class. The first of the calls has three components, as shown in figure 2.1.

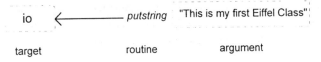

| target | routine | argument |

**Figure 2.1**

The second call is similar, but has no argument. It simply moves the cursor to the next line on the screen.

A call must by definition have a *caller* as well as a *target*. In the above cases the caller is an instance of the root class SIMPLE, and the target is *io*, which is an instance of class STD_FILES, which may be accessed by an instance of any class (see section 2.4). Sometimes an object may call itself. In such cases the target is implied, and a call consists solely of the routine name and any parameters required. The predefined identifier *Current* may be used to make the target explicit.

## 2.4 I-O in Eiffel

Basic input-output facilities in Eiffel are provided by the class library. To do basic input and output using the screen and keyboard in Eiffel we must, as shown already, make a call to an instance of class STD_FILES. In most cases the call is made to *io*,

> *io.putstring;*
> *io.readint*

*io* is defined in class GENERAL. Each class in an Eiffel system automatically inherits from ANY, which itself inherits from PLATFORM, which inherits from GENERAL. In most implementations GENERAL should contain the following entry:

> *io* :STD_FILES **is**
> **once**
>   *!!Result*
> **end** -- io

which returns a shared copy of *io*. In some implementations there may simply be an entry

> *io*:STD_FILES

in which case the creation instruction, !!*io,* must be used before any call is made to it (section 2.8 explains why this is necessary). The following table lists the facilities available for input-output provided by STD_FILES.

| STD_FILES |
| --- |
| **Attributes (Data)**<br>    *lastchar*:CHARACTER<br>    *lastint*:INTEGER<br>    *lastreal*:REAL<br>    *laststring*:STRING<br>    *lastbool*:BOOLEAN<br><br>**Output routines**<br>    *putchar(c*:CHARACTER*)*<br>    *putint(i:*INTEGER*)*<br>    *putreal(r*:REAL*)*<br>    *putstring(s:*STRING*)*<br>    *putbool(b:*BOOLEAN*)*<br>    *new_line*<br><br>**Input routines**<br>    *next_line*<br>    *readbool*<br>    *readint*<br>    *readreal*<br>    *readchar*<br>    *readword* |

The above features have been divided into three categories. The last two categories should be fairly self-explanatory. The first category, the attributes or state variables, are used to store the last item read from the keyboard by the appropriate input routine. So for example

    *io.readchar*

takes a character from the keyboard and transfers it to *lastchar*. To access *lastchar* we must refer to it as

    *io.lastchar*

Some readers may have noted that Eiffel uses the same dot notation for accessing a routine and an attribute. More experienced programmers may wonder why input in Eiffel is handled in this way. It would have been possible to have implemented *lastchar* as a routine which read the keyboard and returned the character immediately to the calling routine. The use of a side-effect in a function is generally considered to be bad practice however, and this solution was deliberately rejected by the language designer. For similar reasons Eiffel provides no call by reference or variable parameters. Readers who wish to pursue this further are recommended to read Meyer (1988) for the discussion of side effects in functions.

It may be noted that there is no state variable for *next_line*. This routine reads the keyboard until it finds the newline character; it is not required to return anything, and so has no associated variable. It is used simply to move the cursor so that subsequent input-output is on the next line.

## 2.5 The assignment instruction

We have already seen how a string of characters may be displayed on the screen using *putstring*. This section illustrates the use of additional i-o facilities and introduces another fundamental instruction, the assignment.

In the example 2.2 the body of the routine *test*, contains a sequence of instructions, which display the product of two integers on the screen. In addition to calls to *io*, the routine *test* now contains two assignment instructions.

```
class SIMPLE;
    creation
        test
    feature
        first,second:INTEGER;
        test is
        -- inputs two integers and outputs their product
        do
            io.putstring("Enter an integer > ");
            io.readint;
            first := io.lastint;
            io.putstring("Enter another integer > ");
            io.readint;
            second := io.lastint;
            io.putstring("Product is :  ");
```

```
                        io.putint(first* second)
                end -- test
        end -- SIMPLE
```

*Example 2.2 Assignment instructions*

The assignment operator, ":=", should be viewed as a left pointing-arrow

first                    io.lastint

which indicates the direction of the data. When executed, it copies the contents of the right-hand operand into the left hand operand. Thus in the example given in figure 2.2, the value 16 is copied from *io.lastint* to the attribute *first*.

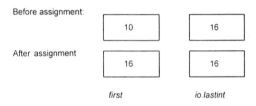

**Figure 2.2**

Readers with experience of other high level languages will have no difficulty with the concept of assignment, which is a core concept of imperative programming. In Eiffel and other OO languages it is more complex, however, as is shown in the fuller discussion of the semantics of assignment in chapter 6.

## 2.6 Class attributes

In any object-oriented language a class is defined in terms of data and action. In Eiffel, both are known as class features. Action in an Eiffel class is encoded in routines (see chapter 4), and data items are known as attributes. This section shows how data is declared in an Eiffel class.

In Eiffel, as in imperative languages, a variable is a user-defined name which refers to a location in the computer's read-write memory. As in other typed languages, an attribute must be declared with a type, as in example 2.2:

*first,second*:INTEGER;

Each variable attribute is allocated an area of memory sufficient to store an item of the attribute's type. The contents of the allocated area of memory may change during execution. So for example, the instruction

*first := second * 2;*

would calculate the result of the expression *second * 2,* and assigns that result to *first* - so that if *second* contained 20, then after execution *first* would contain 40.

Sometimes it is useful to have a data item whose value is guaranteed to remain constant throughout the execution of a program. In Eiffel, constants are declared as shown below:

**feature**
      *message*:STRING **is** *" enter an integer > ";*
      *max_loan*:REAL **is** *1500.00;*
      *months*:INTEGER **is** *12;*
      *male*:CHARACTER **is** *'m';*

and may be accessed on a read only basis:

      *io.putstring(message);*
      *io.putreal(max_loan);*
      *io.putint(months);*
      *io.putchar(male);*
      *any_integer := months;*

The compiler would generate an error if a programmer tried to make *message, max_loan, months* or *male* the target of an assignment instruction.

## 2.7 Basic types

In Eiffel the concepts of class and type may for practical purposes be considered as identical. Every attribute declared in an Eiffel class must have a type. So also must every local variable, every routine argument and every function. The basic types available in the language include

INTEGER    BOOLEAN    REAL    CHARACTER    DOUBLE

The basic type DOUBLE is used to give double precision real numbers. Users who require high precision numbers may wish to use it instead of type REAL. To declare variables of the basic types the following notation is used:

**feature**
>        *age*:INTEGER;
>        *sex*:CHARACTER;
>        *married*:BOOLEAN;
>        *balance*:REAL;

Type indicates the range of values that may be assigned to a variable, it also indicates the operations that may be performed on it. For example we may multiply two integers, but we cannot multiply two chararacters. The following are examples of valid assignments that could be made to each of the attributes declared above:

>        *age* := 23;
>        *sex* := 'm';
>        *married* := *true;*
>        *balance* := − 23.76

As should already be apparent, the basic types are classes, and more advanced programmers may be able to gain an understanding of how to use them simply by studying the listings for classes COMPARABLE, NUMERIC, REAL, INTEGER, BOOLEAN and CHARACTER in the class library.

In Eiffel, as in a number of programming languages, variables of each type are assigned a suitable default value. For Eiffel the initial values assigned are as follows:

|  |  |
|---|---|
| BOOLEAN | false |
| CHARACTER | null character |
| INTEGER | zero |
| REAL | zero |

Chapter 3 discusses the basic types in more detail.

## 2.8 Reference types and creation instructions

Before the introduction to Eiffel types is concluded, it should be pointed out that there are two different kinds of type: expanded types and reference types. The

Eiffel basic types are expanded types. Instances of expanded types contain the actual value or values, and memory for these is allocated by the compiler, as shown in figure 2.3.

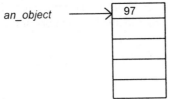

**Figure 2.3**

Instances of reference types contain the addresses of the actual values, and the memory for the actual data must be allocated dynamically (figure 2.4).

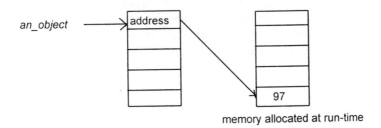

**Figure 2.4**

Instances of reference types require explicit creation instructions, whereas the basic types require no such instructions and are given default values as indicated earlier. It is possible to develop expanded types, by using the heading, **expanded class**. All the examples developed in this text will, however, be reference types.

This section concludes with an example of a creation instruction. Class STD_FILES is a reference type, and we may, if we wish, have our own copy of it, as opposed to the shared one inherited from class GENERAL. To do this we would declare it as with any other attribute:

*my_io*:STD_FILES

but before using it we would need to ensure that memory was allocated to it by using an explicit creation instruction:

*!!my_io*

Unless this was done, the value of *my_io* would be *Void*, as depicted in figure 2.5, and any attempt to reference it by a call such as *my_io.putstring*("*This is my first Eiffel class*") would result in a run-time error. The creation instruction therefore, is necessary in order to allocate memory at run-time to store the data.

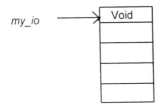

**Figure 2.5**

Finally, for completeness, it should be pointed out that if a reference class has a creation routine specified, then that routine must be invoked when an object of that class is created. So for example, take a class ANY_CLASS, which has a creation routine *make* specified. To create *an_object* of this class requires the following instruction

> *!!an_object.make;*

if *make* required an argument then this would have to be included in the creation instruction, e.g.

> *!!an_object.make(100)*

### 2.9  Strings

Type STRING in Eiffel is not a basic type, but is a special type in the Eiffel system. It is, like STD_FILES a reference type. Strings are denoted in the class source text by using double quotes:

> "*This is a string*".

Examples of their use as output and as constants

> *io.putstring*("*This is my first Eiffel class*")
> *message*:STRING **is** "*enter an integer* > ";

have already been encountered. It is also possible to declare variables of type STRING

>   *name*:STRING

to input strings, and to make assignments to variable attributes of type STRING.

>   *io.readstring*;
>   *name := "Mel Giedroyc"*

It is also possible to use some of the relational operators to compare two strings. Full treatment of this and other aspects of string handling is given in chapter 7.


## 2.10  Special characters

A number of special characters may be used in strings. The most useful of these is perhaps the new line character, which may be appended to a string

>   *io.putstring("This is a string%N")*;

This would ensure that subsequent input-output was on the next line, and so would remove the need to make a separate call to the *new_line* routine.

The use of the '%' character therefore, plays a special role in Eiffel. If this character is to be displayed, it needs to be entered twice:

>   *io.putstring("50% %")*;

Further examples of its use are

>   *io.putstring("%"This is in quotes%"")*;

which would produce the output

>   "This is in quotes"

and

>   %'

which may be used to assign the single quotation mark to a character variable:

*aChar := '% ';*

and

*aChar := '%U';*

to assign a null character to a character variable. A full list of special characters is given in the appendix.


## 2.11 User-defined names

In any programming language a programmer must select names for variables and routines. These should be as meaningful as possible, to aid readability and maintenance of the program, by the author and by subsequent programmers. This is important for all programming, and especially for object-oriented programming which aims to produce reusable, quality code. The reader is recommended to look at the Eiffel class libraries as good models of clarity and consistency.

The rules for forming identifiers in Eiffel are designed to aid the use of sensible names. Identifiers must begin with a letter, and may include digits and the underscore character. There is no limit on length, and programmers are encouraged not to shorten names artificially.The following are all valid:

*test       test5       arithmetic_test       final_year_results*

The convention used by Smalltalk programmers of denoting components of an identifier by an upper-case character is discouraged within the Eiffel community. Although it is legal to write identifiers such as *arithmeticTest* and *finalYearResults*, the use of the underscore character to separate component words is preferred.


## 2.12 Reserved words

Like all programming languages, Eiffel uses some words for special purposes. These words may not be used as identifiers. There are two categories of reserved word:

  1. Keywords
  2. Predefined names

Keywords are in this text written in bold face, according to convention. The ones already introduced include **class, feature, do, end**. Reserved words are by convention always written in lower case although, as mentioned earlier, Eiffel is not case sensitive. Predefined names include the names of special types, such as INTEGER. *Current*, which was introduced earlier in the chapter as the target in cases of self-reference, is also a predefined name. The full list of keywords and predefined names is given in the appendix.

## 2.13  Special symbols

A number of special symbols are used in the language. The text has already introduced the assignment operator, the single quotation marks used to delimit characters and the double quotation mark used to delimit strings.The reader is again referred to the appendix for a full list.

## *Exercises*

1. The following concepts have been introduced in this chapter. The reader is recommended to make notes on each :

| root class | creation routine | | |
| --- | --- | --- | --- |
| feature | attribute | constant | type |
| call | instruction | argument | |
| assignment instruction | | | |

2. Examine the contents of the kernel class library, particularly the universal classes GENERAL, PLATFORM and ANY, and also STD_FILES.

3. Each of the following amendments to class SIMPLE will produce compiler errors; some or all should be tried by those inexperienced in using compilers. Note the error messages produced in each case:
   i) declare an attribute of type CHARACTER; try to perform illegal operations on it (multiplication, addition etc) and to assign it to an integer;
   ii) change the spelling of INTEGER to INTERGER
   iii) change the name of the routine *test* to *start,* but do not alter the entry after **creation**.
   iv) delete the keyword **do**
   iv) delete the keyword **end** which terminates the creation routine
   v)  delete the target of one of the calls
   vi) insert a space between the : and the '=' of the ':=' operator

4. Amend class SIMPLE so that it prompts a user for information as shown below:

>| what is your name | (STRING) |
>| what is your age? | (INTEGER) |
>| what is your gender? | (CHARACTER) |
>| are you married? | (BOOLEAN) |
>| what is your salary? | (REAL) |

Use constant attributes to define the messages that prompt the user for input. Use variable attributes to store the information read from the keyboard. At the end of the input sequence, display the information on the screen. Precede each field with a suitable label, e.g.

>Name: Liz McShane     Age: 43

5. a) Amend example 2.2 as follows, noting what happens when the application is executed on each occasion:

i) declare *my_io* as shown in section 2.8 and try to use it to output an integer to the screen without any creation instruction;

ii) repeat, i) this time using a creation instruction on *my_io*

iii) use a creation instruction on the integer attribute *first;* inspect the contents of *first* using *putint* both before and after the creation instruction;

b) Consider the following:

What is the effect of using a creation instruction on an attribute of a basic type?

Why is it necessary to use an explicit creation instruction for reference types?

# 3  Eiffel Basic Types

The previous chapter has already introduced the basic types supported by Eiffel. This chapter provides examples of operations that may be performed on attributes of the basic types. First, however, it provides an introduction to the concept of type.

## 3.1  Type checking

Type checking is the process which allows the compiler to ensure that a data item is used correctly. To enable this to happen, a programmer must in a typed language such as Eiffel, associate a variable with a type:

>   *age* : INTEGER;

Typing cannot guarantee the correctness of a piece of software, but its presence puts restrictions on what a programmer may do, and allows the compiler to detect a set of errors which would otherwise go undetected and would lead either to run-time errors or to incorrect results.

In Eiffel, as in other typed languages, it is not allowable to assign a value of one type to an attribute of another, so

>   *age := 'B'*

would not be allowable; if it were then consider the results of trying to perform an arithmetic operation on *age*, for example

>   *io.putint(age + 1);*

which would at best yield an indeterminate result. In a typed language a programmer is also prevented from mixing values of different types in an expression, so that

>   25 + 'B'

would not be an allowable expression.

Typing produces problems for object-oriented languages. In typed object-oriented languages the rules for assignment have to be slightly relaxed to take account of inheritance. In such languages we have to differentiate between the

35

*static type* of an entity, which is the type that it is associated with at compile time, and the *dynamic type*, which is the type of the object to which it is attached at run-time. This topic is covered in more detail in chapter 9.

In the case of the Eiffel basic types, however, the rule that an expression of type *t* can be assigned only to a target of type *t* must be adhered to, with one exception, which is discussed in the next section.

## 3.2 Operations on numeric types

The most important numeric types are REAL and INTEGER. For variables of these types the following operators are available:

| REAL and INTEGER | INTEGER only | |
| --- | --- | --- |
| + plus | // | integer division |
| − minus | \\ | remainder after integer division |
| * multiply | | |
| / divide | | |
| ^ raise to power | | |

// and \\ may be used only with integer operands. For example *14 // 5* and *14 \\ 5* are valid, and would yield the results 2 and 4 respectively, whereas *14.5 // 2* and *14 // 2.5* would not be allowed since in each case one of the operands is a real number. The / sign may however, be used with integers, but would yield a result of type REAL. So that *15 / 2* would yield 7.5 whereas *15 // 2* would yield 7. It would of course not be allowable to assign an expression which used the / sign to an integer variable, even if the operands were each of type INTEGER:

> *an_int := an_int / 2*

Eiffel does however allow us to assign an INTEGER expression to a variable of type REAL, since every integer is part of the set of REAL numbers.

When more than one operator is used in an expression, then the order in which each is evaluated depends on the rules of precedence, for example *5+3 // 2* yields 6, not 4, as a casual reading might suggest. But the result of 4 could be obtained by the use of brackets to override the operator precedence: *(5+3)//2*

Precedence is as follows:

High precedence

$$( \ )$$
$$\land$$
$$* \quad / \quad // \quad \backslash\backslash$$
$$+ \ -$$

Low precedence

These operations can now be illustrated in an example. A new feature, the routine, *do_simple_arithmetic*, is to be inserted in class SIMPLE as shown in example 3.1.

```
class SIMPLE
        -- This class has been amended to demonstrate
        -- the use of arithmetic operators
    creation
        test
    feature
        first,second:INTEGER;
        do_simple_arithmetic is
                -- new routine; body still to be added
        do

        end -- do simple arithmetic

        test is
        do
            ...........
            .............
            do_simple_arithmetic;
        end -- test

end -- SIMPLE
```

*Example 3.1 Adding a new routine to SIMPLE*

Note the single instruction added to the creation routine, *test*, which consists of a call to *do_simple_arithmetic*. This is a case of *self-reference*: the target of the call is also the sender. The target could have been made explicit:

*Current.do_simple_arithmetic*

The full code for the new routine is shown in example 3.2.

```
do_simple_arithmetic is
do
    io.putreal(first + second / 12.5);
    io.putreal((first+second) / 12.5);
    io.putint(first+second^3);
    io.putint((first+second)^3);
    io.putreal(first / second);
    io.putint(first // second);
    io.putint(first \\ second);
    io.putint(first+second // first -5);
    io.putint(first+second // (first -5));
    first := first^3 +2 * second;
    io.putint(first);
end -- do simple arithmetic
```

*Example 3.2 Body of new arithmetic routine*

The user may compile and execute class SIMPLE. If the values 10 and 30 are entered then the the sequence of values output should be as follows:

| 12.4 | 3.2 | 27010 | 64000 | 0.3333 |
|------|-----|-------|-------|--------|
| 0    | 10  | 8     | 16    | 1060   |

The following points should be noted from example 3.2:

1. The use of *putreal* instead of *putint* when a REAL result is produced;
2. The use of brackets to change the operator precedence;
3. The assignment instruction:

$$first := first^3 +2 * second;$$

The concept of assignment was introduced in the previous chapter. This example illustrates an important feature of assignment: a variable may be both the target of an assignment instruction, and also appear (more than once if required) on the right-hand side of the assignment instruction. In such cases the target's value is altered; so that if *first* started with the value 2, and *second* with the value 3, after the instruction had executed, *first* would contain the value 14. The value of *second* would of course be unaltered.

## 3.3 Boolean expressions

Variables of type BOOLEAN may have one of two values, *true* and *false*. Boolean expressions may be formed from the relational operators defined in class COMPARABLE.

$$< \quad > \quad <= \quad >=$$

and from the equality/inequality operators

$$= \quad /=$$

both of which are members of the set of special symbols defined for Eiffel.

Issues of equality are potentially complex in object-oriented languages, and this issue is discussed more fully in chapter 6. At this stage it is sufficient to regard Eiffel as providing a single set of relational operators for comparing numbers and characters:

$$< \quad > \quad <= \quad >= \quad = \quad /=$$

The following are examples of boolean expressions using each of the operators:

|  |  |  |  |
|---|---|---|---|
| *17 > 18* | -- false | *17 < 18* | -- true |
| *17 /= 18* | -- true | *17 = 18* | -- false |
| *17 <= 18* | -- true | *17 >= 18* | -- false |
| *18 >= 17* | -- true | *17 >= 17* | -- true |

BOOLEAN expressions are used to form conditions for control instructions (chapter 4). They are also used in assignment statements, and as arguments in procedure calls. Example 3.3 amends class SIMPLE by adding a new routine, *do_comparisons*, which is called from *test*, and also a new variable of type BOOLEAN, *is_true*.

```
class SIMPLE;
            -- this class illustrates the use of boolean expressions
        creation
            test
        feature
            first,second:INTEGER;
            is_true: BOOLEAN;
```

```
              do_comparisons  is
              do


              end -- do comparisons
              do_simple_arithmetic  is
              do


              end -- do simple arithmetic
              test is
              do

                  ..........
                  ..........
                  -- do_simple_arithmetic - will not execute
                  do_comparisons;
              end -- test
        end -- SIMPLE
```

*Example 3.3 Addition of a third routine to SIMPLE*

The reader should note that the routine, *do_simple_arithmetic*, may be left in class SIMPLE, and the call from *test* may either be removed, or commented out so that the compiler ignores it.

Example 3.4 illustrates the use of boolean expressions in an assignment and as arguments to an output procedure.

```
      do_comparisons  is
      do
          is_true := first > second;
          io.putbool(is_true);
          io.putbool(first < second);
      end -- do comparisons
```

*Example 3.4 Boolean assignment and output*

Class SIMPLE may now be recompiled and executed. If at run time the values 17 and 18 are entered then the output should be

   *false*          *true*

We may add to our routine by inputting a boolean value, as shown in example 3.5. The reader is recommended to amend the routine *do_comparisons* as shown, and then to compile and execute it.

```
do_comparisons is
do
        ....
        io.readbool;
        is_true := io.lastbool;
        io.putbool(is_true);
end -- do comparisons
```

*Example 3.5 Boolean input from keyboard*

Finally, more complex expressions need to be considered. These may be constructed using the logical operators defined in class BOOLEAN. We may show the logic of the binary operators, **and, or** and **xor** in the truth tables in figure 3.1.

| *a* | *b* | *a* **and** b |
|-----|-----|---------------|
| t   | t   | t             |
| t   | f   | f             |
| f   | t   | f             |
| f   | f   | f             |

**AND**

| *a* | *b* | *a* **OR** *b* |
|-----|-----|----------------|
| t   | t   | t              |
| t   | f   | t              |
| f   | t   | t              |
| f   | f   | f              |

**OR**

| *a* | *b* | *a* **XOR** *b* |
|-----|-----|-----------------|
| t   | t   | f               |
| t   | f   | t               |
| f   | t   | t               |
| f   | f   | f               |

**Exclusive OR**

**Figure 3.1**

The operand **not** is a unary operator which has the highest precedence of the boolean operators. If *b* is a boolean expression, then **not** *b* is true if and only if *b* is false. The precedence of the operators is as follows:

| high precedence | **not** | | |
|---|---|---|---|
| | **and** | **and then** | |
| | **or** | **xor** | **or else** |
| low precedence | **implies** | | |

The use of each can be illustrated as follows:

| EXPRESSION | RESULT |
|---|---|
| **not** *( 17 > 20)* | true |
| *17 < 20* **and** *17 > 16* | true |
| *17 > 20* **and** *17 > 16* | false |
| *17 > 20* **or** *17 > 16* | true |
| *17 < 20* **or** *17 > 16* | true |
| *17 < 20* **xor** *17 > 16* | false |
| **not** *(17 < 20* **and** *17 > 16)* | false |
| **not** *(17 < 20* **and** *17 > 16)* **or** *10 > 5* | true |
| **not** *(17 < 20)* **and** *17 > 16* **or** *10 > 5* | true |
| **not** *(17 < 20* **and** *17 > 16* **or** *10 > 5)* | false |
| *17 < 20* **xor** *17 > 16* **or** *15 > 6* | true |
| *17 < 20* **xor** *( 17 > 16* **or** *15 > 6 )* | false |
| *17 < 20* **xor** *( 17 > 16* **xor** *15 > 6 )* | true |

The reader may now add the routine given in example 3.5 to class SIMPLE.

```
    do_complex_bool is
do
        ....
        is_true:= not (first > second) and first >25 and second < 30;
        io.putbool(is_true);
        is_true := not (first > second or first >25 ) and second < 30;
        io.putbool(is_true);
    end -- do complex_bool
```

*Example 3.5 Use of logical operators*

The reader should be able to work out some values for 1 and 2 which will generate true for one or other expression. It is not possible, however, to make the above routine yield the output

    *true*       *true*

The reader is encouraged to execute it and try to prove the author wrong!
The following section may be omitted on a first reading.

## 3.4 Semi-strict boolean operators

There are additional boolean operators, known as semi-strict operators :

    **and then**    **or else**    **implies**

The logic and precedence of **and then** and **or else** is the same as **and** and **or** respectively. The difference is that given the following expressions

    *a* **and then** *b*
    *a* **or else** *b*

if *a* is *false* in the first case then *b* is not evaluated, since at that point it is known that the whole expression must be *false*. Similarly, if *a* is *true* in the second case then there is no need to evaluate *b*, since the whole expression must be *true*.

These operators can be useful in conditions when the programmer may not wish to require the second operand to be evaluated because of the chance of a run-time error. For example a terminating condition on a search of a file might be

    *end of file* **or** *key field matches search string*

In this case, when the first operand is *true*, at the end of file, there is no record to compare with the search string, and it is wise to avoid trying to evaluate the second operand. The use of the **or else** would allow us to ensure that the second expression was only evaluated when end of file was *false*.

The operator **implies** has the lowest precedence of the boolean operators. The expression *a* **implies** *b* is the same as **not** *a* **or else** *b*. The expression is true, therefore, if *a* is false, otherwise the result is given by an evaluation of *b*. So, for example, the file search terminator previously discussed, could be rewritten as

**not** *end of file* **implies** *key field matches search string*

so that if the end of file is reached, the expression is true, otherwise the expression is true if key field matches the search string. The truth table for implies is given in figure 3.2.

| a | b | a implies b |
|---|---|---|
| t | t | t |
| t | f | f |
| f | t | t |
| f | f | t |

**Figure 3.2**

The **implies** operator may be further illustrated by considering the statement:

*The sun is shining* **implies** *it is daytime*

which returns the values *true* or *false* as shown below:

| | |
|---|---|
| The sun is not shining and it is daytime | *true* |
| The sun is not shining and it is nighttime | *true* |
| The sun is shining and it is daytime | *true* |
| The sun is shining and it is night time | *false* |

The reader might wish to consider other expressions - e.g.

I have a wife **implies** I am a male
Day of the month greater than 29 **implies** month is not February

## 3.5 Type CHARACTER

In Eiffel, character constants are written using single quotation marks:

'a'    'A'    '@'    '8'    '0'    'o'    'O'    '&'

Characters are ordered, so that each of the following expressions should yield true for any implementation

'a' < 'z'
'A' < 'Z'
'0' < '9'

We may declare variables of type CHARACTER, make assignments to them, read them from the keyboard and output them to the screen. There are few other operations that we would wish to perform on characters.

Each character has an associated integer code which is used as the basis for comparison. This can be obtained by using the routine, *code*, defined in class CHARACTER. The routine shown in example 3.6 may be added to class SIMPLE to enable us to find the integer code of any character in the character set for our implementation.

```
find_character_code is
do
    io.readchar;
    io.putint(io.lastchar.code)
end -- find character code
```

*Example 3.6 Output of integer character-code*

The argument of the last instruction in the routine is worth close examination. It is in fact a chain of calls which is evaluated from left to right:

*io.lastchar*         - returns contents of *lastchar*: a CHARACTER
*lastchar.code*       - calls *code* - target is *lastchar*

The last call returns an INTEGER, which is the type required as an argument to *putint*. The routine may again be called from the creation routine *test*. This can be done by commenting out previous calls. The input-output for the variables *first* and *second,* which are no longer required, may also be commented out, so that the routine test consists of the single call instruction:

*find_character_code*;

***Exercises***

1. Evaluate the following integer expressions:

$15 // 3 * 5 + 3 * 2^2$
$15 + 2^3 * 4 // 3$
$15 + 2^{(3*4)} // 3$
$63 + 15 \backslash\backslash 4 * 2$

2. Evaluate the following boolean expressions:

$17 > 14$ **and** $15 > 20$ **or** $9 > 0$
$17 >= 14$ **and** $(15 > 20$ **or** $9 > 0)$
$15 > 20$ **and** $(17 >= 14$ **or** $9 > 0)$
$15 > 20$ **and** $17 >= 14$ **or** $9 > 0$
$15 < 6$ **or** $7 < 10$ **and** $17 > 20$ **or** $5 < 3$ **or** $1 < 2$
$15 < 6$ **or** $7 < 10$ **and** $(17 > 20$ **or** $5 < 3$ **or** $1 < 2)$

3. The amount an employee receives each month, *net_salary*, is to be calculated as *gross_salary - deductions; taxable_salary* is calculated as *gross_salary - personal_allowance* (4,000); *deductions* consist of the following:

> *tax* - calculated : 25% of taxable salary
> *pension_contributions* - calculated: 6% of gross salary

Amend class SIMPLE so that it allows a user to enter the salary at the keyboard, does the appropriate calculations and displays on the screen the correct values for each of the following:

| | | |
|---|---|---|
| *gross_salary* | *taxable_salary* | *tax* |
| *pension_contributions* | *deductions* | *net_salary* |

4. Consider the following problem. A student passes a unit if the following is attained:

coursework mark >= the minimum allowed for coursework
examination mark >= the minimum allowed for examinations
the total unit mark >= the unit pass mark

The total unit mark is calculated by adding the percentage mark for coursework and exams, and dividing by 2.

Write an Eiffel routine which inputs the following values for coursework and for the examination: actual_mark, maximum, minimum_allowed(%), and which inputs the over-all unit pass_mark (%).

Write a **single boolean expression** to calculate whether a student has passed or failed; store the result in a boolean attribute, *has_passed;* output the boolean variable ( *true* indicates that a student has passed).

# 4 Eiffel Control Instructions

Previous chapters have introduced three types of instruction:

the *creation instruction* used for dynamic allocation of memory to an object;

the *assignment instruction* used to attach the result of an expression to a variable;

the *call*, used to invoke a feature defined in a class.

This chapter introduces the control instructions used to effect sequence, selection and iteration. It begins with a short introduction to structured programming for those for whom this is a new concept. Those who have studied a modern imperative programming language such as Pascal or C may well wish to skip the first section. Subsequent sections provide a quick reference, with short illustrative examples, to the facilities provided in Eiffel for the construction of conditions and loops.

## 4.1 Structured programming

Most current object-oriented developers began by using structured methods and imperative languages. Some would argue that object-oriented development is a new paradigm, and that it is not necessary, and may be harmful, to have any prior knowledge of structured methods which developed within the imperative paradigm. There is probably no right or wrong answer to this: people learn in different ways, and it may well be possible for novice object-oriented developers to remain ignorant about the struggles of their imperative predecessors, whilst others may derive great benefit from an understanding of structured programming.

All the languages of the Algol family, of which Eiffel is a member, provide mechanisms for structuring algorithms using *sequence, selection* and *iteration*. It is well established that no other construct is necessary to solve any problem that is computable.

The concept of sequence or compound statement may be illustrated in the following informal description of an algorithm for reading two integers from the keyboard and dividing the first integer by the second.

1. *print a prompt on screen*
2. *get an integer from the keyboard*
3. *print a prompt on the screen*
4. *get an integer from the keyboard*
5. *display result of first integer divided by the second integer*

The above consists of a sequence of five instructions written in English and readily encodable in any high level programming language. The instructions are intended to be executed in the order given. No variation from the order is allowable.

The alert reader might note that the algorithm cannot be guaranteed to work with every integer. If the user entered 0 when requested to enter the second integer, it would not be possible to provide a result, since we cannot divide by 0. To take account of this we need to introduce the second of our control instructions, selection. We could therefore rewrite the 5th instruction so that it becomes a conditional instruction:

5. **if** *the divisor = 0*
   **then** *display error message*
     **else** *display result of first integer divided by second*
   **end** -- if

The **if** .. **then** .. **else** provides alternative paths through the algorithm depending on the result of the condition.

The revised algorithm could now be coded, and we could be confident that we should not meet the problem of dividing by zero. The full solution would now be the following:

1. *print a prompt on screen*
2. *get an integer from the keyboard*
3. *print a prompt on the screen*
4. *get an integer from the keyboard*
5. **if** *the divisor = 0*
   **then** *display error message*
   **else** *display result of first integer divided by second*
   **end** -- if

This would simply terminate with an error message if the user entered 0 as the divisor.

An even better solution might be to force a user to enter an integer other than 0 as the divisor. To do this we would use the third of our structures: iteration or repetition, implemented in Eiffel as the loop instruction. The sequence of statements would now be amended as follows:

1. *print a prompt on screen*
2. *get an integer from the keyboard*
3. **loop** *until divisor* <> *0*
    1. *print a prompt on the screen*
    2. *get an integer from the keyboard*
    3. **if** *the divisor = 0* **then** *display error message*
        **end** -- if
   **end** -- loop
4. *display result of first integer divided by second integer*

Using the loop, we can now guarantee that instruction 4 will not be executed until an integer other than 0 has been entered.

The above algorithm provides an example of another feature of structured languages, which is the ability to nest control constructs within each other. Thus the loop in the above case contains a sequence of 3 instructions, the third of which is another control instruction. There is no limit on nesting of control instructions, but in the interests of reducing complexity and making software easy to understand and maintain, both imperative and object-oriented programmers need to exercise restraint, and to use the facility only in those cases, such as processing of multi-dimensional data structures, when it provides the most natural solution.

Finally, it should be noted that in this case the selection has no **else**. If the condition is not true the statement is not executed. No alternative needs to be provided. The fourth instruction could have been included as an alternative within the loop, but it is unnecessary: exit from the loop will not take place until a non-zero integer has been entered, so that by the time statement 4 is reached the divisor will not be 0. Each version of the algorithm will now be written in Eiffel as a way of introducing the structures provided. The first to be shown is the sequence.

## 4.2  Compound instruction

In Eiffel a sequence is known as a compound control structure. To illustrate this, a new routine, *do_sequence*, is added to class SIMPLE in example 4.1.

```
        do_sequence is
            local
                integer_1, integer_2 : INTEGER;
    do
            io.putstring("enter an integer > ");
            io.readint;
            integer_1 := io.lastint;
            io.putstring("enter divisor > ");
            io.readint;
            integer_2 := io.lastint;
            io.putint(integer_1 // integer_2)
    end -- do_sequence
```

*Example 4.1 Sequence of instructions*

It will be noted that there is now a sequence of seven instructions. The additional instructions

```
integer_1 := io.lastint;
integer_2 := io.lastint;
```

are required by Eiffel to assign the integer from the variable *io.lastint* to the local variable locations defined for the purpose. The use of local data items is explained in chapter 5.

The syntax of a compound can be defined using the meta language introduced in chapter 2, as

instruction {";" instruction }

It may be recalled that { } indicates an iteration. Symbols enclosed in " " are special symbols which appear in the class text. The above definition indicates that a compound instruction in Eiffel consists of at least one instruction, followed by an iteration (0 or more) of instructions. The semi-colon is used to separate instructions. An alternative representation is given in figure 4.1. The ";" is in fact optional, but it is good practice to use it as a separator, and this practice is followed throughout the text.

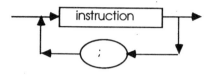

**Figure 4.1**

## 4.3 Selection

Eiffel provides standard facilities for selection. It provides an **if** ... **then** ... **else** instruction and also provides for multi-way selection using the **inspect** (see section 4.5). Example 4.2 amends the previous example to include the **if** ... **else** instruction.

```
do_selection is
       local
               integer_1, integer_2 : INTEGER;
       do
       io.putstring("enter an integer > ");
       io.readint;
       integer_1 := io.lastint;
       io.putstring("enter divisor > ");
       io.readint;
       integer_2 := io.lastint;
       if integer_2 /= 0
               then io.putint(integer_1 // integer_2)
       else io.putstring("cannot divide by zero")
       end -- if
end -- do_selection
```

*Example 4.2 If .. else instruction*

The routine's change of name should be noted.

Wherever there is a single instruction there could be more than one. The **else** marks the end of the sequence of instructions to be executed when the condition is true, and the **end** is required to terminate the sequence of instructions to be executed when the condition is false.

The syntax of the **if** may be defined more formally as follows

**if** condition
    **then** compound
{**elseif** condition **then** compound }
[ **else** compound ]
**end**;

The else-if part, {**elseif** condition **then** compound }, indicates that there may be 0 or more occurrences of an **elseif** as shown below. The [ **else** compound ] indicates that the item enclosed is optional. Given the above syntax definition, each of the following would be legal constructs:

**if** condition-1
    **then** compound-1
**end** -- if

**if** condition-1
    **then** compound-1
**elseif** condition-2
    **then** compound-2
**elseif** condition-3
    **then** compound-3
**end** -- if

**if** condition-1
    **then** compound-1
**elseif** condition-2
    **then** compound-2
**elseif** condition-3
    **then** compound-3
**else** compound-4
**end** -- if

**if** condition-1
    **then** compound-1
**else** compound-2
**end** -- if

A syntax diagram for the **if .. else,** is shown in figure 4.2.

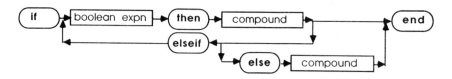

**Figure 4.2**

As already indicated, control instructions may be nested. A compound could itself be an **if** instruction, so that we are able to nest **if** instructions. An **if** instruction of the following form would therefore be legal, but perhaps not desirable:

```
if condition-1
    then if condition-2
        then if condition-3
            then  compound
                                    -- executes if conditions
                                    -- 1,2 ,3 are true
                    else compound   -- executes if 1,2 are true
                                    -- and condition 3 is false
            end; -- inner if
        else compound               -- executes if 1 is true and 2
                                    -- is false
        end                         -- middle if
    else compound                   -- executes if condition 1 is false
    end;                            -- outer if
```

### 4.4 Iteration

Eiffel is designed to be a small language, so that whereas other languages typically provide three or four different ways of structuring repeated statements, Eiffel provides a single multi-purpose loop instruction. This is illustrated in example 4.3, which returns to the algorithm introduced in section 4.1.

```
do_iteration is
    local
            integer_1, integer_2 : INTEGER;
    do
        io.putstring("enter an integer > ");
```

```
                    io.readint;
                    integer_1 := io.lastint;
                    from
                         integer_2 := 0;
                    until
                         integer_2 /=  0
                    loop
                         io.putstring("enter divisor > ");
                         io.readint;
                         integer_2 := io.lastint;
                         if integer_2 /= 0
                              then io.putint(integer_1 // integer_2)
                              else io.putstring("cannot divide by 0%N")
                              end -- if
                    end -- loop
              end -- do_iteration
```

*Example 4.3 Use of Eiffel loop*

The from-part of the loop is used to set initial values; it may consist of more than one instruction. It may also be left empty e.g.

```
     from
     until integer_2 /= 0
```

and indeed, in example 4.3 it is not strictly necessary to initialise the variable *integer_2*, since it will automatically be set to its default value, which is 0. It makes good sense, however, to give variables explicit initial values, particularly when they are being used to control loops.

It should be noted that if the from-part had read

```
     from integer_2 := 1
```

then the loop would not have executed: the loop makes the test before entry, not afterwards, so that it in such situations it never enters the loop body.

It would be possible to produce a slightly more elegant solution using the read ahead technique. This would remove the **if** instruction. The reader should carefully compare example 4.4 with the previous example.

```
              do_iteration is
                    local
                         integer_1, integer_2 : INTEGER;
          do
```

```
              io.putstring("enter an integer > ");
              io.readint;
              integer_1 := io.lastint;
          from
                  io.putstring("enter divisor > ");
                  io.readint;
                  integer_2 := io.lastint;
          until
                  integer_2 /=  0
          loop
                  io.putstring("cannot divide by 0 : enter again >");
                  io.readint;
                  integer_2 := io.lastint;
          end -- loop
          io.putint(integer_1 // integer_2)
      end -- do_iteration
```

*Example 4.4 Use of Eiffel loop with read-ahead*

Particular care has to be taken to ensure that the loop does not exit before the task has been completed. This is illustrated by a short piece of code in example 4.5, which is designed to print out each number in the range 1 to 12 multiplied by 12.

```
          do_multiply is
          local
              multiplier, multiplied : INTEGER;
      do
              from multiplier := 1;
                    multiplied  := 12
              until integer_2  = 12;
                    io.putint(multiplier);
                    io.putstring(" *   ");
                    io.putint(multiplied);
                    io.putstring(" = ");
                    io.putint(multiplier * multiplied);
                    io.new_line;
                    multiplier = multiplier + 1
              end -- loop
      end -- do_multiply
```

*Example 4.5 Loop which iterates 11 times only*

The output from this would in fact be

```
1  *  12  =  12
.............
10 *  12 =  120
11 *  12 =  132
```

because on the 11th iteration the value of *multiplier* would initially be 11, and would therefore output 132. *Multiplier* would then be incremented, and would become 12, which is the exit condition, without having produced the final output required. For a correct solution the reader should use either of the alternatives given in example 4.6.

---

a)

**from**
  *multiplier := 0*
**until**
  *multiplier = 12*
**loop**
  *multiplier := multiplier +1;*

  .........................

  .........................
**end** -- loop

b)

**from**
  *multiplier := 1*
**until**
  *multiplier > 12*
**loop**

  .........................

  .........................
  *multiplier := multiplier +1*
**end** -- loop

*Example 4.6 Loops which execute 12 times*

---

The syntax of the loop instruction may be defined as follows:

**from**
  Compound

```
[invariant
        Assertion]
[variant
        Integer_expression]
until
        Boolean_expression
loop
        Compound
end
```

The [ ] indicates that the invariant and variant parts are optional. They are in fact an important part of design by contract, and are more fully covered in chapter 8. The equivalent diagram is shown in figure 4.3.

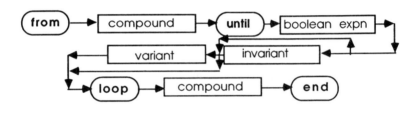

**Figure 4.3**

### 4.5 Multi-way selection

All modern structured languages provide a construct to express multi-way selection. In practice, this construct is not used a great deal in object-oriented programming, but there are occasions when it is useful.

We may take the case when we are required to take a set of actions dependent on the run-time evaluation of an integer expression $x + y$. This could have an infinite number of values at run-time, depending on the contents of $x$ and $y$. If $x = 2$ and $y = 3$ then the result would be *5*, if $x = 6$ and $y = 7$ then the result of evaluating the expression would be *13*, and so on.

The inspect structure provides a relatively simple construct which allows each possible value to be catered for, as example 4.7 shows.

```
inspect  x + y
    when  0  then  compound
    when  25, 67,87 then  compound
                        -- executes when x + y  = 25 or 67 or 87
    when  1..10 then compound
                        -- executes when x + y in range 1  to 10
    when  11..20, 31..40 then compound
                        -- executes when in range 11 to 20 or 31 to 40
    when 90..100  then  compound
                        -- executes when in range 90 to 100
    else compound
                        - executes when  no  previous conditions true
end -- inspect
```

*Example 4.7 Outline of inspect instruction*

It would of course be possible to produce the same logic using the **if ..elseif ..
else** construct, but it would require the repetition of the full condition:

```
if x + y = 0
    then .......
elseif ( x + y = 25)  or (x + y =67) or (x + y = 87)
    then .......
elseif ......
```

and so on.

A good example of the use of multi-way selection would be a menu. If for
example a menu required a user to press a key to indicate the selection required,
we could code this as shown in example 4.8.

```
menu is
do
    io.readchar
    inspect  io.lastchar
        when 'A', 'A' then  io.putstring("amend selected")
        when 'd', 'd' then  io.putstring("delete selected")
        when 'r', 'R' then io.putstring("retrieve selected")
        when 's', 'S' then io.putstring("save selected")
        when 'q', 'Q' then io.putstring("quit selected")
        else io.putstring(" invalid selection")
    end -- inspect
end -- menu
```

*Example 4.8 Inspect instruction*

In a real application the compound instruction following each **then** would of course perform the function requested rather than display a string on the screen - but implementing the selection in this way by putting in stubs rather than actual code is a useful technique which allows the menu logic to be tested before the functions are coded. At a later stage the stubs may be replaced by code which performs the functions required.

The syntax of the inspect statement may be defined as follows:

    **inspect** expression
       { **when** Choice {  "," Choice} **then** Compound}
      [ **else** Compound]
    **end**

A Choice may be either a constant value of any type, e.g. "X", 15, 2.3 or an interval e.g. 5..10. The equivalent syntax diagram for the inspect instruction is given in figure 4.4.

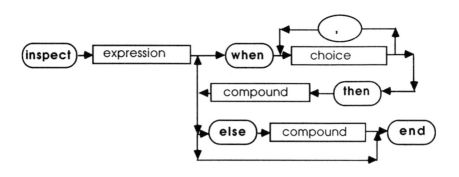

**Figure 4.4**

### Exercises

1. Write a routine, for insertion in class SIMPLE, which asks a user to indicate how many real numbers are to be entered; the routine then allows the user to enter each number; at the end it displays the mean and the sum of the numbers entered. (Hint: use a loop, make sure that it can handle an input of 0 numbers.)

2.Write a routine, using **inspect**, which allows a user to enter an integer, and prints out the month of the year, e.g. if 1 is entered then *January* is output. If an invalid month is entered, then an error message should be displayed.

3. Amend the first exercise so that the maximum and minimum are also output at the end. (Hint: read first number outside loop, and set *max* and *min* to this number before entering the loop; make sure that it can still handle 0 numbers.)

# 5 Eiffel Routines

The routines introduced in the preceding chapters have been introduced mainly to illustrate features of the Eiffel language. The role of a routine in object-oriented programming ought now to be clarified:

in the context of object-oriented development the routine is a secondary concern, whereas in the context of process-oriented development it has a major role in decomposing a problem into manageable small tasks;

in object-oriented software development, data is given a more privileged position, whereas functions and sub-functions are the primary organising idea in traditional software development;

the primary focus in object-oriented software development is on the classes of objects in the system being modelled;

classes provide a combination of state and behaviour, and externally may be viewed as collections of data and services;

in the context of Eiffel, routines are features of a class which if public, are used to provide the services required by clients, or if private are used to perform auxiliary tasks necessary to satisfy the requests of clients;

in pure object-oriented languages such as Smalltalk and Eiffel, routines, or 'methods' as they are known in Smalltalk, are associated with a particular class, and can be invoked only when sending a message to an instance of that class.

This chapter introduces the syntax of routines in the Eiffel language, distinguishes between routines which do and do not return a result, and covers local variables and arguments, creation routines and once routines. It also introduces ideas of recursion.

Those readers with experience of other high-level languages may well be able to skip much of what follows.

## 5.1 Routines which do not return a result

In many languages routines which do not return a result are known as procedures. We may define a procedure as a sequence of instructions, referenced by name, and designed to perform some action as part of a larger program. Additionally procedures have the following characteristics:

have no state but may hold data temporarily;

may have inputs, variously known as arguments or parameters;

in object-oriented programming they often cause a change in the state of the object for which they are invoked

In Eiffel, the syntax of a routine which does not return a result may be given as follows:

```
<routine_name> [ formal argument list ] is
        [preconditions]
        [local declarations
do
        compound instruction
        [postconditions]
end
```

(See figure 5.1 for the syntax diagram). The above indicates that a routine begins with its name - formed according to the same rules as other user-defined names. It optionally has arguments, and likewise may have some local variables. The reserved word **is** follows the arguments and precedes the local declarations. The preconditions and postconditions, which are optional, are covered in chapter 8. The body of the routine, which is where the action is encoded, is delimited by the reserved words **do** and **end**, and consists of a compound instruction, which, as indicated previously, is a sequence of instructions.

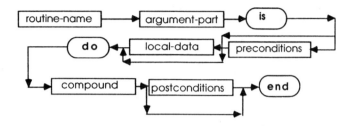

**Figure 5.1**

The argument part of a routine may be defined as

"(" entity declaration list ")"

and an entity declaration list may be defined as

*<identifier >* {"," *< identifier >*} ": " type
{";" *<identifier* { "," *<identifier>* } :" type }

or diagrammatically as shown in figure 5.2.

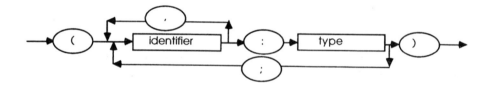

**Figure 5.2**

The use of arguments allows the action performed by a routine to be varied according to a value or values passed in at run-time. Good examples of this may be found in the Eiffel libraries. For example STD_FILES includes the following routines, with formal arguments of types BOOLEAN, CHARACTER and INTEGER:

*putbool* (*b*:BOOLEAN);
*putchar* (*c*:CHARACTER);
*putint* (*i*:INTEGER);

The formal argument of *putint* is therefore

*i*:INTEGER

and whenever **putint** is called the caller must supply a single integer expression as an actual arguument. This means that if at run-time it is called with an argument of *7 + 16*, the value 23 would be output; likewise, if called with an argument of *95//2*, the value 47 would be displayed on the screen.

The type of a formal argument will usually be a type identifier such as STRING, INTEGER, CUSTOMER, but alternatives are sometimes used, as a look at the class libraries soon reveals:

> *copy(other* **like** *Current)* -- in class GENERAL
> *copy(other*: ARRAY[G]*)* -- in class ARRAY

The first is an anchored declaration, which in this case indicates the the actual argument must be the same type as the target object. The second is a formal generic parameter (see chapter 10).

In a typed language, such as Eiffel, the compiler will check to ensure that the actual arguments are the same type as the formal arguments declared in the routine, so that for a routine with the following heading:

> *make(c*:CHARACTER,*i*:INTEGER);

it would check that the actual arguments consist of a character and an integer in the same order as the declaration. The following would therefore be valid calls:

> *make('B', 17);*
> *make(io.lastchar, io.lastint\*10);*

In the first case the arguments are explicit values of the correct types; in the second case they are expressions which yield the correct types - but whose value cannot be known until run time.

If a programmer tried to call *make* with the following actual arguments, then compilation errors would result:

> *(17,'B');*
> > -- arguments in wrong order
> > -- so types would not match those
> > -- of formal arguments
> *('B');*
> > -- not enough arguments

*(io.lastint,io.lastchar)*
　　　　-- arguments in wrong order
*(io.lastreal)*
　　　　-- insufficient arguments
　　　　-- also wrong type

Unlike languages such as Pascal and Ada, Eiffel does not allow values to be passed back to a caller from a routine using *variable parameters* or *call by reference*. Arguments are read only, so it is not possible to use an argument as the target of an assignment instruction, and an attempt to do so would yield a compilation error. It is allowable, however, to alter the state of the argument by making it the target of a call.

We may give a simple example of two routines with arguments defined as features in class BANK_ACCOUNT, shown in example 5.1. This class has four attributes: *id_no, balance, credit_limit, name,* and two routines which may be used to change the value of *balance* and *id_no.*

Both the routines in example 5.1 illustrate a common occurrence in object-oriented programming: using a routine to alter the contents of an attribute - this type of routine is often described as a *transformer*, in that it transforms the state of the target object. Attributes are read only for clients, so it is not possible to alter an attribute externally unless a suitable transfomer has been defined.

The first routine, *debit_amount,* has a single formal argument, *amount*:REAL, which is used to pass in the amount to be debited from the account. It also has a body, consisting of a single line which subtracts *amount* from *balance*. The second routine has two arguments: it compares the first argument with the attribute *id_no*, and if they match, then it changes *id_no*; if not, then it writes an error message.

```
class BANK_ACCOUNT
    feature
        id_no: INTEGER;
        balance: REAL;
        credit_limit: REAL;
        name: STRING;

        debit_amount(amount:REAL) is
        do
            balance := balance - amount;
        end -- debit_amount;
        change_id(old_no, new_no:INTEGER) is
        do
```

```
        if old_no = id_no
            then id_no := new_no
        else io.putstring("invalid current id")
        end -- if
    end -- change_id
end -- BANK_ACCOUNT
```

*Example 5.1 Transformer routines with arguments*

As previously indicated, the compiler will check that the actual arguments match the formal arguments: in the first case the caller must pass in a single actual argument of type REAL; in the second case the caller must pass in two arguments, both of type integer.

Example 5.2 shows class CONTROLLER, which is a client of class BANK_ACCOUNT through its declaration of the attribute *account*. The example shows some legal calls to each of the routines defined in class BANK_ACCOUNT.

```
class CONTROLLER
    creation
        test
    feature
        debit:REAL;
        id :INTEGER;
        account:BANK_ACCOUNT;

        test is
            -- shows some legal calls to an instance
            -- of class BANK_ACCOUNT
        do
            ----------
            account.change_id(id,1002);
            account.debit_amount(20.50);
            account.debit_amount(debit);
            ----------
        end -- test
end -- CONTROLLER
```

*Example 5.2 Examples of calls to routines with arguments*

It should be noted that the target of each call is *account*, which is an instance of class BANK_ACCOUNT. The type and number of the actual arguments matches the formal argument list specified in the corresponding routine declarations in class BANK_ACCOUNT. The result of the first call would be to change the *id_no* of *account* to 1002 - assuming that the value of *id* matched *account*'s *id_no*.The second and third call would debit 20.5 from *account*'s attribute, *amount_owing*, and would then deduct whatever value was held in the attribute, *debit*.

## 5.2 Local data

In common with Pascal and other block-structured languages, Eiffel allows programmers to declare data which is local to a routine. A local data item has the following characteristics:

it is visible only within the routine in which it is declared;

it is purely temporary in duration: it is stored only whilst the routine is executing.

With regard to the last point it should be remembered that a routine may have inputs but, unlike an instance of a class, it does not have a state. Local data is not allocated a permanent place in memory, but is held on a stack, and is recreated each time that a procedure is called. The contents of a local variable are therefore lost on exit from the procedure.

Local data should therefore be used only for storing information whose contents are not considered part of the state of the current object. Good examples would be a variable used to control a loop, or a variable required to store an item temporarily during a calculation. Such data items should not be made features of a class.

The syntax for local variables may be defined as follows:

    **"local "**    *< local_name >*   { ","   *< local_name >* } ":" type
    { ";"   *< local_name >*   { ","   *< local_name >* } ":" type }

Or diagrammatically they may be represented as in figure 5.3.

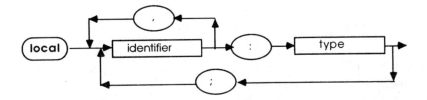

**Figure 5.3**

As with arguments of routines, and indeed with attributes, the type of a local may also be an anchored declaration or a parameterised generic type.

Example 5.3 gives an illustration of the use of local data in a routine. In this instance the local variable *count* is used to control the loop. If this routine were called with the parameters ('*', 25) then it would produce the following output:

**************************

```
write_char_n_times(char:CHARACTER;n:INTEGER) is
        local
                count:INTEGER
do
        from count := 1
        until count > n
        loop
                io.putchar(char);
        count := count + 1
        end -- loop
end -- write_char_n_times
```

*Example 5.3 A routine which uses a local variable*

## 5.3 Routines which return a result

It is often useful to make a distinction between a procedure and a function. The terminology used by various modern languages can be confusing. C and C++ allow us only to write functions. Pascal allows us to write functions and procedures. Modula-2 allows us to write procedures and procedure-functions. Smalltalk uses the term 'method'.

A function may be defined as a procedure which returns a result. That should be its sole purpose. In the context of object-oriented programming, a function is an *accessor*, a routine which allows a client to query the state of an object. It should not, therefore, be used to perform actions which alter the contents of attributes. Sometimes it might seem more efficient to allow a function to change the state of an object by a 'side-effect' - i.e. something which is not its main purpose. Such practices can, however, be a nightmare to debug, and this practice is strongly discouraged, even though the Eiffel language does not prevent a programmer from doing it. The rule should always be to use a procedure, not a function, to alter the state of an object.

We may now look at some Eiffel routines, firstly in order to understand the difference between a routine which returns a result (a function), and one which does not (a procedure). For those who are unclear as to what a function is, perhaps the best place to look is in the SINGLE_MATH class in Eiffel. Here we will find some familiar, and perhaps not so familiar mathematical functions, including the following:

> *cos(r*:REAL*)*:REAL;
> *floor(r*:REAL*)*:REAL;
> *ceiling(r*:REAL*)*:REAL;
> *rabs(r*:REAL*)*:REAL;

In each case the routines have a single argument of type REAL, the input to the routines; and they also return a result of type REAL.

```
class SIMPLE
    feature
        fn:SINGLE_MATH;
        maths_examples is
        do
            !!fn;
            io.putreal(fn.floor(125.76))
                -- displays -126 on screen
            io.putreal(fn.ceiling(-125.76))
                -- displays -125 on screen
            io.putreal(fn.cos(15.5))
        end -- maths_examples
end -- SIMPLE
```

*Example 5.4 Using routines as arguments to other routines*

To use these functions we must either inherit from or become a client of SINGLE_MATH. If we take the latter course then we must use a creation instruction as shown in example 5.4. It should be noted that since a function returns a result it may only be called either as an argument to another routine, or in other cases when an expression might be used. Example 5.4 illustrates the use of routines which return a result as parameters to other routines. Example 5.5 shows their use in assignment instructions or as parts of conditions.

```
class SIMPLE
    feature
        fn:SINGLE_MATH;
        maths_examples is
            local
                a_real:REAL
    do
            !!fn;
            io.readtreal;
            a_real := fn.floor(io.lastreal);
            io.readreal;
            if fn.floor(io.lastreal) > a_real
                then
                        io.putreal(io.lastreal);
                        io.putstring(" is larger")
            end -- if
        end -- maths_examples
    end -- SIMPLE
```

*Example 5.5 Using routines in assignment instructions and conditions*

We are now in a position to consider how we construct our own routines which return a result. We may begin with the syntax:

```
<routine_name> [ arguments ]  ":"  < result_type >  is
    [local variables]
    {preconditions}
do
    compound instruction
    [postconditions]
end
```

which, as illustrated in the shaded part of figure 5.4, differs only in one respect: the routine must be declared with a result type, which immediately precedes the reserved word **is** and is separated from the argument part by a colon.

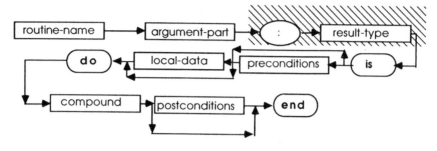

**Figure 5.4**

---

*amount_available*: REAL **is**
**do**
    *Result := credit_limit + balance*;
**end** -- amount_available

*Example 5.6 A routine which returns a REAL result*

---

Example 5.6 provides an accessor routine which may be added to class BANK_ACCOUNT. This function which has no argument, returns the result of a simple calculation. The use of the predefined identifier *Result* should be noted: with every function declaration there is an implicit *Result* which has the same type as the function. *Result* may be regarded as a local variable, and is both readable and writable, as is illustrated in example 5.7. It has the same initial default value as the routine's type. So in the above case its initial value would be 0. If the routine's type was CHARACTER then the value would be *nul,* and if it were a reference type then its default value would be *void.*

---

*factorial(i:*INTEGER*)*:INTEGER **is**
    **local**
        *count:*INTEGER
**do**
    **from**
        *count := 0*;
        *Result := 1*;
    **until**
        *count = i*
    **loop**
        *count := count + 1;*
        *Result := Result * count*;
    **end** -- loop
**end** -- factorial;

*Example 5.7 A routine which returns an INTEGER result*

At the time when control is passed back the value currently held in *Result* is passed back to the caller.

## 5.4 Creation routines

Creation routines have been introduced in earlier chapters. As previously indicated, a root class must have a creation routine. It is this which is first executed when the executable file is loaded into the computer's memory. For classes not intended to be root classes, a creation routine is optional. If one is defined then it must be invoked in the creation instruction:

*!!an_obj.a_routine(an_argument)*

The main use of a creation routine is to give attributes initial values. Creation routines may or may not have arguments.

Creation routines are written in the same way as ordinary Eiffel routines. They are declared as creation routines in the early part of the class prior to the declaration of any features. This is illustrated in the case of BANK_ACCOUNT, which, is shown in example 5.8, with a creation routine, *make*, which has three arguments. The purpose of this routine is to provide initial values for the attributes *id_no*, *credit_limit* and *name*. This would allow each customer that is created to be given a unique *id_no*, and also to have the *name* and *credit_limit* attributes individually initialised. All customers will certainly not have the same name, and this routine allows customers to be given differing credit limits from the outset. The attribute *balance* is intended to be the same initially for all customers, the default value, 0.

```
class BANK_ACCOUNT
    creation
        make;
    feature
        id_no: INTEGER;
        balance: REAL;
        credit_limit: REAL;
        name: STRING;
        make(cust:STRING;limit:REAL;id:INTEGER) is
        do
            name := cust;
            credit_limit := limit;
            id_no := id;
```

```
                   end -- make
                ............................
        end -- BANK_ACCOUNT
```

*Example 5.8 A creation routine with arguments*

Example 5.9 illustrates how an instance of BANK_ACCOUNT could be instantiated using the creation routine *make*.The reader might be puzzled by the use of the function *clone* in the last instruction. This is a necessary safeguard because STRING is a reference type, and *clone* ensures that an independent copy of *io.laststring*, rather than simply a reference to *io.laststring*, is passed as an argument. Were this not done, any subsequent call to *io.readstring* would change the name stored in *account*. It is not necessary to clone *io.lastreal* and *io.lastint* which are values rather than references. Issues of copying and cloning are discussed further in chapter 6.

```
        class CONTROLLER
            creation
                test
            feature
                account:BANK_ACCOUNT;
                init_account is
                do
                    io.putstring("enter customer number >")
                    io.readint;
                    io.putstring("enter customer name >");
                    io.readstring;
                    io.putstring("enter credit limit >");
                    io.readreal;
                    !!account.make(clone(io.laststring),
                                    io.lastreal, io.lastint);

                    ----------

                end -- init_account
        end -- CONTROLLER
```

*Example 5.9 Invoking a creation routine with arguments*

## 5.5 Recursive routines

Like most modern computer languages, Eiffel supports recursion. Recursion is a well understood technique for solving certain types of problem, and in some cases may be used as a more elegant alternative to loops, especially for processing lists and trees, which are naturally recursive data structures.

A recursive routine is a routine which calls itself. When a routine is invoked recursively a stack of activation records is kept. An activation record consists of local variables, arguments, and a return address, which is the instruction following the original call. This is illustrated in figure 5.5.

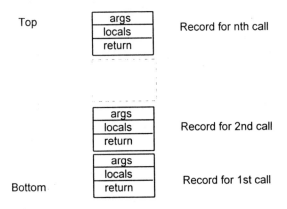

**Figure 5.5 Stack of activation records**

A recursive routine consists of at least one of each of the following:

> a base case which can be solved directly
> a recursive call
>> e.g.
>>> **if** *base case*
>>>> **then** *solve problem*
>>> **else** *solve smaller problem*

The reader should be able to identify the base case and the recursive call in example 5.9, which returns a factorial.

```
factorial(n:INTEGER ):INTEGER is
do
    if n = 0
        then Result := 1
        else Result := n * factorial(n-1)
    end;
end -- factorial;
```

*Example 5.10 A recursive routine*

An English description of this might be:

>   *the factorial of 0 is 1*
>       *the factorial of a positive integer n is n multiplied*
>           *by the factorial of n minus 1*

To take an example, the factorial of 3 may be calculated as follows:

>   *3 * factorial 2;*

factorial 2 is calculated as        *2 * factorial 1;*

factorial 1 is calculated as        *1 * factorial 0*

factorial 0 is          *1.*

So the result, working backwards, is *1 * 1 * 2 * 3*, which is *6*.

This introduction to recursion concludes with an example of a recursive routine which does not return a result (5.11). Other examples of the use of recursion will be found in later chapters.

```
print_seq(i:INTEGER; n:INTEGER) is
do
        if i < = n
            then
                    print_seq(i+1,n);
                    io.putint(i);
            end -- if
end -- print_seq
```

*Example 5.11 A routine that prints a range of positive integers in reverse order*

### 5.6 Once routines
(Non-advanced readers are recommended to skip this section)

Once routines are routines which execute once only. On any subsequent call they return exactly the same result. Their main use is to provide an application with shared or global objects. An example of the use of a once routine was introduced in chapter 2, when it was indicated that the following feature in class GENERAL provides a shared instance of STD_FILES.

---

*io* :STD_FILES **is**
**once**
     *!!Result*
**end** -- io

*Example 5.12 Once routine, providing shared copy of io*

---

Each class inherits automatically from GENERAL, so every object in an Eiffel application shares the same copy of *io*.The first time *io* is called it executes the creation instruction

     *!!Result*

which creates an instance of STD_FILES which is returned to the caller. On each subsequent call, from whichever object the call is made, it returns the same instance. How the Eiffel system does this is beyond the scope of this text, suffice it to say that the memory location of all once routines must be independent of any single object, and the system must keep some kind of record that indicates whether the routine has previously been called. This happily is a matter for language implementors rather than application programmers.

If a programmer wishes to provide for an instance of a class to be shared among many objects, a once routine needs to be placed in a separate class, from which each class that needs access to the shared object may inherit. As an example, consider an application simulating the passage of customers through a supermarket: the objects in the system would consist of customers, checkout-tills and so on. Each customer object might, on leaving the store, need to update the simulation statistics; other objects would also need to access the statistics. To allow this a class SIM_STATS might be developed. Such a class is shown in example 5.12. It consists of two attributes only: *count,* which is used to keep a tally of the number of customers passing through the checkout, and a time counter, *secs,* which is used to record the total queueing time of all the customers.

```
class SIM_STATS
    feature
        count:INTEGER;
        secs:REAL;
        inc(t:REAL) is
            -- increments count and adds t to secs
        do
            count := count+1;
            secs := secs + t
        end -- inc
        average_time :REAL is
            -- returns average time
        do
            Result := secs / count;
        end -- average_time

end -- SIM_STATS
```

*Example 5.13 Class designed to store simulation statistics*

The next stage would be to create a class SIM_GLOBALS as shown below. Class CUSTOMER, and any other class in the simulation that needed access to the stats would simply inherit SIM_GLOBALS.

```
class SIM_GLOBALS
    feature
        stats: SIM_STATS is
        once
            !!Result
        end -- stats

end -- SIM_GLOBALS
```

*Example 5.14 Once routine, providing shared copy of SIM_STATS*

Examples of the use of once routines to provide global variables are given in the second case study in chapter 14.

The use of once routines needs to be treated with caution. A shared object is inherently less secure. Even in the case of *io* the programmer may find unanticipated results: the attributes used to store the state of *io* will be altered by any call to an input routine, and if any of its instance variables are referred to after a delay, then the results may well be affected by calls made from other objects in the intervening time.


## 5.7 External routines
(Readers are advised to skip this on a first reading)

Eiffel is a high-level programming language, but sometimes it is necessary to access low-level, system-dependent routines, and sometimes it is beneficial to be able to reuse existing well-tried code written in another language. To support this, Eiffel provides external routines, which may be used to call C routines. An external routine will have a form as shown in example 5.15.

The alias is optional, and is used to provide the actual name of the C routine. C routines may begin with an underscore as shown in example 5.15. Detailed coverage of external routines is beyond the scope of this text, and the programmer who wishes to use such routines will need to consult the installation manual for more information.

```
any_routine( arg1: INTEGER; arg2:REAL) is

external
     "C"

     alias "_c1"
end -- any_routine
```

*Example 5.15 An external routine*

This completes the coverage of routines, apart from preconditions, post-conditions and the rescue instruction, which are covered in chapter 8.


## *Exercises*

1. Rework exercise 2 in chapter 4 to provide the following routine:

   *month_as_string(month:INTEGER):STRING*

2. If the following routines are not available in the class library

   *greater_than(x,y:INTEGER):INTEGER;* -- returns greater of x ,y

*smaller_than(x,y*:INTEGER):INTEGER;
*abs(x*:INTEGER):INTEGER; -- converts negative x to positive

then write your own, then implement and test them.

3.Fully implement class BANK_ACCOUNT, and class CONTROLLER.
a) BANK_ACCOUNT should contain additional routines to those already given:

*pay_in* (*amount*:REAL)
   -- adds *amount* to *balance*
*is_over_drawn*:BOOLEAN
   -- returns true if *balance* < 0
*can_issue_cash(amount_requested:REAL)*:BOOLEAN
   -- returns true if  *amount_requested* > *amount_available*
*print_details*
   -- outputs full account details to the screen

b) CONTROLLER should have a creation routine, *test,* and should have an attribute of class BANK_ACCOUNT, *account;* the routine *init_account* should be   invoked by *test* to initialise the account; *test* should then perform the following operations on account

     print account details
     change credit limit to 100
     print account details
     add 200 to *account*
     print account details
     withdraw 250 from  *account*
     query *account* to see if 51 can be withdrawn from it
     pay in 1
     query account to see if 51 can be withdrawn from it

4. Work out what the output of the routine *mystery* would be if the following sequence of 10 characters was entered at the keyboard:  "sdrawkcab "

*mystery* **is**
  **local**
    x:CHARACTER;
  **do**
      *io.putstring("enter character>");*
      *io.readchar;*

```
    x := io.lastchar;
    if x /= ' '
    then
            mystery;     --**
            io.putchar(x);   --**
        end -- if
end -- mystery
```

5. Work out the result using the same input as in question 4 if the lines of code marked with --** were reversed so that they read:

```
io.putchar(x);
mystery;
```

# 6 Classes, Objects and Instantiation

Chapters 2 to 5 have introduced the lower level features of the Eiffel language. The reader should now have enough grasp of the language to return to the basic ideas of object-orientation introduced in chapter 1. This chapter explores the relationship between classes and objects, introduces the Eiffel facilities for data hiding, and discusses issues of memory allocation, object copying and object comparison.

## 6.1 Classes and objects

Object-oriented programming may be regarded as simulation or model-building. When software is developed in an object-oriented way, we begin by identifying 'things' in the external world being modelled (a customer, an account, an employee) and also parts of the computer support required to implement the model (e.g. a file, a window, a menu). When the objects to be modelled have been identified, we must then identify which attributes of an object are to be modelled, and also what requests other object will make to that object.

Object-oriented applications consist of collections of interacting objects. Objects interact by sending messages/requests to each other and by responding to those messages/requests. Communication between objects is by invocation of one of the methods or services provided by an object. The response of an object to a message will at run-time be determined both by any inputs which accompany the message, and by the state of the object when it receives the message.

When we talk of object-oriented programming in Eiffel and indeed in most 'object-oriented' languages, we are more accurately talking of 'class oriented' programming. Eiffel allows us to write only classes. There is no such construct for object. An object is an instance of a class dynamically created during the execution of a software system. Any object must belong to a class, even if it is the only member of that class.

A class is, therefore, a template from which objects may be created. The code for a class specifies the data to be held by all instances of a class and also the functionality which will be common to all instances of that class.

Some of these concepts may be illustrated by looking at a simple object, a person called JIM. JIM has a name, JIM, he is 31 years old, he is male, and has an address, 31, Panjim Road, Dona Paula, Goa, India. There is of course much more to JIM than that - height, weight, marital status and so on, but that is enough for the moment. Likewise in our model JIM responds to three messages only:

*increment your age*
*change your address*
*display yourself*

although in real life he does lots of other things, and will not respond sensibly to any of these messages.

Now if we were going to model JIM using Eiffel or indeed most object-oriented languages we have no choice but to create a class, and it would be more sensible to create a class PERSON ,with JIM stored in an attribute (*name*) rather than JIM being the name of the class. In practice our application would be unlikely to require just JIM alone, but might require hundreds, even thousands of people like JIM.

Happily, creating a class PERSON means that we do not need to write a separate piece of code for each: we may create as many instances of the class as we wish. The features of PERSON are shown in figure 6.1.

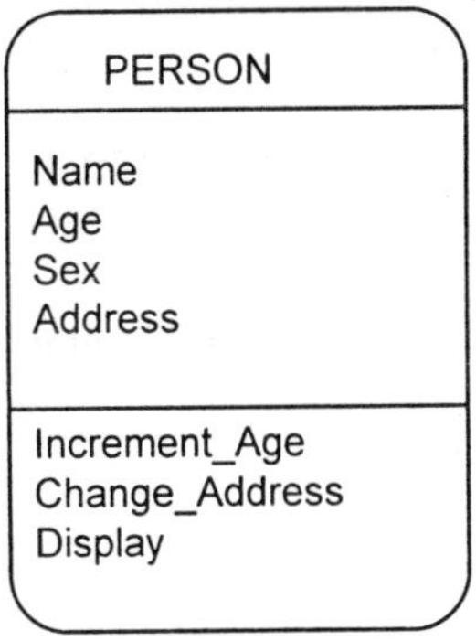

**Figure 6.1**

It may be recalled that the attributes or data are listed in the middle sector of the box, and the services, or messages to which an object of class person will respond, are listed in the lower part of the box.

For each of these messages, PERSON has a method or routine which enables it to respond in a predefined way. Routines can conveniently be divided into three categories: constructors, transformers, accessors. The first two routines above can be described as transformers: they change the state of the recipient. We shall normally need one transformer for each public attribute of an object, but in this case we have not provided one for sex or name. Person cannot be instructed to change sex or to change name. We have assumed that these are immutable. The third message can be described as an accessor. It does not affect the state of a Person, but provides access to each of the state variables. There is no example of a constructor in the above list (but see section 6.6).

The effect of the first message will be determined by person's state. If we tell Person "increment your age" and the current contents of the age variable are 30, then the new state of the age variable will be 31.The effect of the *change your address* message will be dependent solely on the inputs sent with the message:

*change your address to "15, Park Lane, Cheetham Hill, Manchester, U.K."*

The effect of the *display* routine will be dependent on the contents of each statevariable, which will simply be displayed on the screen:

```
Jim Perera      Male      31

15 Park Lane,
Cheetham Hill,
Manchester,
U.K.
```

We can now write Class PERSON in Eiffel (example 6.1). It has eight features: four attributes and four routines. A creation routine, *make*, has been added. This is used when an object is instantiated, to set the unchangeable attributes, *name* and *sex* and to give *age* an initial value.

```
class PERSON
    creation
        make
    feature
        age: INTEGER;
        sex: CHARACTER;
        name: STRING;
        address: STRING;

        change_address(new_address:STRING) is
        do
            address := new_address;
        end -- change_address
        inc_age is
        do
            age := age +1;
        end -- inc_age
        display is
```

```
        do
            io.putstring(name);
            if sex = 'm' or sex = 'M'
                    then io.putstring("Male")
            elseif sex ='f' or sex = 'F'
                    then io.putstring("Female")
            end -- if
            io.putint(age);
            io.new_line;
            io.putstring(address);
            io.new_line;
        end -- display
        make(p_name:STRING;m_or_f:CHARACTER;
                p_age:INTEGER) is
        do
            name := p_name;
            age := p_age;
            sex := m_or_f;
        end -- make
end -- PERSON
```

*Example 6.1 Encapsulation of person in an Eiffel class*

We can now show how, in a client class, objects of class PERSON could be declared and created.

## 6.2 Instantiation

The term instantation means *to create an instance of a class*; this is the process by which objects are allocated memory. In Eiffel, unless we specify otherwise, any class that we write will be a reference type. This means that instances must be created dynamically, at run-time. Thus the declaration

  *p1*:PERSON

simply produces a reference or pointer, with an initial default value *Void*.

In example 6.2, three attributes of class PERSON are declared, but until they are created dynamically they do not exist: they have no data and they can respond to no messages. It should be pointed out that a compiler will not detect whether or not an object has been created. An attempt to invoke a call on an entity which has the default value *Void* will therefore result in a run-time error.

```
    class CONTROLLER
        creation
            test
        feature
            p1, p2, p3 : PERSON;

            test is
            do
                !!p1.make("Jim Perera", 'M',31);
                !!p2.make("Anne Jones", 'F',27);
                !!p3.make("Robert Bruce", 'M',56);
                .....
            end -- test
    end -- CONTROLLER
```

*Example 6.2 Creation instructions*

Before any messages can be sent to *p1* for example, it must first have memory allocated to it. This is done by the creation instruction, which in the case of *p1*, whose class has a creation routine, *make*, specified, is of the form

*!!p1.make((... )*

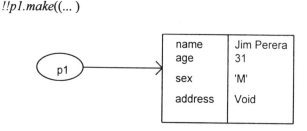

| name | Jim Perera |
| age | 31 |
| sex | 'M' |
| address | Void |

**Figure 6.2**

The effect of this is to allocate memory, and to initialise all fields of the new instance with either default values, or values set in the creation procedure, as shown in figure 6.2.

It should be noted that address has the value *Void*, which is the default value of all reference types.

## 6.3 Object destruction

In C++ the programmer is responsible for managing memory, and therefore must take care of memory deallocation as well as allocation. In Eiffel, as in Smalltalk, no explicit deallocation of memory is required. It is perfectly acceptable for example to make assignments such as the following:

*p2:= p1;*
*p1 := void*

without having to make any provision for deallocating the memory to which either *p2* or *p1* was previously attached.

All Eiffel run-time systems include a garbage collector, which keeps a track of memory that is no longer required, and reallocates it when necessary. So that in the case shown in figure 6.3, the memory containing "Anne Jones", to which *p2* was previously pointing, would be a candidate for reclamation by the garbage collector, provided that no other attribute of any object in the system was attached to it.

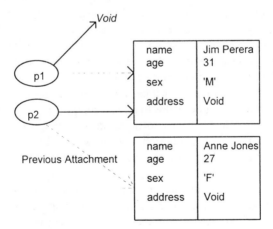

**Figure 6.3**

The final section of the chapter returns to the issue of pointer semantics when it covers equality and copying.

## 6.4   Data abstraction and feature visibility

The concept of data abstraction is fundamental to object-oriented programming. Classes are abstract entities which should hide implementation details from potential users. A well written class should have a simple interface:

>   not too many public features;

>   public routines should have few arguments.

In order to provide this abstract view of a class, we need to hide information - to be able to provide a private and a public view. In some languages it is necessary to write a class interface and a class implementation. One of the problems with this is that when a change is made to the interface, it must also be made to the implementation; this can be very time consuming. Eiffel makes no such distinction; a single text defines a class, and a tool is used to produce a **short**, external view of the class. This means that implementation details and private features of a class are filtered out by the tool, and the user can view the class abstractly. It also means that any change has to be entered once only.

The concept of visibility is similar to the concept of scope which is commonly used in block structured languages such as Pascal to describe the contexts in which an identifier will be recognised by a compiler. The scope or visibility of a global variable is unrestricted. Its contents may therefore be accessed freely within a software system. Global variables stand at the opposite pole to information hiding, and their use has long been discouraged in the OO community. Eiffel in fact does not allow a programmer to define global variables, although Smalltalk does. It is possible however to use once routines to provide shared instances of a class (see chapter 5).

Even outside the OO community it has long been recognised that control over the scope or visibility of names helps to reduce complexity in software systems - it reduces the dependence between software units, helping to produce software units which exhibit that 'high cohesion' and 'loose coupling' which is a feature of quality software development, and which is perhaps more easily attainable using object-oriented methods.

So far as feature visibility is concerned, the most important issue is the visibility of attributes outside the class in which they are declared. All object-oriented languages provide some mechanisms to control their visibility. In Smalltalk instance variables (attributes) are not visible outside their class, and cannot therefore be read or updated from outside. In C++ there are facilities for defining public, protected and private fields within a class, although it is still possible to have read-write access from outside the class in which the field has been declared.

The default in Eiffel is for all class features to be public. This affords limited protection in that it is not possible for a client to alter the state of any attribute by assignment. Assuming declarations in a client class of

*p1, p2, p3* : PERSON

The compiler would not allow us to write

*p1.name := p2.name;*
*p1.age := 17;*

because the attributes of an Eiffel class are considered read-only for clients. It would however be possible to write the following

*p1.name.copy(p2.name)*

which would achieve the same purpose as *p1.name := p2.name*.

It is possible within Eiffel to provide protection for data by making features private, or by limiting access to specified client classes. This facility is achieved by specifying access in the feature clause:

| | |
|---|---|
| **feature** | -- features are public |
| **feature** {NONE} | -- features are private |
| **feature** {} | -- features are private |
| **feature**{A} | -- features available to class *A* only |
| **feature** {A,B} | -- features available to classes *A,B* only |

Class PERSON, shown in example 6.3 with additional features to those previously defined, shows how the features of an Eiffel class may be restricted.

```
class PERSON
      creation
            make
      feature EMPLOYER,BANK}
            salary: REAL;
            change_salary(p_salary:REAL) is
            do
                  salary := p_salary;
            end -- change_salary
```

```
feature {BANK}
        overdraft_limit:REAL;
        change_overdraft(p_overdraft:REAL) is
        do
                overdraft_limit := p_overdraft;
        end -- change overdraft
feature {}
        net_assets : REAL;
        change_assets(p_assets:REAL) is
        do
                net_assets := p_assets;
        end -- change_assets
        inc_age is
        do
                age := age +1;
        end -- inc_age
feature
        sex: CHARACTER;
        name: STRING;
        address: STRING;
        age:INTEGER;
        change_address(new_address:STRING) is
        do
                address := new_address;
        end -- change_address
        make(p_name:STRING;
                m_or_f :CHARACTER;
                p_age:INTEGER) is
        do
                name := p_name;
                age := p_age;
                sex := m_or_f;
        end -- make
end -- PERSON
```

*Example 6.3 Restrictions on export of features*

Instances of class BANK have read-only access to the attributes *salary, name, sex, address* and *age*, may call the routines *make, change_salary, change_overdraft* and *change_address,* and so may both read and alter the contents of *salary, address*, and *overdraft_limit*.

For completeness it should be pointed out that it is quite common for a class to be a client of itself, and this can cause unanticipated problems when restrictions are placed on the visibility of a feature. A class may become a client of itself whenever one or more of the following occurs:

it contains an attribute or local entity of its own class
it contains a function which returns a result of its own class
it contains a routine which has a formal argument of its own class

As an example we might consider the addition to class PERSON of a routine

    *is_older(p*:PERSON*)*:BOOLEAN

which returns *true* if *Current* is older than the argument *p*. In this case PERSON is now a client of itself. Likewise we might add the routine shown in example 6.4 which is designed to return *true* if *Current* is richer than *p*.

---

    *is_richer(p*:PERSON*)*:BOOLEAN **is**
  **do**
    *Result := Current.net_assets > p.net_assets*
  **end** -- is_richer

    *Example 6.4 Class PERSON as client of itself*

---

In this case the routine would not compile because of the restrictions on the visibility of *net_assets* (see example 6.3). The compiler would not allow the feature call *p.net_assets,* but would allow the self reference to *net_assets.*


### 6.5 Issues of assignment and equality

These issues can be quite difficult at the beginning, and the reader might chose to come back to this section at a later stage. These are important issues however, and unless understood will sooner rather than later lead to unanticipated results.

As indicated earlier, Eiffel provides the standard Pascal-like equality and assignment operators. It should be borne in mind. however, that for objects of reference types, assignment is actually pointer assignment, and equality is pointer equivalence. The effect of a statement *p1 := p2* is as shown in figure 6.4.

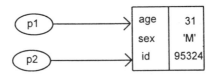

**Figure 6.4**

As a result of pointer assignment, *p1* and *p2* point to the same area of memory. Also the equality operation *p1* = *p2* yields true. Now consider the case shown below: each field contains identical information, and *p1* and *p2* are therefore structurally equivalent. Since they are separate objects however (see figure 6.5), the boolean expression, *p1* = *p2* would yield false.

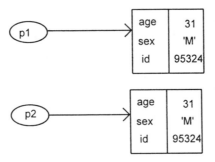

**Figure 6.5**

In order to test structural equivalence as opposed to pointer equivalence, Eiffel provides two routines in class GENERAL that allow objects to be compared :

> *is_equal*(*other*:**like** *Current*):BOOLEAN;
> *equal*(*some*:ANY;*other*:**like** *some*):BOOLEAN;

so that

> *p1.is_equal(p2)*

and

> *equal(p1,p2)*

would both yield *true* in the above case.

Unfortunately, comparing objects is still more complex than the above example indicates. If any of the objects' attributes are themselves of a reference type, then *is_equal* and *equal* will simply compare the addresses to which the attributes point, and will yield *true* only if they point to the same address, as figure 6 illustrates. Here the problem is that one of the attributes is itself a reference type, and although the value of *name* is, in each case, 'Jim Perera', the address of each will differ. The routines *is_equal* and *equal* will not do a deep comparison of two structures, but will compare only the first level of each structure. So whereas *p1.name.is_equal(p2.name)* yields *true*, what is critical is that *p1.name = p2.name* yields *false*, and therefore *p1.is_equal(p2)* yields *false*.

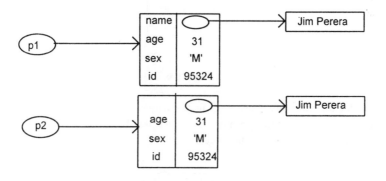

**Figure 6.6**

To do a recursive comparison of classes, the following routines must be used:

> *is_deep_equal(other:**like** Current)*:BOOLEAN.
> *deep_equal(some:ANY;other:**like** some)*:BOOLEAN.

These functions will expand all the references and so do a field by field structural comparison, so that

> *p1.is_deep_equal(p2)*

would yield *true*.

There are similar difficulties with *copy*. So for example *p1.copy(p2)* would produce two objects which each shared another object of type STRING; so that the condition *p1.name = p2*.name would yield true, and *p1.is_equal(p2)* would also yield *true*, as shown in figure 6.7.

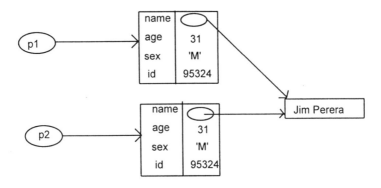

**Figure 6.7**

In order to avoid any sharing of memory there is a *deep_copy* so that the call *p1.deep_copy(p2)* would produce two completely separate objects, each of which contained the same data values.

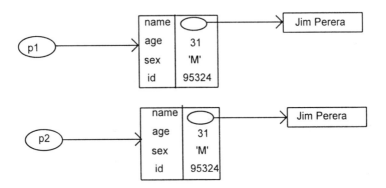

**Figure 6.8**

In the case shown in figure 6.8 the following would yield *true*:

> *p1.is_deep_equal(p2);*
> *deep_equal(p1,p2)*
> *p1.name.is_equal(p2.name)*

but the following would yield *false*:

*p1.is_equal(p2);*
*equal(p1,p2);*
*p1=p2*
*p1.name = p2.name*

## 6.6 Cloning objects

In order to copy one object to another, the target must already have been instantiated: a call may not be made to a target that does not exist. Eiffel provides routines in class ANY which enable us to avoid this problem, and to combine the actions of creation and copying in one operation:

*clone(other:*ANY): **like** *other*;
*deep_clone(other:*ANY): **like** *other*;

*Clone* and *deep_clone* are functions which return new objects which are copies/deep_copies of the object passed in as an argument. They are normally used on the right hand of assignment statements, e.g.

*p1 := clone(p2);*

and in such cases the target of the assignment may be *void*. These functions may also be used as arguments to other routines. For example the following

*any_target.any_routine(clone(an_obj))*

would ensure that *an_obj* was unaffected by any action performed internally by *any_routine*, since what was being passed in would be a copy of *an_obj*, rather than *an_obj* itself. The use of *deep_clone* would of course be even safer.

## Exercises

1. Examine the example in 6.3 and work out the following:

a) Which attributes of Class PERSON cannot be read by any client class?
b) Which attributes of Class Person cannot be altered by any Client class?
c) Which attributes does employer have read only access to?
d) Which attributes is class employer able to alter?

2. a) Look in class GENERAL at the routines available for comparing, copying and cloning objects. Make notes on the difference between the deep and the shallow versions of these;

b) *Clone* is a constructor; *copy* is a transformer; explain the difference between a *constructor* and a *transformer*;

c) Implement classes PERSON and CONTROLLER. Declare and create two instances of PERSON. Assign the same data to each, and investigate the results of using: =, *is_equal, is_deep_equal, copy,* and *deep_copy.*

# 7 Classes STRING and ARRAY

Strings and arrays are fundamental to programming. In Eiffel they are not a part of the languages, but are provided in class libraries. There are some differences between the libraries for STRING and ARRAY produced by different vendors, but fortunately there is a great deal of standardisation. The author has moved relatively freely between ISE Eiffel and Eiffel/S in preparing this chapter.

## 7.1 Class STRING

Strings have already been briefly introduced in chapter 2, where it was shown how strings could be written in a class source, how attributes and constants could be declared, how assignments could be made, and how strings could be output to the screen. Treatment of strings in this chapter begins with comparison of strings, then considers problems of assignment, and concludes by looking at other string handling facilities. In order to take full advantage of the facilities available for string handling the reader is encouraged to study the class listing.

## 7.2 String comparison

Strings are ordered: class STRING inherits from class COMPARABLE, and the standard relational operators which are defined there are available:

>     >=     <     <=

The following expressions yield the boolean values indicated:

```
"Smith" < "Simon"      -- false
"Smith" >= "Smith"     -- true
"Simon" < "Smith"      -- true
"Robert" <= "Smith"    -- true
```

The test for equality follows the same rules as those for other reference classes. The = operator yields *true* only if the two strings being compared are actually the same string. In the case shown in figure 7.1, in which the entities *a_string* and *b_string* are attached to the same object *a_string* = *b_string* would yield true.

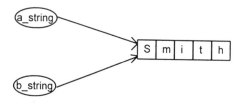

**Figure 7.1**

In the next case, shown in figure 7.2, the expression *a_string = b_string* would yield *false*.

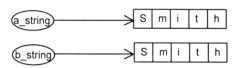

**Figure 7.2**

When testing two strings for equality therefore, it is necessary to use the *is_equal* routine, inherited from ANY and redefined for class STRING. The boolean expression

    *a_string.is_equal(b_string)*

would yield *true* in both the cases shown above.


## 7.3 String creation and assignment

As for other reference types, memory is dynamically allocated for instances of class STRING. It is also possible however, to do this at compile time by declaring its contents in an assignment instruction:

    *c_string := "Patel"*

Unless this is done, the default value for a string is *Void*. To create a string at run-time, a creation instruction is used with the creation routine *make*:

    *!!a_string.make(10);*
    *!!b_string.make(6)*

This would create two strings, the first with the capacity to hold 10 characters, the second with the capacity to hold 6. Each string would be filled with blanks. Despite the requirement to set the capacity initially, a string is automatically resized if it requires more space.

If after creation, either a_*string* or b_*string* were to be used as the left hand of an assignment then the blank object created would be lost, and the strings would be pointing to a new object. So for example the result of

a_string := c_string

would be as shown in figure 7.3.

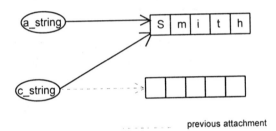

**Figure 7.3**

Since STRING is a reference type, a_*string* would now be pointing to the same object as the entity on the right-hand side of the assignment statement. The object to which it was previously attached would now be lost.

If we wished to attach a_*string* to a separate object containing the same characters as c_*string* then there are two alternatives available:

a_string := clone(c_string);
a_string.copy(c_string);

It may be remembered that the routine *clone* is a constructor defined in class GENERAL, and available to instances of all classes. It creates a new instance, which contains a copy of its argument. The routine *copy* is a transformer routine, redefined for class STRING, which copies its argument to the target of the call. In the case of *clone*, the target of the assignment may be *void*; in the case of *copy*, the target of the call must not be *void*, otherwise a run-time error will occur.

## 7.4 String manipulation

This section provides a brief guide to the operations available in class STRING. There are a number of useful transformer operations that may be performed on instances of class STRING.

| Class STRING: | Transformer Routines |
|---|---|
| *append* | -- places a string after target string |
| *prepend* | -- places a string before target string |
| *precede* | -- places a character before target string |
| *extend* | -- places a character after target string |
| *put* | -- places a character at *i*-th position |
| *fill_blank* | -- fills target string with blanks |
| *head* | -- removes all but first *n* characters |
| *tail* | -- removes all but last *n* characters |
| *left_adjust* | -- removes leading blanks from target string |
| *right_adjust* | -- removes trailing blanks from target |
| *remove* | -- removes *i*-th character from target |
| *remove_all_occurrences* | |
| | -- removes all occurrences of a specified character |
| *to_lower* | -- converts target to lower case |
| *to_upper* | -- converts target to upper_case |

There is also a constructor routine, *substring*, which returns a copy of all the characters between *n1* and *n2*. For example, if *c_string* was attached to an string object containing the letters "anabolic steroids", then

> *io.putstring(c_string.substring(6,10))*

would display on the screen:

> lic s

and

> *c_string :=c_string.substring(10,17))*

would attach *c_string* to an object containing "steroids". It would also be possible to have a chain of calls to *substring* as follows:

> *io.put_string(c_string.substring(3,10).substring(3,6).substring(2,4));*

which, given the original attachment,"anabolic steroids" would display on the screen the three letters: lic

There are also features which may be used to query the state of a string:

> *count*   -- returns actual number of characters in a string
> *empty*   -- returns true if count = 0

So that *io.putint(c_string.count)* would display 17 on the screen.

This brief treatment of class STRING concludes with a solution to the following problem:

A text analyser wishes to be able to analyse the occurrence of pairs of characters in a string - for example the character pair "an" occurs four times in the following string:

"Smalltalk is an object-oriented language and so are CLOS, Self and Actors "

Note that "an" "AN" "An" "aN" are considered equal. So we must either convert both arguments to upper, or both to lower case. If this is not done then when we compare characters of different case, e.g. "A" and "a" they will not be interpreted as being equal.

In the solution given below both arguments have been cloned. Had this not been done, tthen the instructions

> *a_string.lower*
> *a_string.upper*

which change each of the arguments to lower case, would have changed the strings in the caller, with possible undesirable consequences. It is necessary to change the strings either to lower or to upper case for reasons already given. Once this has been done, the algorithm uses a loop which begins at the first character in the string *s*, and compares it and its successor character with *character_pair*. If they are equal then it increments *Result*. This process continues until the counter *i* is equal to the size of the string *s*, at which point the loop terminates and the value in *Result* is passed back to the caller.

```
occurs(a_string:STRING; character_pair:STRING)
                    :INTEGER is
    local
            i:INTEGER;
            s,c:STRING
    do
            s := clone(a_string); -- copies arguments to avoid side effects
            c := clone(character_pair);
```

```
    c.to_lower;            -- transforms to lower case
    s.to_lower;
    from i = 1
    until i = a_string.count
    loop
        if s.substring(i,i+1).is_equal(c)
            then Result := Result + 1
        end -- if
        i := i + 1;
    end -- loop
end -- occurs
```

*Example 7.1 Routine which counts character pairs in a string*

The reader may try this by inserting it in an existing root class such as SIMPLE. The routine could then be called as follows:

*io.putint(occurs("Smalltalk is an object-oriented language*
*and so are CLOS, Self and Actors","an"));*

which should output the integer 4.


## 7.5  Class ARRAY

Facilities for handling arrays are provided by class ARRAY which is part of the basic cluster of classes. As with STRING there are some differences between implementations, but the basic facilities provided for insertion and accessing arrays are fairly standard.

An array is best viewed as a variable capable of holding a sequence of values of the same type, often described as its *element type*. Its advantage as a data structure is the speed of retrieval and insertion made possible by an index or subscript which contains the relative address of the element being accessed. For example if an array begins at address 10000, and each element takes 2 words of memory, then the absolute address of the 20th element in the array is readily calculated as 10038.

An array of Integers, I, which holds 7 values is shown in figure 7.4.

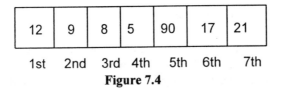

**Figure 7.4**

If we wished to reference the 5th element we would, depending on the program language, refer to it as

I(5) or I[5],

because a standard keyboard does not allow us to write

$I_5$.

In order to use an array in Eiffel, a class must either inherit from or be a client of class ARRAY. This chapter deals only with the client relationship. ARRAY is the first **generic** class that we have covered so far; this is denoted by its heading:

**class** ARRAY[G]

The [G] is a formal parameter, and indicates that we can instantiate an array with any class as the actual parameter - we can have an array of INTEGER, REAL, PERSON and so on (see chapter 10 for further discussion of genericity). Such arrays could be declared as shown below:

**feature**
   *names* :ARRAY[STRING];
   *employees* : ARRAY[PERSON]
   *sensor_readings*: ARRAY[REAL];


**7.6 Array creation**

Before any operations may be performed on an array, it must first be allocated memory using a creation instruction. For class ARRAY a creation routine is defined as shown below:

*make( minindex:INTEGER; maxindex:INTEGER)*;

An instruction such as

*!!employees.make(1,100)*

would allocate memory for 100 instances of class PERSON. It should be noted that we do not have to use 1 as the minimum index. It could, for example, have been set to 0, and the maximum index to 99; one or both could have been set to negative integers. We must of course ensure that the second argument is not smaller than the first. The minimum size of an array is 1.

Amongst the other features of class ARRAY which are available are those which provide information about its size:

| | |
|---|---|
| *count* | -- returns the length of the index interval; |
| *lower* | -- returns the lower index bound |
| *upper* | -- returns the upper index bound |

Given our initial creation instruction, *lower* would return 1, *upper* would return 100, and *count* would return 100. If we used different arguments with *make*, e.g. *!!employees.make(-5,20)*, as shown in figure 7.5.

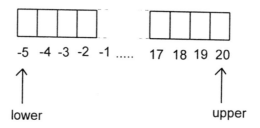

**Figure 7.5**

*lower* would now return -5, *upper* would return 20, and *count* would return 26, (*upper* + 1 -*lower*).

## 7.7 Array insertion and retrieval

As indicated already, basic array operations involve direct insertion and retrieval of elements. To insert an element in an array in Eiffel we may use the routine *put,* and to retrieve an element we may use the routine *item,* or its infix form "@" :

*put ( element : G; index : INTEGER)*;
**infix** *"@"* , *item (index :INTEGER) : G;*

*Put* requires two arguments, the element to be inserted, and the index position at which it is to be inserted. *Item* returns a result of whatever type the array contains; it requires a single argument, the index position of the element to be retrieved.

We may illustrate the use of these routines with the array of integers shown earlier, which we would declare in Eiffel as follows:

I:ARRAY[INTEGER]

To access the 5th location we would write the following

*I.item(5)*

or, using the infix form:

*I @ 5*

To insert the value 3 at the 6th position , and the value 99 at the 7th position we would write the instructions

*I.put(3,6);*
*I.put(99,7)*

Our array would now be updated as shown in figure 7.6.

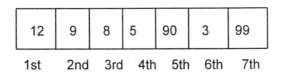

| 12 | 9 | 8 | 5 | 90 | 3 | 99 |
|----|---|---|---|----|---|----|
| 1st | 2nd | 3rd | 4th | 5th | 6th | 7th |

**Figure 7.6**

The values 17 and 21, which were previously stored at the 6th and 7th positions would, as indicated, have been replaced by the values 3 and 99.

We may now look at the root class ARRAY_EXAMPLE defined in example 7.2. This class contains an array of INTEGER, *store*. It contains three routines: the creation routine *start*, a routine which fills the array with elements entered at the keyboard, and a routine which prints them out in order.The reader should note the use of *upper* and *lower*. It is sensible to use this rather than the integers 1 and 7: if the size of the array was changed, no other change would be required to any instruction other than the creation instruction.

The reader should note the use of the routine *put* to insert an element in the array, and of *item* to retrieve it. In the case of each loop used, *index* has been set to *lower −1*, and the exit point defined as *upper*. Had *index* been initially set to *lower*, then the exit point would be > *upper*, and the instruction which increments *index* would need to be placed at the end of the loop.

```
class ARRAY_EXAMPLE
    creation
        start
    feature
        store:ARRAY[INTEGER];

    fill_array is
        -- fills array with integers entered from keyboard
        local
            index:INTEGER;
        do
            from index = store.lower -1
            until index = store.upper
            loop
                index := index + 1;
                io.readint;
                store.put(io.lastint,index);
            end -- loop
        end -- fill_array
    print_array is
        -- displays contents of array on screen
        local
            index:INTEGER;
        do
            from index := store.lower − 1
            until index = store.upper
            loop
                index := index + 1;
                io.putint(store.item(index));
            end -- loop
        end -- print_array
    start is
        do
            !!store.make(1,7);
            fill_array;
```

> *print_array;*
> **end** -- star t
> **end** -- ARRAY-EXAMPLE
>
> *Example 7.2 Arrays:insertion and retrieval*

Should the reader wish to use this with STRING, then fill_array should be amended as follows: *clone* should be used to insert a copy of *io.last_string.*

## 7.8 Dynamic array operations

Although the creation routine requires an array's size to be specified, it is possible to make the array grow during program execution. This may be done either by explicit resizing, or by using the routine, *force*, which automatically resizes the array if it is necessary.

The routine, *resize*, allows us to alter the size of an array by specifying new upper and lower indices. For example

   *store.resize(0 ,15)*

would set new *upper* and *lower* indices with the results indicated:

   *store.count* -- would now return 16
   *store.lower* -- would now return 0
   *store.upper* -- would now return 15

The feature *force* which may be used instead of *put* to insert items in the array has the effect of automatically resizing the array if the specified index falls outside the current bounds. So that if we have an array with 7 elements, as previously specified, and we make the call

   *I.force(2,8)*

then the array would automatically be resized to allow the value 2 to be inserted at the 8th position.

## 7. 9 Sorting an array

This section provides an example of the use of Eiffel array handling facilities to sort an array.

```
class ARRAY_EXAMPLE;
    creation
        start
    feature
        store:ARRAY[INTEGER];
        -- fill_array
        -- print_array

        sort_array is
            -- sorts array in ascending order
            local
                sorted:BOOLEAN;
                temp_item: INTEGER
                index, last :INTEGER;
        do
            from
                last := store.upper ;
                sorted := false;
            until sorted or else last = store.lower
            loop
                from
                    sorted := true
                    index := store.lower -1
                    last := last-1
                until
                    index = last
                loop
                    index := index + 1;
                    if store.item(index) > store.item(index+1)
                    then
                        -- swap element with successor element
                        temp_item := store.item(index+1);
                        store.put(store.item(index),index+1);
                        store.put(temp_item,index);
                        sorted := false;
                    end -- if
                end -- loop
            end -- loop
        end -- sort_array
        start is
        do
```

```
    ↘!!store.make(1,7);
    fill_array;
    sort_array;
    print_array;
end -- start
end -- ARRAY-EXAMPLE
```

*Example 7.3 Sorting an array*

The *sort_array* routine (example 7.3) has one loop nested within the other. The inner loop does the work: it checks that each element is smaller than its successor, and if not it swaps them. The effect of one iteration of the inner loop is to guarantee that the largest element is in the last position. Once this is done, *last* is then decremented by the outer loop, and the process starts again. It continues until either the inner loop makes a complete pass without finding any element out of order, or until *last* becomes equal to *store.lower*. The use of *upper* and *lower* has the advantage that it allows us to sort an array of integer of any size. We should, however, only get the full benefit of using an object-oriented language if we could write it so that it could sort arrays of any ordered type (any type which inherits from class COMPARABLE) including types STRING and CHARACTER. This could be done by rewriting the routine header, and making *store* a formal argument instead of a feature, as shown in example 7.4.

```
class SORT_ROUTINES
    feature
        sort_array (store:ARRAY[COMPARABLE]) is
            local
                temp_item:COMPARABLE;
            --------
                -- sorts array in ascending order
                -- remainder of code unchanged - see example 7.3

    end -- sort_routines
```

*Example 7.4 Header for a reusable sort routine*

The major change required is that of the first line, as indicated above. The new formal argument declaration requires an array as the actual argument; the element type of the array must be a class which inherits from class

COMPARABLE. Also the local variable, *temp_item,* would need to be declared as

*temp_item*:COMPARABLE

to allow elements of any type to be assigned to it during the swap operation. The routine has been placed in a separate class, SORT_ROUTINES, and could be declared and used in a client class as shown in 7.5. It could of course also be inherited.

```
class ANY_CLASS
    feature
        s:ARRAY[STRING];
        sorter: SORT_ROUTINES;

        any_routine is
        do
            !!sorter;
            sorter.array_sort(s);
        end -- any_routine
    end -- ANY_CLASS
```

*Example 7.5 Calling reusable sort routine*

A better solution to this problem is given in chapter 10, which shows how a generic class, SORTABLE_ARRAY, could be constructed.


## 7.10  Manifest arrays

In the same way that it is sometimes useful to be able to initialise a string at compile time, so it may also be useful to be able to describe an array by listing its contents. Eiffel allows us to do this by declaring a *manifest array*. The original integer array given in figure 7.4 could have been initialised as follows:

$I :=$    <<  12,  9,  8,  5,  90,  17,  21  >>

This is certainly simpler than the sequence of calls which would otherwise be necessary.

*!!I.make(1,7);*

*l.put(12,1);*
*l.put(9,2);*
*l.put(21,7);*

It is also possible to use a manifest array as an actual argument to a routine. Given for example a routine defined as

*print_array(a:ARRAY[INTEGER])*

it would be permissible to write the actual call as

*print_array( << 12, 9, 8, 5, 90, 17, 21 >>)*


## 7.11 Matrices and *n*-dimensional arrays

So far this chapter has covered single dimension arrays. Frequently, however, we need an array with two or more dimensions. In some cases a two-dimensional array may be included in an Eiffel class library, but if not it would be relatively simple to construct. We shall begin by showing how in Eiffel we can declare and manipulate a matrix such as that shown in figure 7.7, using the facilities provided by class ARRAY.

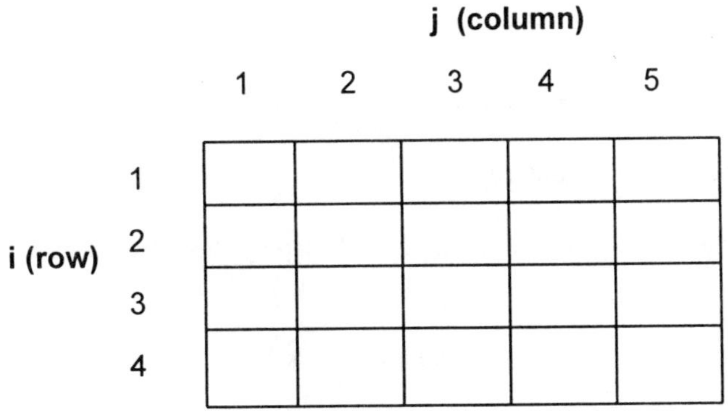

**Figure 7.7**

The Eiffel declaration would be written as follows:

*matrix* :ARRAY[ARRAY[INTEGER]]

It is therefore an array of array of integer, as shown in figure 7.8. It is therefore also an array of references, each of which points to an array of integers.

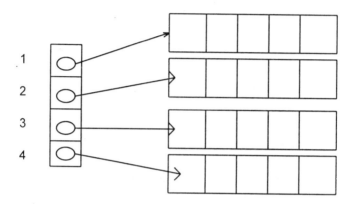

**Figure 7.8**

To store an item 10 in position 4,3 therefore we first have to retrieve the 4th array, and then to place the item in the third position:

*matrix.item(4).put(10,3)*

To put the element 15 at row 3 column 5 we would similarly write

*matrix.item(3).put(15,5)*

and to write an instruction which would display the element at 1,3 we would write

*io.putint(matrix.item(1).item(3))*

It should be noted that as with one dimensional arrays, the declaration tells the compiler nothing about the size of the array. This is done when it is created at run-time. To create *matrix* it is necessary to allocate memory for the array of arrays, and then for each of the four arrays of INTEGER.

It would be sensible to use constants to define the number of rows and number of columns, and to use a loop to allocate memory to each row, as shown in example 7.6. This would make modification easier should we later require a matrix with different dimensions.

```
class MATRIX_EXAMPLE
    creation
        make
    feature
        matrix :ARRAY[ARRAY[INTEGER]];
        rows: INTEGER is 4;
        columns: INTEGER is 5;

        make is
            local
                index:INTEGER;
                temp: ARRAY[INTEGER]
        do
            !!matrix.make(1,rows);
            from index := 0
            until index = rows
            loop
                index := index + 1;
                !!temp.make(1,columns);
                -- this ensures that a different array is
                -- created each iteration
                matrix.put(temp,index);
            end -- loop
        end -- make
end -- MATRIX_EXAMPLE
```

*Example 7.6 Creating an array of array*

It should be noted that *make* uses a local one-dimensional array, *temp*, and that memory is allocated to this on each iteration of the loop; unless new memory is allocated each time, the underlying memory allocation would be as shown in figure 7.9.

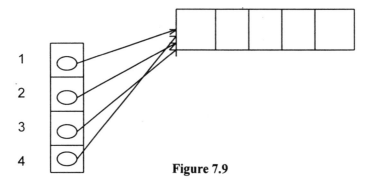

**Figure 7.9**

To perform searches or sequential retrieval of the elements in our two-dimensional array we should need to use nested loops, as shown in the print routine defined below.

```
class MATRIX_EXAMPLE
    creation
        make
    feature
        -- matrix and make as before
        print_matrix is
            local
                row_index,col_index :INTEGER;
        do
            from row_index := 0
            until row_index = rows
            loop
                row_index := row_index + 1;
                from col_index := 0
                until col_index = columns
                loop
                    col_index := col_index + 1;
                    io.putint(matrix.item(row_index).item(col_index));
                end -- loop
                io.new_line
            end -- loop
        end -- print_matrix
end -- MATRIX_EXAMPLE
```

*Example 7.7 Traversing a two-dimensional array*

It is possible to create arrays with greater than two dimensions. For example we might think of a data structure which is used by a retailing company to keep the daily sales details of each department within each of its stores. The company has 120 stores, and each store has 10 departments. We will assume that each store opens 52 weeks in a year and 6 days in a week. When it is not open the value 0 will be inserted as its sales figure. The data structure will be used to calculate responses to queries such as:

> *which was the best store in week 6?*
> *which hardware department did best in week 6?*
> *which of the 10 departments did best in all stores in weeks 5 to 10?*
> *what were the total sales of a given store for the whole year*
> *what were the total sales for all stores in week 52?*

To store the information we need a four-dimensional array. The dimensions of the array are:

52 weeks  X  6 Days  X  120 stores  X  10 departments

This gives a total of 374400 cells , each of which contains a real number.

| Week | Day | Store | Department | |
|------|-----|-------|------------|--------|
| 1 | 1 | 1 | 1 | 1209.60 |
| 1 | 1 | 1 | 2 | 345.55 |
| 26 | 6 | 120 | 10 | 937.50 |
| 27 | 1 | 1 | 1 | 1012.34 |
| 52 | 6 | 120 | 9 | 800.23 |
| 52 | 6 | 120 | 10 | 763.25 |

**Figure 7.10**

From figure 7.10 it can be deduced that the first item in the array will be the sales total for department 1 in store 1 on day 1 of week 1, namely 1209.60. The next will be the sales for department 2 - same week, day and store - 345.55.The last item in the array will be the figure for department 10 of store 120, on day 6 of week 52 - 763.25.

To implement this in Eiffel we would declare an array as follows:

*group_sales*: ARRAY[ARRAY[ARRAY[ARRAY[REAL]]]]

To process this would require a nested loop structure which reflects the structure of the array itself. This is shown in the following solution for the creation procedure, and as with the matrix shown earlier in this section, would be true of any process requiring sequential interrogation of the whole array.

```
class STORE_SALES
    creation
        make
    feature
        max_store : INTEGER is 120;
        max_week: INTEGER is 52;
        max_day: INTEGER is 6;
        max_dept: INTEGER is 10;
        group_sales: ARRAY[ARRAY[ARRAY[ARRAY[REAL]]]]

        make is
            local
                dept_sales:ARRAY[Real];
                store_sales:ARRAY[ARRAY[REAL]];
                day_sales:ARRAY[ARRAY[ARRAY[REAL]]];
                week, day, store, department:INTEGER;
        do
            !! group_sales.make(1..max_week);
            from
                week := 0
            until
                week = max_week
            loop
                week := week + 1;
                !!day_sales.make(1,max_day);
                from
                    day := 0
                until
                    day = max_day
```

```
        loop
                day := day + 1;
                !!store_sales.make(1,max_store);
                from
                        store := 0
                until
                        store = max_store
                loop
                        store = store + 1;
                        !!dept_sales.make(1,max_dept);
                end -- store loop
                store_sales.put(dept_sales,store)
        end -- day loop
        day_sales.put(store_sales,day)
    end -- week loop
    group_sales.put(day_sales,week)
  end -- make
end -- STORE_SALES
```

*Example 7.8 Traversing a four-dimensional array*

It should be appreciated from example 7.8 that for every iteration of the outer loop, the day loop iterates 6 times; and for every iteration of the day loop, the store loop iterates 120 times. A representation of the array is given in figure 7.11.

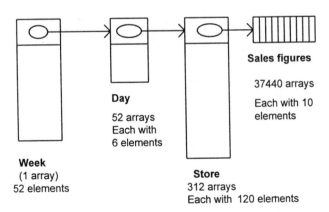

**Sales figures**

37440 arrays

Each with 10 elements

**Day**

52 arrays
Each with
6 elements

**Week**
(1 array)
52 elements

**Store**
312 arrays
Each with 120 elements

**Figure 7.11**

Clearly, this is a very complicated underlying structure. To access the sales return of the 10th department for store 1 on day 2 of week 17 we would write

*group_sales.item(17).item(2).item(1).item(10)*

Normally, we would not wish to create such a complex structure, and if we wished to use an array to store items organized in that way we would usually map them on to a one-dimensional array. This would enable us to access the element we required using more conventional notation, e.g.

*group_sales.item(week,day,store,dept)*

This would be conceptually simpler to understand and implement - and it would also offer greater potential for reuse. This will be further explored in the next section.

## 7.12  Mapping an *n*-dimensional array on to a vector

Multi-dimensional arrays are usually mapped on to the computer's memory in row-major order. For example the elements in a 4 X 5 matrix would normally be mapped as shown in figure 7.12.

| | | |
|---|---|---|
| 0 | | row 1  col 1 |
| 1 | | row 1  col 2 |
| 2 | | row 1  col 3 |
| 3 | | row 1  col 4 |
| | | |
| 18 | | row 4 col 4 |
| 19 | | row 4  col 5 |

**Figure 7.12**

Example 7.9 shows how this could be done in Eiffel, using mapping functions to transform the column and row coordinates into a single subscript .

```
class INTEGER_MATRIX
    creation
            make
    feature
            matrix:ARRAY[INTEGER]
            columns: INTEGER;
            rows:INTEGER;

            put(element :INTEGER; row,col:INTEGER) is
            do
                    matrix.put(element, (row-1)* columns+col-1)
            end -- put
            item(row,col:INTEGER):INTEGER is
            do
                    Result := matrix.item((row-1)*columns+col-1)
            end -- item
            make(n_row,n_col:INTEGER) is
            do
                    !!matrix.make(0, n_row*n_col-1);
                    columns := n_col;
                    rows := n_row;
            end -- make
end --INTEGER_MATRIX
```

*Example7.9 Mapping functions for accessing a matrix*

We can illustrate how this works with a 4 X 5 matrix. A client class which declares an attribute

*integer_store* :INTEGER_MATRIX

would use the creation instruction, *!!integer_store(4,5).make(4,5)*. This would allocate space for a one-dimensional array with a lower bound of 0 and an upper bound of 19. The instruction *!!integer_store.put(17,2,2)* would store 17 in location 5. The mapping function would calculate this as follows: $(2-1) * 4 + 2 -1$. Likewise, the call, *integer_store.item(4,5)*, would access the element at location 19, the upper location in the array. In this case the mapping function would calculate as follows: $(4-1) * 5 + 5 -1$,

This matrix is reusable for any size of integer matrix. To develop a truly reusable matrix, a generic class must be written. Discussion of how to do this is postponed until chapter 10.

### 7.13  Comparing and copying arrays

The routines *copy* and *is_equal* are redefined for class ARRAY to allow arrays of arrays to be copied and compared. This works well as long as the elements stored in the arrays are basic types or other expanded types, but if instances of reference types are stored in the arrays then *copy* will result in each array sharing the same data. In this situation *deep_copy* and *is_deep_equal* should be used.

### *Exercises*

1. a) Write a constructor routine
     *replace_with(old_char,new_char*:CHARACTER; *s*:STRING): STRING
   which returns a string so that, for example,
        *io.putstring(replace_with("a","*","alcoholics anonymous"))*
   would output *"*lcoholics *nonymous"*;
   b) what changes would need to be made to convert the above routine into a transformer? (Assume that the class of which it is a feature, has an attribute, *s*:STRING )

2. Implement ARRAY_EXAMPLE so that it stores and sorts strings.

3. Amend ARRAY_EXAMPLE to allow it to use class SORT_ROUTINES.

4. Given the array of array shown in example 7.6, write Eiffel code which would do the following:

   a) put the value 17 in cell 4, 2;
   b) retrieve the item in cell 3, 6;
   c) retrieve the whole of row 3
   d) replace the existing row 3 with the values, 12, 10, 9, 15, 31
      (Hint, use a temporary variable and a manifest array)

5. Write the following routines for class STORE_SALES:

   a) *best_store(wk*:INTEGER):INTEGER; -- returns best store for *w*
   b) *weekly_sales(wk*:INTEGER):REAL;--returns total sales for *wk*
   c) *daily_sales(wk,day*:INTEGER):REAL;-- returns total for *wk* and day

# 8 Assertions and Software Correctness

Software systems have been beset by errors since the dawn of the computing age. Type checking has enabled a number of potential errors to be eliminated at the compilation stage. There are, however, many other sources of error which a compiler cannot detect, and the more complex the system the harder it is to eliminate all potential errors.

A philosophy which promotes the building of software systems from components ought to reduce the amount of errors. The more tried and tested components are re-used, the more certain that software will perform correctly - provided that we understand how to use those components, and do not push them beyond their limits. This requires an accurate specification of what a component will do, as well as the constraints on its use - a contract between the supplier and the user of the component.

Eiffel is unique among object-oriented languages in that it was designed from the outset to enable a programmer and a system builder to produce a formal contract for a software component. If properly used, an Eiffel class is a formal specification of what an instance of that class will do, and of how it should be used. The language designer has drawn on abstract data type theory and formal approaches to software design to provide Eiffel with a set of facilities for making assertions about the correctness of classes, routines and loops. These can be switched on during the testing stage and can prove an important aid to testing and debugging.

The use of assertions in Eiffel is illustrated with two case studies, one of which has already been introduced. Later sections provide brief introductions to exception handling and debugging facilities.

## 8.1 Preconditions and postconditions

In chapter 5 the syntax of a routine was defined as shown below:

```
<routine_name> [ formal argument list ] [ ":" <result-type> ] is
        [preconditions
        [local declarations]
    do
        compound instruction
        [postconditions]
    end
```

As this syntax indicates, each may have a precondition and a postcondition. These are boolean expressions which are compiled and may be checked at run-time. Preconditions and postconditions derive directly from a view of software development as a contract between the client and the provider of services. A precondition defines the client's responsibility: it stipulates those conditions that must be met at the point when a routine is called. The postcondition is the supplier's part of the contract: it stipulates what will be true on exit from a routine, provided that the preconditions were met on entry. It says nothing about what will happen if preconditions are not met. The supplier is not required to take action to deal with a client's failure to meet preconditions, and indeed is discouraged from doing so. At first sight this may seem odd, but it is a deliberate attempt to break away from 'defensive programming' which can lead to duplication of checking by users and suppliers of routines, to consequent inefficiency, and more importantly perhaps, to confusion as to who is responsible for what.

The syntax for preconditions and postconditions in the Eiffel language may be defined as follows:

Precondition:
**require [else]**
    Assertion_clause {";" Assertion_clause}

Postcondition:
**ensure [then]**
    Assertion_clause {";" Assertion_clause}

An assertion clause may be defined as

[ *Identifier* ] ":" (*Boolean expression* | *Comment*)

Syntax diagrams for each of these are given in figures 8.1 and 8.2.

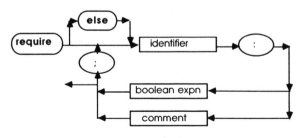

**Figure 8.1**

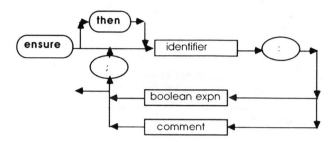

**Figure 8.2**

The optional **else** and **then** relate to the redefinition of inherited features and the effecting of deferred features. These are more advanced topics which are covered in chapters 11 and 12.

A precondition comes immediately after the **is** in the routine declaration, and the postcondition comes in the body of the routine, after the instructions. Example 8.1 returns to class BANK_ACCOUNT, which was first introduced in chapter 5, and which the reader was recommended to develop as an exercise.

```
class BANK_ACCOUNT
    creation
        make
    feature
        id_no: INTEGER;
        balance: REAL;
        credit_limit: REAL;
        name: STRING;

        make(cust:STRING;limit:REAL;id:INTEGER) is
        do
            name := cust;
            credit_limit := limit;
        end -- make
        debit_amount(amount:REAL) is
        do
            balance := balance - amount;
        end -- debit_amount;
        amountt_available: REAL is
        do
            Result := credit_limit + balance;
        end -- amount_available
```

```
change_id(old_no, new_no:INTEGER) is
do
        if old_no = id_no
            then id_no := new_no
        else io.putstring("invalid current id")
        end -- if
    end -- change_id
end -- BANK_ACCOUNT
```

*Example 8.1 Class BANK_ACCOUNT*

The transformer routine, *debit_amount*, may now be amended as shown in example 8.2, by the addition of two preconditions and one postcondition.

The first precondition indicates that the argument, *amount*, must be a non-negative real number - and also not 0, since it makes no sense to deduct 0 from an account. This ensures that a client will not pass in a value such as minus 1000, on the assumption that a debit is naturally a minus figure. The second precondition requires that the amount being debited does not exceed the money available.

```
debit_amount(amount:REAL) is
        require
            amount > 0;
            amount <= credit_available;
do
        balance := balance - amount;
        ensure
            old balance = balance + amount
    end  -- debit_amount;
```

*Example 8.2 Preconditions and postconditions*

It is permissible to precede each assertion with a tag; the tag is displayed on the screen if a violation is triggered during debugging. So the precondition could have been written as shown below.

```
require
        non_negative :
            amount > 0;
        credit_limit_not_exceeded:
            balance-amount >= credit_limit
```

The use of tags clearly aids readability, as well as providing additional information at run-time.

The postcondition of the above routine indicates that provided the precondition is met, *amount* will be subtracted from *balance*. To do this it uses the keyword **old** to precede *amount*; **old** *amount* refers to the value stored in *amount* at the time when the routine was entered. Again a tag could have been used:

> **ensure**
>> *has_been_debited*: **old** *balance* = *balance* + *amount*

Clearly, this is a relatively simple example, but even so the writing of preconditions and postconditions has forced us to clarify precisely what the routine does, and to put it in a machine readable form that can trap possible errors at debug time. In particular, we have avoided the possibility of a programmer writing a line such as

> *debit_amount(-1000)*

which would soon be disastrous for the financial health of the bank.

Example 8.3 gives the preconditions and postconditions for a new transformer routine, *credit_amount*, which adds money to an account.

---

> *credit_amount(amount*:REAL*)* **is**
>> **require**
>> *non_negative: amount > 0*
>
> **do**
>> *balance := balance + amount*;
>> **ensure**
>>> *is_updated*: **old** *balance* = *balance* - *amount*
>
> **end** -- credit_amount;

*Example 8.3 Further preconditions and postconditions*

---

These may be tested from class CONTROLLER. To do so the reader should ensure that preconditions and postconditions are switched on. This will require an amendment to the ACE file. The following should be inserted after the **default** keyword:

> assertion(**all**)

```
    class CONTROLLER
        creation
            test
        feature
            account:BANK_ACCOUNT;
            test is
                --tests preconditions and postconditions
            do
                !!account.make("Milton Obote",500.00, 9999);
                account.credit_amount(20.00);
                account.debit_amount(520.50);

                ----------
            end -- test
    end -- CONTROLLER
```

*Example 8.4 Testing a precondition*

Example 8.4 should generate an exception after the *debit-amount* call, because the 520.50 exceeds the amount available. The reader may care to make other tests, for example introduce a deliberate error into the *debit_amount* body, such as, *balance := balance + amount,* and see whether the postcondition generates an exception.


## 8.2   Class invariants

A class invariant is another kind of assertion, in this case an assertion about the state of an instance of a class. The assertions defined in the class invariant clause must be true on entry and on exit. The invariant comes at the end of the class, and is formed similarly to preconditions and postconditions:

**invariant**
    Assertion_clause {";" Assertion_clause}

We can now add two  invariants to class BANK_ACCOUNT as shown in example 8.5.

```
class BANK_ACCOUNT
    feature

        ...........................

    invariant
        limit_is_negative:  credit_limit  <= 0;
        is_within_credit_limit :  balance >= credit_limit;
end -- BANK_ACCOUNT
```

*Example 8.5 Class invariants*

The invariants that have been selected perhaps need some explanation. The *is_within_credit_limit* condition is related to the precondition for *debit_amount*. It guarantees that at all stable times the value in *amount* will not be smaller than *credit_limit*. Likewise the assertion, *limit_is_negative*, tells us that the credit limit on any account will either be zero (no credit) or a negative value, and that any attempt to alter this to a positive number will be a violation of the invariant and will trigger an exception if the class invariant check is switched on. The reader might object that this is a curious way to store a credit limit, but the assertion mechanisms have made us reason about it and produce a consistent set of routines, and a class that can be demonstrated to be safe.

## 8.3  Case study: class CLOCK

This section illustrates how assertions may be used in developing a new class, CLOCK, which will be taken from the early stages of specification through to implementation and testing. Class CLOCK is depicted in figure 8.3. As can be seen this is rather a strange kind of clock. In fact it is not really a clock at all, but simply a device which stores the time that we input, and displays it on request. It has an on off button, currently set to off, and a small screen for displaying the time. There are three buttons for manipulating the clock - one sets the time, one displays the time stored in the clock, the other increments the clock by one second. At the bottom there is a keyboard for inputting the time after the set button has been pressed. The buttons include one for entering a colon between numbers e.g. 15:24:50.

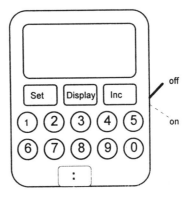

**Figure 8.3**

Three INTEGER attributes are needed to store the state of an instance, *hour,*
*minute and second,* and four services must be offered. Each of the services now
needs fuller discussion.

| **display** | -- *displays state of the clock on the screen* |
|---|---|

| **set** | -- *a transformer*<br>-- *sets time to  hh:mm:ss   as input via keyboard*<br>-- *hh must be <  24;  mm <=59  ss <= 59*<br>-- *no effect on screen* |
|---|---|

| **increment** | -- *a transformer*<br>-- *advances clock by one second*<br>-- *ensure that  ss 59 changes to 0 and increments mm*<br>-- *ensure that when mm 59 and ss 59, hh is incremented*<br>        *and hh and mm are set to 0*<br>-- *time must be < 23:59:59*<br>-- *no effect on screen* |
|---|---|

| **switch-on** | -- *internal time set to 0:0:0*<br>-- *time displayed on screen* |
|---|---|

There is no switch-off button: we have no interest in the state of a clock when
it is switched off.

This is a reasonably comprehensive description which hopefully answers all our questions. Now it is possible to specify preconditions and postconditions for some of the routines.

Neither *display* nor *switch_on* needs a precondition, but *switch_on* might be given a postcondition which makes explicit the initial state of the clock:

   *time_initialised: hour = 0* **and** *min = 0* **and** *sec = 0;*

The routine *set* requires further consideration.

We may require a user to input a valid time, which is any time between 0:0:0 and 23:59:59, and we could guarantee that if preconditions are met the time stored in the machine would be the same as the time input. We make no commitment as to what we shall do if the time is not valid. An alternative strategy would be to have no precondition, but simply a postcondition which ensures that the time set on exit from the routine would be either the old time or the new time if it were valid. We shall stick to the first strategy, although there might be arguments for the second. The assertions for the routine *set* are given in example 8.6.

---

   *set(hh,mm,ss*:INTEGER*)* **is**
        **require**
              *valid_hours: hh < 24*  **and**  *hh >= 0 ;*
              *valid_mins :  mm < 60*  **and**  *mm >= 0;*
              *valid_secs :  ss < 60* **and** *ss >= 0;*
   **do**
           **ensure**
              *time_has_been_set:*
              *hour = hh* **and**  *min = mm* **and**   *sec = ss*
        **end** -- set

   *Example 8.6 Assertions for routine* 'set'

---

We can now write the assertions for increment. The only precondition is that time is smaller than 23:59:59. The postcondition needs, however, to ensure that the internal state of the clock has been correctly incremented, which is not a trivial task, as shown in example 8.7.

```
            increment is
                  require
                        below_max_time :
                              sec < 59 or  min < 59 or  hour < 23
      do
            ensure
                        time_correctly_updated :
                        old sec < 59
                              and sec = old sec + 1
                              and min = old min
                              and hour = old hour
                        or sec = 0
                              and old sec = 59
                              and ( min = old min +1
                                          and  hour = old hour
                              or min = 0
                                          and old min = 59
                                          and hour = old hour +1)
      end -- increment
```

*Example 8.7 Assertions for routine 'increment'*

The complete class, with a class invariant, is shown in example 8.8.

```
      class CLOCK
            creation
                  switch_on;
            feature
                  hour,min,sec : INTEGER;

      display is
      do
            io.putint(hour);
            io.putchar(':');
            io.putint(min);
            io.putchar(':');
            io.putchar(sec);
      end -- display
      set(hh,mm,ss:INTEGER) is
            require
                  valid_hours:  hh < 24 and hh >= 0 ;
```

       *valid_mins* : *mm* < 60 **and** *mm* >= 0;
       *valid_secs* : *ss* < 60 **and** *ss* >= 0;

**do**

      *hour* := *hh*;
      *min* := *mm*;
      *sec* := *ss*;
      **ensure**
          *time_has_been_set*:
             *hour* = *hh* **and** *min* = *mm* **and** *sec* = *ss*

**end** -- set
*increment* **is**
   **require**
      *below_max_time* :
        *sec* < 59 **or** *min* < 59 **or** *hour* < 23

**do**

*hour* := *hour* + ( *min* + ( *sec* + 1 ) // 60 ) // 60;
*min* := (*min* + (*sec* + 1) // 60 ) \\ 60;
*sec* := (*sec* + 1 ) \\ 60;
   **ensure**
      *time_correctly_updated* :
            **old** *sec* < 59
                **and** *sec* = **old** *sec* + 1
                **and** *min* = **old** *min*
                **and** *hour* = **old** *hour*
             **or** *sec* = 0
                **and old** *sec* = 59
                **and** ( *min* = **old** *min* +1
                    **and** *hour* = **old** *hour*
                    **or** *min* = 0
                        **and old** *min* = 59
                        **and** *hour* = **old** *hour* + 1)

**end** -- increment
*switch_on* **is**
**do**
   *display*
   **ensure**
      *time_initialised*:
        *hour* = 0 **and** *min* = 0 **and** *sec* = 0;
**end** -- switch_on

**invariant**

```
                upper_limit: hour < 24 and min < 60 and sec < 60;
                lower_limit: hour >= 0 and min >= 0 and sec >= 0;
        end -- CLOCK
```

*Example 8.8 Class CLOCK*

The reader might notice that there is some overlap in the assertions, and that the source code could be simplified by the addition of an auxiliary routine,

*is_valid_time(h,m,s*:INTEGER):BOOLEAN;

which could be used in the preconditions for *set* and in the class invariant (but not in *increment*). This was not anticipated at the beginning, but the reader should see that such a routine would both simplify the source code and provide an additional service for clients.

Next we shall consider how we would test this class, with the precondition, postcondition and class invariant switches on. To do this requires a root class, CLOCK_TESTER, with a creation routine, *test_clock*. This routine tests class CLOCK without violating preconditions - there is no point in doing otherwise unless we wish to test that the preconditions have been properly defined and are triggered as expected.

```
    class CLOCK_TESTER
        creation
            test_clock
        feature
            test_clock is
                local
                    clock1 :CLOCK;
        do
                !!clock1.switch_on;          -- 0:0:0 expected
                clock1.increment;
                clock1.display;              -- 0:0:1 expected
                clock1.increment;
                clock1.display;              -- 0:0:2 expected
                clock1.set(22,59,59);
                clock1.increment;
                clock1.display;              --23:0:0 expected
                clock1.set(22,0,59);
                clock1.increment;
                clock1.display;              --22:1:0 expected
```

```
              end -- test_clock
      end -- CLOCK TESTER
```

*Example 8.9 Harness for testing class CLOCK*

The above tests have been designed to check the critical cases when the seconds and minutes on the clock are individually or jointly set to 59. If the class satisfies the above tests it then with confidence be submited to a final test: devise a routine which increments the clock until it is set to 23:59:59, and which displays the clock at the beginning and at the end, and whenever both minutes and seconds are set to zero. To ensure that the clock is incrementing correctly a loop counter may be included which counts the number of times the clock is incremented; this can also be displayed at periodic intervals, and should finally have the value 86,399. This example is concluded later in the chapter when loop invariants and variants are covered.

Looking back over the development of class CLOCK, the reader might well object that the assertions require a lot of work for a class with so few lines of executable code. We know from experience, however, that the building of software from hastily constructed components does not in the long run save time. We should also appreciate that if we wish to offer classes for reuse, we must be even more confident that a class works as specified, and that its correct use is clear to both producer and potential users.

## 8.4 The check instruction

Whereas preconditions, postconditions and class invariants enable us to make assertions about the state of an instance of a class on exit and on entry, check instructions enable us to make assertions at any point in the internal code. Check instructions may, like the previous facilities, be switched on and off. They are are particularly useful in the debugging stage, but may also be used, when following the 'design by contract' philosophy, as assertions about the conditions that must be satisfied before a particular instruction is executed. We might for example be writing a routine which increments an instance of class CLOCK, *clock1*. We could in this case use the *check instruction* as follows to show that we are aware of the constraints on our use of CLOCK.

```
    check
           can_be_incremented: clock1.sec < 59
                or  clock1.min < 59
                or  clock1.hour < 23
```

**end** -- check
*clock1.increment;*

If the check does not trigger an exception, but an error occurs when the call is made to *increment,* we can be confident that we as users of class CLOCK have met our side of the contract, and that the error lies with the suppliers.

The syntax of the check instruction has the following form

**check**
    *<identifier>* ":"   *boolean_expression* ";"
    *<identifier>* ":"   *boolean_expression* ";"
    ........
**end**

As indicated, there may be more than one assertion, and the check instruction is delimited by an **end**.

## 8.5 Loop variant and invariant

Programmers with any experience at all soon become aware of the kinds of errors that loops produce; few if any programmers can have gone through a career without constructing a loop which never terminates. Unfortunately, using Eiffel cannot guarantee that such a thing will never happen again, but it does at least offer facilities which may be used to make assertions about loops, and which can be used at run-time to debug them if there is a problem.

The use of an loop *invariant* and *loop variant* is illustrated in example 8.10. The invariant asserts that at initialisation and throughout the execution of the loop, the local variable *count* will be less than or equal to *p*. If this facility is switched on at run-time and the assertion is at some point untrue, then an exception will be triggered.

```
exp(n:REAL, p:INTEGER):REAL is
    require
        non_neg_args:  p >= 0 and n > 0
    local
        count:INTEGER
do
  from
        Result := 1;
        count := 0;
```

> **invariant**
>    *count* < *p* + *1;*
> **variant**
>    *p* − *count*
> **until**
>    *count* = *p*
> **loop**
>    *Result* := *Result* \* *n;*
>    *count* := *count* + *1;*
> **end** -- loop
>    **ensure**
>          -- returns n to power of p
> **end** -- exp

*Example 8.10 Loop invariant and variant*

The variant must be an integer expression which, at initialisation and on each iteration of the loop, yields a non-negative value; the variant must decrease on each iteration, which ensures that it will at some point terminate. In the above case we intend the loop to iterate *p* times, which is guaranteed by the variant chosen. If, for example, the routine is called with arguments as follows:

*exp(3,4)*

then on initialisation *p* - *count* will yield 4, and the assertion *count* < *p* +*1* will yield true; on the next iteration the variant will yield 3 and the invariant will remain true; at the beginning of the final iteration the invariant will remain true, and the variant will yield 1 - on exit the invariant would remain true and the variant would be 0. If for some reason another execution were to take place then an assertion violation would be triggered.

Having introduced loop invariants and variants, the clock case study may now be concluded (example 8.11). A loop has been inserted in CLOCK_TESTER. As indicated previously, a clock set to 0:0:0 will, if incremented 86,399 times, have reached 23:59:59, which is the terminating condition of the loop, so that the variant should yield 0 on the last iteration. The assertion that count must always be below 86400 will likewise be true. Just to be sure that the calculation is not an over-estimate, *count* may be output on the screen on exit from the loop. Also the clock ought to be displayed at the end to ensure that it has the expected value: 23:59:59.

```
class CLOCK_TESTER
    creation
        test_clock
    feature
        test_clock is
            local
                clock1 :CLOCK;
                count:INTEGER
        do
            from
                !!clock1.switch_on;
                count := 0;
            invariant
                count < 86400;
            variant
                86399 - count
            until
                clock1.hour = 23
                    and clock1.min = 59
                    and clock1.sec = 59
            loop
                count := count +1;
                clock1.increment;
                if clock1.sec = 0
                    and (clock1.min = 30
                        or clock1.min = 0)
                then
                    clock1.display;
                    io.putint(count)
                end -- if
            end -- loop
            clock1.display;
            io.new_line;
            io.putint(count);
        end -- test_clock
end -- CLOCK TESTER
```

*Example 8.11 Loop variant and invariant for testing class CLOCK*

As will be noticed, example 8.11 also provides for the clock and the counter to be displayed at regular intervals throughout the test. The reader is recommended to try this example, and also to alter the variants and invariants to trigger an exception - e.g. alter the invariant so that it reads *count* $<$ *86399*.

The following section may be omitted on a first reading.

## 8.6 Exception handling

An exception is an unexpected hardware or software fault which may result in system failure. If an exception occurs - for example an attempt to open a file fails - then usually the system fails too, and important data may be lost. In safety critical systems, failure may of course be quite literally a life and death matter, and provision has to be made to deal with failure in a way which minimises the consequences.

Few languages have in the past offered support for handling exceptions. One language that does is Ada, which allows a programmer to provide an exception handler for each software unit. The Eiffel mechanisms for exception handling are defined at routine level. The Eiffel approach to exception handling may be summarised as follows:

i) a routine either fails or succeeds

ii) if a routine fails it must not pretend that it has succeeded

iii) it should either try again or report failure to the client

iv) if it tries again and still fails then it should so far as possible leave the environment stable

v) failure is reported upwards through the chain of routine calls until either the error is dealt with or - if it gets to the root - it causes system failure.

The mechanisms that the Eiffel language provides are a *rescue clause* and a *retry instruction*. The rescue clause, if used, must be inserted at the end of a routine, after the postcondition:

<*routine_name*> [ formal argument list ] [ ":" <*result-type*> ] **is**
    [ preconditions]
    [local declarations ]
  **do**
    compound instruction
    [postconditions]
    [rescue clause]
  **end**

The rescue clause consists of

**rescue**
compound instruction

It is executed only if an exception occurs in the body of the routine. It cannot therefore be used to deal with violations of preconditions. Its main purpose is to return the current object to a stable state so that invariants are satisfied. It may also attempt to re-execute the body of the routine. This may be accomplished by a retry instruction. This instruction, which consists simply of the reserved word **retry,** may be used only in a rescue clause.

The use of **retry** is illustrated in class STATIC_QUEUE, which is implemented using an ARRAY (example 8.12). The front element is stored in location 1, and *last* indicates the rear of the queue, as shown in figure 8.4.

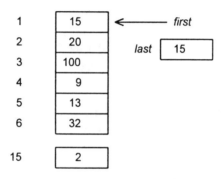

**Figure 8.4**

When an item is removed, then all the elements must be moved up and *last* decremented; when an item is added, then *last* is incremented and the new item inserted at the location stored in *last* (in the above case the next item would be added to location 16). When an element is added to a full array, an exception will occur. This is dealt with by resizing the array as shown in the rescue clause of *add.*

```
class STATIC_QUEUE;
    creation
        make;
    feature { }
        list:ARRAY[INTEGER];
        size : INTEGER;
    feature
        is_empty : BOOLEAN is
```

```
do
     Result := size = 0
end -- empty
add(element:INTEGER) is
     local
          has_tried:BOOLEAN;
do
     size := size + 1;
     list.put(element,size)
     ensure
          is_inserted: list.item(size ) = element;
     rescue
          list.resize(1,list.upper+10);
          old size := size -1;
          if not has_tried
               then has_tried := true;
                    retry;
          end -- if
end -- add
front: INTEGER is
     require
          not_empty : not empty
do
     Result := list.item(1);
end -- front
rear: INTEGER is
     require
          not_empty : not empty
do
     Result := list.item(size);
end -- rear
remove is
     require
          not_empty : not empty
do
     list.remove(1);  -- available in Eiffel/S but not ISE Eiffel
     size := size -1
end -- remove
make is
do
     !!list.make(1,100);
```

```
        ensure
            empty: is_empty
    end -- make
end -- STATIC_QUEUE
```

*Example 8.12 Use of **rescue** and **retry***

In example 8.12 a rescue clause is used to provide automatic resizing (allocating another 10 locations) if an exception is triggered when a client tries to add an element to the queue. It should be noted that the attribute *last,* which points to the rear, is in this case set to the value it had on entry to the routine. The routine is then asked to try to execute its body.

As pointed out in the comment in the source code, a *remove* for class ARRAY is available in Eiffel/S, but not ISE Eiffel. In practice this does not matter, since the exception handling may be tested without removing a single element from the queue. ISE users may either comment out the call, not implement a *remove* routine in STATIC_QUEUE, or write their own substitute for the Eiffel/S *remove*, which moves every element one place to the left.

To test example 8.12, the reader should write a root class which is a client of STATIC_QUEUE, and should insert in it a test routine which triggers the exception - for example a loop which iterates 1000 times, and on each iteration adds its own index to the queue - an unlikely scenario, but one which allows the programmer to experiment with exception handling.

It should be emphasised that other and arguably better strategies could have been chosen to implement a static queue, including

1. a precondition which required the client not to add an item if the queue was full (this would have required an *is_full* routine to be supplied);
2. the use of *force* instead of *put,* which would have automatically resized the array whenever required.

Had the first strategy been chosen, then the rescue clause would not have been appropriate. A rescue clause cannot deal with the failure to meet a precondition; it deals with failure in the body of a routine.

Finally, it should be pointed out that other facilities for exception handling are available in the class library. Readers who wish to pursue this should look at class EXCEPTIONS in the class library.

The following two sections deal briefly with facilities available to detect the causes of error in an Eiffel application.

## 8.7 The debug instruction

The debug instruction is an instruction designed, as the name suggests, for tracing errors. It allows us to insert instructions in a piece of code during debugging, and to switch them off when they are no longer required. It is possible to switch all debugging on or off, or to switch individual debug statements or sets of statements on or off. This is done either by specifying at run-time which classes in a system are to be switched on, or by appending a key or keys to the keyword **debug,** which allows the system to execute selectively a specified debug or set of debug instructions.

The debug instruction has the following form:

> **debug**
>> *instruction*
>> *instruction*
>> ....................
>
> **end**

or with a debug key:

> **debug** ("INCREMENT")
>> *instruction*
>> *instruction*
>> ....................
>
> **end**

In the second case, the keyword **debug** is followed by a string; this allows debug instructions to be turned on and off more selectively. If the reader wishes to use the debug facilities then alterations may have to be made to the ACE file. The ACE file should include entries such as the following to indicate whether debug should be turned on, off, on selectively, or whether a debug key should be turned on.

> **debug**(no)
> **debug**(yes)
> **debug**(yes):CLOCK, CLOCK_TESTER
> **debug**("INCREMENT")

It should be made clear that debug instructions are designed for debugging and not for testing classes. The two terms are often confused: testing is a process designed to establish the existence of errors; debugging is the process of locating errors and correcting the code which is causing them. Sometimes the source of an error can be located simply through code inspection; quite often the violation of an assertion will give the programmer a good clue as to where the error is occurring. If the exact source of an error cannot be detected from source code inspection and from assertion violations, then the use of output statements to check key attributes is a technique which should be used. So, for example, to return to class CLOCK, if at some point the clock appears to be updating incorrectly, the debug instruction might at one or more points be used to view the attributes of CLOCK:

> *io.putint(hour);*
> *io.putint(min);*
> *io.putint(sec);*

It is also sometimes useful to make a program execute step by step; an instruction sequence such as

> *io.putstring("Press key to continue");*
> *io.readchar;*

will accomplish this.


### 8.8 Trace

A trace facility is provided as part of the run-time support for Eiffel. This may be used during debugging to trace the flow of control in a system; it will help a programmer to ensure that routines are being called in the order expected. The trace facility may be switched on in ACE files, for individual classes, for all classes, and for none. If switched on it generates information about calls to, and returns from, routines of specified classes. Like the debug instruction this can be very useful in tracing the causes of error. Readers who wish to use this facility are advised to switch it on only for a limited number of classes. If this is not done it will trace the flow of execution through all the low level classes; this will produce much unnecessary information, and the large number of i/o operations generated can also result in very slow execution speeds.

## Exercises

1. a) Implement and test class BANK_ACCOUNT;
b) write a precondition for *change_id* to ensure that the current id and the new id are not the same;
c) write a transformer, *change_credit_limit(new_limit:REAL);* supply a suitable precondition to ensure that class invariants are not violated by *new_limit;*

2. a) Implement classes CLOCK and CLOCK_TESTER; implement the function, *is_valid_time,* and use in assertions as appropriate;
b) make a slight alteration to the body of increment, and test with the postconditions switched on;
c) make changes to CLOCK_TESTER to trigger an exception as suggested in section 8.5.

3. a) Write an invariant and variant for the loop shown in example 5.6.
b) Examine the loop in example 4.3. Why is there no point in using a variant and invariant in this case?

4. A stack is a last in first out data structure; the function, *top,* returns the top item on the stack, but leaves the stack unaltered; *push(i:ANY)* places i on the stack, so that it becomes the new top; *pop* removes the item on the top of the stack; *pop* and *top* must never be used when the stack is empty. There are also accessor routines, *size*:INTEGER and *is_empty*:BOOLEAN.
Write a suitable set of preconditions and postconditions for

> *top:ANY;*
> *pop;*
> *push(i:ANY);*

# 9 Inheritance

This chapter introduces single inheritance; it also covers the concept of polymorphism, the rules for conformance in Eiffel, and the related topic of reverse assignment. It concludes with a discussion of when inheritance is and is not appropriate.

## 9.1 Inheritance for specialisation

The most important use of inheritance is for specialisation. The use of inheritance often results in the development of classes linked in tree-like structures, with an abstract root, and more specialised descendants. As an example we could model the people in a typical university, as in figure 9.1.

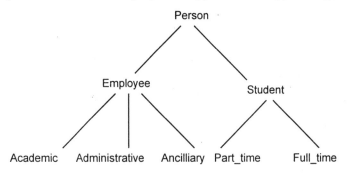

**Figure 9.1**

At the top of thehierarchy is as general a class as we can model: Person. An employee is a specialisation of Person, and a student also is a specialisation of Person. We have in the above diagram continued our specialisation to the next level: an academic is a specialisation of Employee, and a Full_time is a specialisation of Student. The specialisation relationship is often described as an *is_a* relationship; so if we look at the above hierarchy we can make the following observations among others:

> a Full_time *is_a* Student
> a Full_time *is_a* Person
> an Administrative *is_a* Employee
> an Employee *is_a* Person
> an Ancilliary *is_a* Person

We would also say that class ACADEMIC is a descendant of class EMPLOYEE and through EMPLOYEE is also a descendant of class PERSON. Class EMPLOYEE is a descendant of PERSON only.

We may now consider the kinds of attribute that might be required by each of the classes in the above hierarchy. Clearly we do not need to model all attributes about people in the university - for example, height, weight, even hair colour change over time, and are, as far as the author is aware, of little interest to university authorities. There, are however, certain attributes which are common to all people in the university, and which an information system would need to contain. The following are some fairly obvious attributes: name, sex, date_of_birth, home_address, next_of_kin, telephone_number.

At the next level we have decided to group the people in the university into two categories: employees and students. Employees will have common attributes of interest to the university: employee_number, start_date, salary, bank_account (this assumes that all the employees are paid directly into a bank account).

Employees have been further subdivided into three kinds. The first two should be self explanatory. In the third category are grouped together various kinds of function necessary in a modern university: catering, security, buildings, technical support. It should be noted that we have not created a separate class for each. This is unnecessary: we can indicate their actual function by an attribute. Similarly, we have not provided a class for each academic department. Our university may have an academic structure such as that depicted in figure 9.2.

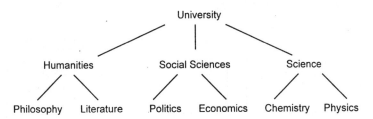

**Figure 9.2**

Here academic departments are grouped into faculties such as humanities, social sciences and so on. But we should not confuse the two hierarchies. Each academic in the university will be attached to a department, and each academic in our hierarchy will have an attribute indicating his/her department. We might if we were building an information system for the university wish to create a class DEPARTMENT, but it would have no place within our hierarchy. The relationship between an academic and a department is a *has_a* relationship: class ACADEMIC is a *client* of class DEPARTMENT.

Students have been divided into two categories - perhaps a less obvious dividing line in some universities - those who attend full-time, and those who are on part-time courses. All students will have common attributes: *course, year, commencement_date.* Full-time students will have additional attributes - *term_time_address, term_time_phone, funding_body.* Part-time students will typically, in the UK at least, have an *employer,* an *address* and a *phone-number* at their place of work.

In figure 9.3 certain attributes have been specified for each class.

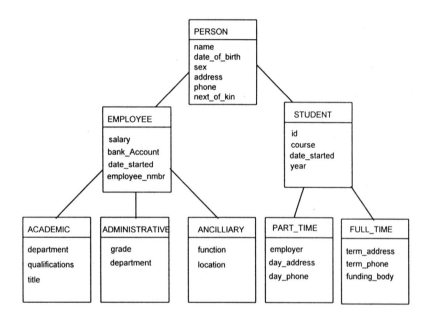

**Figure 9.3**

It should be emphasised that any descendant automatically inherits the attributes of all its ancestors. We can illustrate this by looking at class ANCILLIARY. In addition to the attributes *function* and *location,* which are special to ANCILLIARY, any instance of this class would inherit the attributes, *salary, bank_account, date_started,* and *employee_nmbr,* from EMPLOYEE, and would inherit *name, date_of_birth, address, sex,* and *next_of_kin* from class PERSON. Likewise class PART_TIME would inherit all the attributes from class PERSON, and would in addition inherit *id, course, year,*and *date_started* from class STUDENT, and would also have the attributes *employer, day_address,* and *day_phone.*

The functionality or services of each class have not been modelled; but the rules for inheritance would apply to them in the same way as the data. If therefore class PERSON has the following routine

*make*(*nme*:STRING;*date_of_birth*:INTEGER;*gender*:CHARACTER)

then that routine will be available to all its descendants. The next section continues this example, and shows how the inheritance relationship is declared in Eiffel.

## 9.2   Single inheritance in Eiffel

The following example shows how class ADMINISTRATIVE would be written in EIFFEL. This class inherits all the features of EMPLOYEE, and through EMPLOYEE, all the features of PERSON.

```
       class ADMINISTRATIVE
           inherit
               EMPLOYEE
           creation
               make
           feature
               grade:INTEGER;
               department:STRING;
               change_grade(g:INTEGER) is
               do
                   grade := g
               end -- change_grade
               change_dept(dept:STRING) is
               do
                   department := d
               end -- change_dept
       end -- ADMINISTRATIVE
```

*Example 9.1 Inheritance in Eiffel*

It may be noted that a creation routine has been declared, and that, *make* which has been inherited from PERSON, has been chosen. To create an instance of class ADMINISTRATIVE it would, therefore, be necessary to supply a name, a date of birth, and the person's sex, as shown in example 9.2.

```
class INFORMATION_SYS
    creation
        start
    feature
        admin_1,admin_2:ADMINISTRATIVE;
        start is
        do
            !!admin_1.make("Long Tran",220365,'m');
            !!admin_2.make("Sai Ming Lee",190567,'m');
            !!admin_1.change_dept("Law");
            !!admin_2.change_dept("Registry");
            !!admin_1.change_grade(2);
            !!admin_2.change_grade(3);
            io.putstring(admin_1.name);
            io.putstring(admin_1.department)
            ..................
        end -- start
end --  INFORMATION_SYS
```

*Example 9.2 A client of class ADMINISTRATIVE*

This example cannot of course be executed without implementing classes PERSON and EMPLOYEE. This is left to the reader (see the exercises at the end of the chapter).

Finally this brief introduction to single inheritance in Eiffel should be concluded with an update to the syntax of an Eiffel class, showing the inheritance part.

```
class <class_name>
    [inherit
        type]
    [creation
        <routine_name>]
    feature
        {routines | attributes}
end
```

It should be pointed out that this is still incomplete - and in particular it takes no account of feature adaptation and multiple inheritance (chapters 11,13).

## 9.3 Inheriting for reuse

This section returns to class CLOCK (see chapter 8) to illustrate a common occurrence - the need to enhance the functionality of an existing class. In such a case there are two alternatives - either the existing class is altered, or a new descendant class is developed to allow existing attributes and functionality to be reused. We shall assume that class CLOCK is now stable, and is being used by clients who are quite happy with it. So in this situation it is sensible to develop a new class, DELUXE_CLOCK, as a descendant of CLOCK.

Class DELUXE_CLOCK will have the following added functionality, but no new attributes.

| add_seconds | *-- a transformer routine*<br>*-- adds s seconds to target*<br>*-- adding s must not advance time beyond*<br>*23:59:59* |
|---|---|

| add_clock | *-- a constructor routine*<br>*-- returns a new clock with time stored that of target + clock c*<br>*-- no side effects: target and c are unchanged*<br>*-- result of adding must not advance time beyond*<br>*23:59:59* |
|---|---|

| time_in_seconds | *-- accessor routine*<br>*-- returns time stored in seconds* |
|---|---|

| smaller_than | *-- compares clock c with target*<br>*-- true if the time stored in target is less than that held in c* |
|---|---|

It may be noted that a *smaller_than* routine has been specified, but an equality routine has not. It should be remembered that class CLOCK inherits from ANY, and that we can use the *is_equal* routine inherited from GENERAL. The reader should recall our discussion of this in chapter 6. In this case it is perfectly safe to use *is_equal* since the attributes are all type INTEGER. If class CLOCK had any reference types then it would be necessary to use *is_deep_equal.*

In outline the new class will be as presented in example 9.3. The inherited routine, *switch_on*, has been selected as the creation routine. A descendant class does not automatically inherit a creation routine. Often a descendant has additional attributes, so that further initialisation may be required, and a new creation routine defined for that purpose. In this case there are no further attributes, and it makes sense to reuse the creation routine already specified.

The class invariant defined in class CLOCK automatically applies to class DELUXE_CLOCK; an additional invariant may be added, but the inherited invariant cannot be weakened. Any new invariant will therefore simply be added to inherited invariants.

```
class DELUXE_CLOCK
      inherit
            CLOCK
      creation
            switch_on
      feature
            time_in_seconds:INTEGER
                  -- returns time in seconds

            add_seconds(s:INTEGER)
                  require
                        time_in_seconds + s < 24*60*60
                  ensure
                        correct_time:
                              time_in_seconds= s + old time_in_seconds

      infix "+" , add_clock(c:DELUXE_CLOCK)
                              :DELUXE_CLOCK
            require
                  not_void: c/= void;
                  time_in_seconds + c.time_in_seconds < 24*60*60
            ensure
                        Result /= current;
                        time_in_seconds + c.time_in_seconds
                              = Result.time_in_seconds
      infix "<" , smaller_than(c:DELUXE_CLOCK)
                              :BOOLEAN
            require
                  c /= void
      end DELUXE_CLOCK
```

*Example 9.3 Class DELUXE_CLOCK in outline*

The use of the **infix** should be noted. It is permissible to give a routine two names, as in the case of *smaller_than* and *add_clock*. The infix allows us to use the "<" and "+" with two operands of class DELUXE_CLOCK:

> **if** *a_deluxe_clock* < *another_deluxe_clock*
>     **then** ...

and

> *a_deluxe_clock* := *a_deluxe_clock* + *another_deluxe_clock;*

We may now implement each routine, as shown in example 9.4.

```
class DELUXE_CLOCK
    inherit
        CLOCK
    creation
        switch_on
    feature
        time_in_seconds:INTEGER is
        do
            Result := hour * 3600 + min * 60 + sec
        end -- time_in_seconds
        add_seconds(s:INTEGER) is
            require
                    time_in_seconds + s < 24*60*60
        do
            hour := hour + (min + ( sec + s )// 60 ) // 60;
            min := ( min + ( sec + s ) // 60 ) \\ 60;
            sec := ( sec + s ) \\ 60;
            ensure
                correct_time:
                    time_in_seconds
                        = s + old time_in_seconds
        end -- add_seconds
        infix "+", add_clock(c:DELUXE_CLOCK)
                            :DELUXE_CLOCK is
                require
                    not_void: c/= void;
                    time_in_seconds + c.time_in_seconds
                            < 24*60*60
        do
                Result := clone(Current);
```

```
                    Result.add_seconds(time_in_seconds(c));
                ensure
                    Result /= Current;
                    time_in_seconds + c.time_in_seconds
                              = Result.time_in_seconds
            end -- add_clock
            infix "<" ,smaller_than(c: DELUXE_CLOCK)
                              :BOOLEAN is
                require c /= void
            do
                Result := time_in_seconds < c.time_in_seconds
            end -- smaller_than
    end -- DELUXE_CLOCK
```

*Example 9.4 Class DELUXE_CLOCK*

The reader should note the coding of the routine *add_clock* in which the current object has been cloned, and *time-in_seconds*, and *add_seconds*, already defined in the class, have been used. This provides a neat solution to the problem, and avoids unnecessary duplication of code.

Instances of class DELUXE_CLOCK now have the following set of features: *hour, min, sec, display, increment, set, switch_on, time_in_seconds, add_seconds, add_clock , smaller_than.*

It should be emphasised that class CLOCK has been extended through inheritance, it has not been altered. None of the new features may be used with entities of class CLOCK. It should be added that the decision to create DELUXE_CLOCK was not one that would be taken were we designing class CLOCK from scratch again. It would indeed make sense to incorporate all the facilities defined in class DELUXE_CLOCK in class CLOCK. As was stated out the outset, it is not a good idea to replace classes that are currently in use. Inheritance allows us to reuse what has been done before without any danger of affecting those who are already using a class.

It may also be pointed out that designing a class for subsequent reuse is difficult to achieve. As object-oriented developers we should not expect to be able to get the best solution first time. The conventional engineering paradigm which envisages software development as an ordered sequence - specification, followed by design, then by implementation - was always more an aspiration than an accurate model of how software is actually constructed, and it will not enable us to produce systems that are easy to maintain, let alone to develop reusable code.

## 9.4 Polymorphism

The concept of polymorphism causes a great deal of unnecessary confusion, and it is probably true to say that it is possible to learn object oriented programming without a clear idea of what people mean when they use the term. The reason for the confusion is that there are at least three possible contexts in which the term is used.

Firstly, it is often associated with overloading - allowing the same name to be used for different features.

Secondly, it is used in the context of generic data structures - sometimes known as 'parametric polymorphism', which is explored further in chapter 10.

Thirdly, it is used in the context of inheritance in a typed language. It is this context which we shall now explore.

Inheritance introduces the possibility that an entity may, at some time during execution, be attached to an object of a different type from the entity's type. We must, therefore, distinguish between the *static type* of an entity, which is that known at compile time, and the *dynamic type*, which is the type of the object to which an entity is attached at a given instant during run-time.

The ability to have more than one type may be referred to as *inheritance polymorphism*. Such polymorphism is a fundamental feature of object-oriented software development, because it allows algorithms to be defined at an abstract level, for many types, and to be adapted lower down the class hierarchy if necessary. In dynamically bound languages such as Smalltalk, all entities are potentially polymorphic, and there is no restriction as to the kind of object to which an entity may be attached during execution. In a typed language such as Eiffel, polymorphism is possible only within the framework of inheritance. At one extreme, an entity whose static class was ANY, could be attached to an object of any class within the Eiffel library, or indeed to an object of any programmer-defined class. Normally, however, the conformance rules (see next section) greatly restrict the number of possible types to which an entity may be attached.

## 9.5 Conformance

The conformance rules govern assignment, the allowed types of actual arguments, and attribute and routine redefinition. The issues involved may be stated as questions.

**assignment**:
   - may an object of type *T1* be attached to an object of type T2*?*

**actual arguments:**
- may an actual argument of type T1 substitute a formal argument of type T2 ?

**attribute redefinition:**
- may an attribute of type T2 be redefined as type T1

**routine redefinition:**
- may a formal argument of type T2 be replaced by one of type T1?
- may a result-type of type T2 be replaced by one of type T1?

Eiffel allows each of the above, provided that T1 conforms to T2. The rules for conformance in Eiffel may be summarised as follows:

T1 conforms to T2
if they are the same or if T1 is a descendant of T2

This may be illustrated by returning to the examples developed earlier in the chapter: inituitively we would say that an EMPLOYEE is a PERSON, but we would not say that a PERSON is an EMPLOYEE; also, a DELUXE_CLOCK is a CLOCK, but a CLOCK is not a DELUXE_CLOCK. This is precisely how conformance works in Eiffel: EMPLOYEE conforms to PERSON and DELUXE_CLOCK conforms to CLOCK.

The conformance rules allow us therefore to assign an entity of a class DELUXE_CLOCK to an entity of class CLOCK. So, assuming the following declarations:

*clock1*:CLOCK;
*del_clock1*: DELUXE_CLOCK;

the assignment *clock1 := del_clock1* would be allowable, but *del_clock1:= clock1* would not be allowed.

The same rule applies for arguments to a routine. So for example had the routine *add_clock*, been specified with a formal argument of type CLOCK, we could still have used an actual argument of type DELUXE_CLOCK. Again, the reverse is not true: we cannot use an actual argument of type CLOCK with the *add_clock* routine as it is defined in example 9.4 (further discussion of redefintion will be found in chapter 11).

## 9.6 Reverse assignment attempt

Section 9.5 has indicated that an entity of type T1 may only be assigned to an entity of type T2 if its class type conforms to that of the target. This can cause problems. Object-oriented languages, as we have seen, allow an entity to be attached at run-time to an object of a different type from that of its static type. Nevertheless, given the following declarations

> *clock1*:CLOCK;
> *del_clock1, del_clock2*: DELUXE_CLOCK;

the rules of conformance would not allow us to make the second of the following sequence of assignments

> *clock1 := del_clock1;*
> *del_clock2 := clock1;*

It may be obvious that after the first instruction *clock1* is attached to a DELUXE_CLOCK, but the compiler makes only static checks, and does not attempt to trace the history of attachments to work out the type to which an entity would be attached at a given time. In any case it would not be possible to do this in every situation.

To be able to do what we wish, we have in effect to override the rules of conformance. To achieve this Eiffel provides the reverse assignment attempt. Therefore if we have a situation in which we believe that *clock1* may at a certain point be attached to a DELUXE_CLOCK, we could make an attempt to assign *clock1* to *del_clock2* as follows:

> *del_clock2 ?= clock1;*

The syntax is similar to assignment, but the ? indicates that the compiler cannot be sure that the attempt will succeed, and so must make provision in case it does not.

If at run-time the attempt succeeded - i.e. if *clock1* was attached to an object whose type conformed to DELUXE_CLOCK, then the assignment would take place, and *del_clock2* would be attached to the same object as clock1 as depicted below. Attachments of *clock* and *deluxe_clock2* before and after the reverse assignment attempt, *del_clock2 ?= clock1* are shown in figures 9.4 and 9.5.

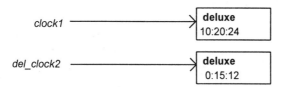

**Figure 9.4**

**Figure 9.5**

A failed attempt is shown in figures 9.6 and 9.7.

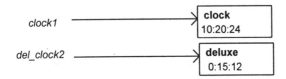

**Figure 9.6**

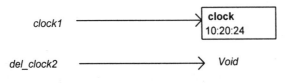

**Figure 9.7**

Sometimes, we do not wish to make an assignment, but merely to check on the type of an object. In this case the routine

*conforms_to (other* **like** *Current)* :*BOOLEAN*

from class GENERAL may be used to test if the dynamic type of the target conforms to the dynamic type of *other*. So for example the expression *clock1.conforms_to (del_clock1)*

would yield true only if *clock1* was attached to a DELUXE_CLOCK, or a descendant of DELUXE_CLOCK.

Occasionally, we have a situation in which an entity could potentially be attached to an object of many possible types, in which case there is no easy solution using any of the standard Eiffel facilities. If, for example, an entity is of CLASS_A, and CLASS_A has six descendant classes:CLASS_B, CLASS_C, CLASS_D, CLASS_E, CLASS_F, and CLASS_G, then it would require a fairly complex and laborious piece of coding to ascertain the actual type of the argument passed in at run-time. Example 9.5 which provides a routine

*find_class(a:CLASS_A);*

illustrates how this could be done. The reader should appreciate that according to the rules of conformance, the actual argument may be of CLASS_A or any descendant of CLASS_A.

```
find_class(a:CLASS_A) is
        local
                b:CLASS_B; c:CLASS_C;
                d:CLASS_D; e:CLASS_E;
                f:CLASS_F; g:CLASS_G;
do
        b ?= a;
        if b = Void
        then  c ?= a
             if c = void
             then  d ?= a
                  if d = Void
                  then  e? = a
                       if e = Void
                       then  f ?= a
                            if f = Void
                            then  g ?= a
                                 if g= Void
                                 then
                                 -- must be type A
                                 else
                                         -- is type G
                                 end -- if
```

```
                        else  -- is type F
                        end -- if
                    else -- is type E
                    end -- if
                else -- is type D
                end -- if
            else -- is type C
        end -- if
        else -- is type B
        end -- if
    end -- find_class
```

*Example 9.5 Complex reverse assignment attempt*

As an alternative ISE Eiffel provides a routine in class INTERNAL ,

*class_name(object:*ANY*):*STRING

which returns the class name of an object. A class which inherited from
INTERNAL could therefore use this routine to determine whether two classes
were the same:

**if** *class_name(clock1).is_equal(class_name(del_clock1))*
**then** ...

Happily, the cases when we need to do anything such as that shown in
example 9.5 are relatively rare.

## 9.7  When to inherit

Inheritance is a powerful and very useful mechanism; as a result many students
when they first come across it tend to over use it. There are clearly different
viewpoints as to the proper use of inheritance. The author tends to the view that
inheritance should be a last resort. Too often, perhaps, it is the first resort, with
the result that there is a danger that inheritance will become the GO TO of the
1990s. There is also some current concern that indisciplined use of inheritance
makes the testing of new classes very difficult.

It ought to be emphasised that inheritance is not *the* defining feature of
object-oriented software development. In his classic study of object-oriented
software construction, Bertrand Meyer defined seven steps to object-oriented
happiness, of which single inheritance was step five (Meyer 1988). Some of the

preceding steps are more important to the design of object-oriented systems - and it is particularly important that we do not lose sight of the fundamental - that systems must be modularised around data structures rather than functions.

Of the examples in this chapter, the PERSON, EMPLOYEE hierarchy illustrates the use of inheritance in designing a set of related classes from scratch. CLOCK and DELUXE_CLOCK, is an example of inheritance for reuse: it would have been better to have redesigned CLOCK from scratch with the additional features; the decision to inherit in this case was taken because of the assumption that the class was currently being used, and it was safer not to alter it. At some point a decision has to be made that a class may not be altered any more: Meyer refers to this as the open-closed principle (Meyer 1988).

We may now introduce a further example, class SENSOR_READINGS which stores readings from a sensor at timed intervals during the day, and is required to perform calculations on these using mathematical functions such as *log, exp, sqrt*. Since it is required to store more than one reading, we need access to the functionality of a linear data structure. Having chosen the data structure from the library, (we have selected ARRAY), we now must chose whether to inherit ARRAY, as in example 9.6, or to make SENSOR-READINGS a client as shown in example 9.7.

```
class SENSOR_READINGS
       inherit ARRAY[REAL]
       feature
             count:INTEGER;
             calc_result:REAL  is
             do

             end -- calc_result
             .........
end -- SENSOR_READINGS
```

*Example 9.6 Inheriting class ARRAY*

```
class SENSOR_READINGS
       feature
             store:  ARRAY[REAL]
             .........
end -- SENSOR_READINGS
```

*Example 9.7 Client of class ARRAY*

In this case the use of inheritance seems better to the author for the following reasons: SENSOR_READINGS is a collection of data; the *is_a* relationship seems to make sense. There is an added reason. A client will need to put information into its instance of data readings. SENSOR_READINGS should logically act as a passive repository of data, not an active collector of data, otherwise it needs a complete reconsideration. A client would presumably have a feature such as:

*readings*:SENSOR_READINGS

If a client class is to put data in *readings*, and perhaps retrieve it, then it seems preferable for a client to be writing shorter call such as

*readings.put(some_reading,reading_number)*

as opposed to the kind of chain that would be needed for the user to access the array:

*readings.store.put(some_reading,reading_number)*

If on the other hand we were going to define special transfomer and accessor routines for SENSOR_READINGS, then there is good justification for taking the second path, of declaring a client instead of inheriting. In this case we would be able to hide the implementation from the client, and not require the client to know anything about arrays at all.

```
class SENSOR_READINGS
    feature {NONE}
        store: ARRAY[REAL]
    feature
        count:INTEGER;
        calc_result :REAL is
        do
              ......
        end -- calc_result
        insert_at(r:REAL; index:INTEGER) is
        do
            store.put(r,index);
        end -- insert_at
        append(r:REAL) is
        do
```

> *store.put(r, count+1);*
> *count := count +1;*
> **end** -- append
> *retrieve(index:*INTEGER*):*REAL **is**
> **do**
> *Result := store.item(index);*
> **end** -- retrieve;
> **end** -- SENSOR_READINGS
>
> *Example 9.8 Client of ARRAY, with own insertion and retrieval routines*

The arguments for inheriting or becoming a client of ARRAY seem in this case to be finely balanced, although others may disagree. The client solution with the new insertion and retrieval routines requires slightly more work from the developer, but produces a class which seems easier and safer for a client of SENSOR-READINGS to use. As an alternative, it would be possible to inherit ARRAY and to use the re-export features of the language to hide array operations from a client (see chapter 11).

When we have decided whether to inherit ARRAY or not, and then begin writing the calculation routine, we find that the functions required are defined in class SINGLE_MATH in the library. Again there is a choice of the inheritance or client relationship. The most common solution appears to be to use inheritance. This is a different category of inheritance from those previously encountered. It is a case of using inheritance simply to acquire functionality. Clearly in this example SENSOR_READINGS would fail the *is-a* test, as would almost any other class one may think of, except for the case, similar to DELUXE_CLOCK, when we wish to create a new class which extends the current collection of maths routines.

As an alternative, we could declare an attribute,

*fn*: SINGLE_MATH

which would allow the functions defined in SINGLE_MATH to be accessed by prefixing *fn*:

*fn.log*
*fn.cos*

and so on. One disadvantage with this is the need to use a creation instruction before any of the functions may be accessed, unless of course a once routine which returned a shared copy of *fn* was defined somewhere in the class hierarchy.

It may be seen that the question of when to inherit, as opposed to becoming a client of a class, is often not as clear-cut as in the case of the example with which the chapter began. It is worth re-emphasising the points made earlier in this section of the chapter:

- The purpose of object-oriented software development is not to devise as many ways as possible of using inheritance.

- The purpose is to develop quality software, which is easy to understand and maintain.

- Over-use of inheritance can add to the complexity of software, and can incidentally make testing much more difficult.

- Inheritance is an essential technique, but it should be used with caution.


### *Exercises*

1. This chapter has introduced concepts of *polymorphism*, *conformance* and *reverse assignment*. Make notes on each of these.

2. a) draw a diagram to represent the following: CLASS_H inherits from CLASS_D, CLASS_D and CLASS_E inherit from CLASS_B, CLASS_B and CLASS_C inherit from CLASS_A; CLASS_F and CLASS_E inherit from CLASS_C.
b) given the following attributes:
     a:CLASS_A; b:CLASS_B; c:CLASS_C; ...
    and so on, which of the following are legal assignments?
    a := d;  c := g;  f :=c;   d := b;  d := h;  d:= a;  e := f
c) given a routine, *x(r:CLASS_B)*, which of the following actual arguments would be valid?
         a    e    h    b    f

3. The following exercises involve classes PERSON, EMPLOYEE, ACADEMIC and AMINISTRATIVE, which should first be implemented and tested: select appropriate types for the attributes, and provide a transformer for each; write a root class, e.g. INFORMATION_SYS, for testing each class as it is developed.

a) Write a routine in the root class which enables data for instances of ACADEMIC and ADMINISTRATIVE to be entered from the keyboard;

b) write a class, STAFF_LIST, which inherits from ARRAY; make the root class a client of STAFF_LIST, and add the employees entered from the keyboard to a STAFF_LIST; (Hint: STAFF_LIST is an array of EMPLOYEE)

c) write a *display* routine in EMPLOYEE, and write a *display* routine in STAFF_LIST; the former needs to output two or three attributes only; the latter should be a standard array traversal, which calls the *display* defined in employee; test this routine from the root class, e.g. given the declaration, *staff* : STAFF_LIST, it may be tested by the call, *staff.display;*

d) in class STAFF_LIST write constructor routines, which return arrays of staff as suggested by the routine name;

> *academic_list*: STAFF_LIST
> *administrative_list*:STAFF_LIST

each of the above should traverse the array of EMPLOYEE, and return the appropriate employees found in the array. (Hint: use reverse assignment); consider whether *clone* or *deep_clone* should be used to put elements in the new arrays; test these routines (Hint - *display* may be used)

e) both routines in question 2d) exhibit duplication of code; write a single routine to do this task. (Hint: use an argument, which will enable the type required to be determined dynamically.)

# 10 Generic Classes

The term genericity is clearly related to the word 'general', and when we talk of genericity in the context of software construction we are talking about the capacity to produce components which have a general use. Such components are essential if we are to promote the reuse of code through the development of class libraries.

The development of the technique of genericity has been in response to the need in typed languages to provide container classes or data structures which may be used for any type.

The idea of a generic class was first introduced in chapter 7 where it was shown how class ARRAY could be used to store integers, reals, strings, or indeed any class of object. This chapter introduces another generic class, LINKED_LIST, and shows how programmers may develop their own generic classes. The chapter begins by introducing container classes and the concept of genericity. This is followed by a brief introduction to LINKED_LIST, and then a brief section on alternatives to genericity, which may be of interest to those with experience of other object-oriented languages. The rest of the chapter shows how reusable classes may be developed in Eiffel using unconstrained and constrained genericity.

## 10.1 Container classes

Any object-oriented language should include an extensive class library of data structures such as sets, stacks, lists, trees, queues, ordered lists, tables and so on. Such classes are often referred to as container classes. To be useful, and to meet the goal of reusability, container classes must be as general purpose as possible, and must therefore, be able to allow the storage of objects of any type.

For an untyped language, such as Smalltalk, this was never a problem. The Smalltalk class library from its inception provided an impressive number of container classes which could be used to store any object. The problems in managing structures which may contain any kind of object are in Smalltalk left to the programmer, and the consequences of programmer error may not appear until execution-time.

For typed languages, the 'container problem', as it has sometimes been known, has presented the challenge of how to combine reusability and generality with safety and static type checking. The solution, which Eiffel was the first object-oriented language to adopt, is referred to as *parametric polymorphism* or more commonly, *genericity*. This solution allows us to develop class templates.

The decision as to the class type or types to be contained in a generic data structure is postponed until compile time, when the programmer who is using a generic class is required to supply the name or names of the types to be used.

For languages which do not support parameterised classes the best solution is to define a base element class, preferably an abstract class, and make all actual element types inherit from it, as shown in section 10.3.

## 10.2 A generic class: LINKED_LIST

A generic class is a template from which actual data structures may be derived. So if we look at class LINKED_LIST in the EiffelBase library, we will find that it is declared as

**class** LINKED_LIST [G]

The [G] is known as a formal generic parameter. G is now the most widely used formal parameter, but the rules of Eiffel allow any identifier. By convention a single letter is used, which is likely to avoid the use of a class name. The following declarations would not be allowed:

**class** LINKED_LIST[ANY];
**class** LINKED_LIST[INTEGER],

since ANY and INTEGER are both classes.

A class may derive a type from a generic class either by becoming a client, as shown below

**feature**
*customers*:LINKED_LIST[CUSTOMER]

or by supplying an actual parameter with the inheritance part:

**class** CUST_LIST
**inherit** LINKED_LIST [CUSTOMER]

In both cases an actual class must be provided - CUSTOMER in the above cases; this is called an *actual generic parameter*.

The main advantage of a linked list is that it is a dynamic data structure, the size of which is increased and decreased as elements are added and removed. Each element in the list, apart from the first and the last, has a predecessor and a successor. The kind of operations performed on a linked list are similar to an array: add an element; remove an element; traverse the list; search for an element. A linked list in Eiffel has a distinguishing feature that is absent from most of the standard textbook explanations of lists, a cursor, which indicates the current position in the list (see figure 10.1). Access to the list is determined by the state of the cursor.

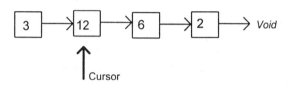

**Figure 10.1** An Eiffel LINKED LIST with Cursor

In the case shown in figure 10.1, the call, *item*, would retrieve the value, *12*, the call, *forth*, would move the cursor to the next element; *item* would then retrieve the value 6. The call, *back*, would move the cursor back to the 2nd element. To move the cursor to the first element there would, at that point, be three choices: *start*, *go_to_ith(1)*, or *back*.

A selection of the basic features in the Eiffel LINKED_LIST are summarised below.

| **Transformers** | |
| --- | --- |
| *forth* | -- moves cursor forward one element |
| *back* | -- moves cursor back one element |
| *start* | -- moves cursor to first element |
| *finish* | -- moves cursor to last element |
| *go_to_ith (i:*INTEGER*)* | -- moves cursor to ith element |
| | |
| *put_left(v:* **like** *item)* | -- adds element to left of cursor position |
| *put_right (v:* **like** *item)* | -- adds element to right of cursor position |
| *remove_left* | -- removes element to left of cursor position |
| *remove_right* | -- removes element to right of cursor position |
| *remove* | -- removes element at cursor position |

| **Accessors** | |
| --- | --- |
| *before* :BOOLEAN | -- is cursor pointing before the list? |
| *after*:BOOLEAN | -- is cursor pointing after the list? |
| *off*:BOOLEAN | -- *before* **or** *after* |
| *isfirst*:BOOLEAN | -- is cursor pointing to first element? |

| | |
|---|---|
| *islast*:BOOLEAN | -- is cursor pointing to last element? |
| *item* : G | -- returns element at cursor position |
| *first_element:* **like** *item* | -- returns first element |
| *last_element:* **like** *item* | -- returns last element |
| *previous:* **like** *item* | -- returns element before cursor |
| *next:* **like** *item* | -- returns element after cursor |

The features are grouped into four sections: those which alter the cursor, those which alter the contents of the list, those which query the state of the cursor, and those which access items in the list.

The use of the generic parameter, G, as in the type of the accessor, *item:* should be noted. This indicates that the type of the object returned will be the type with which the class is derived. Similarly, the anchored declarations which follow, indicate that the other accessors will return objects of the same type as *item*. It is this which gives the generic class its flexibility: at compile time the compiler is able to supply an actual class name as the parameter. It can at the same time check that only elements which conform to that class will be put into the list.

This brief introduction to generic linked lists concludes with an example of a simple list_traversal algorithm (10.1). The reader is left to implement the routine which adds elements to the list.

```
class CONTROLLER
    creation
        start
    feature
        int_list:LINKED_LIST[INTEGER];
        fill_list is
        do

        end -- fill_list
        start is
        do
            !!int_list.make
            fill_list;
            from int_list.start
            until int_list.after
            loop
                io.putint(int_list.item);
                int_list.forth
```

```
                    end -- loop
                end -- start
        end -- CONTROLLER
```

*Example 10.1 Using LINKED_LIST*

Our view of the syntax of an Eiffel class may now be updated to show how classes may be defined with formal generic parameters, and how classes which have formal generic parameters are inherited. It can be seen that after the name of the class there is the provision for optional formal generic parameters. More than one such parameter is allowed.

```
class <class_name> [ "[" formal generic parameters "] " ]
    inherit
        <class_type> [ "[" actual generic parameters "] " ]
    creation
        <routine_name>
    feature
        {routines | attributes }
end
```

## 10.3 Non-generic solutions to writing container classes

In Eiffel it would be possible to emulate Smalltalk and write a library of classes which allowed any item to be added to a list. To do this we would simply make the formal arguments of the routines of type ANY, so that the signatures of the routines for adding and removing lists would be as follows:

```
add (an_obj:ANY);
remove(an_obj:ANY);
```

At first sight this might seem an attractive solution. We cannot provide a more general facility than this. The problem is that it is unsafe; it makes static type checking impossible - for example it does not allow the compiler to guarantee that if we wish to have a list of integers, the list will contain integers and only integers. Such an approach to building a library would certainly be inconsistent with the Eiffel philosophy, which includes reliability as well as reuse. Eiffel container classes require us to specify the type of elements that are to be put in the data structure, and in return we can rely on static checks to ensure that only elements which conform to that type will ever get into the structure.

A similar solution, used in hybrid languages which contain no generic facility, and no general class from which all classes automatically inherit, would be to declare a base class designed to serve as a template for all classes whose instances may be added to the data structure. Such a base class would have virtual methods, that is to say methods designed to be overridden and to be bound at run time - and any object which was to be added to the data structure would have to conform to this base class. So, for example, we might declare a class LINK_OBJECT, with a single attribute, *link*, which is a pointer to a LINK_OBJECT, and a routine, *smaller*, to ensure that objects in the list can be compared (figure 10.2).

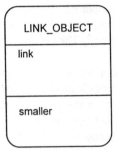

**Figure 10.2**

Class LINKED_LIST would have a single attribute, *first*, a pointer to a LINK_OBJECT, and the signatures of its routines would be as follows:

>*add(an_element*:LINK_OBJECT);
>*remove(an_element*:LINK_OBJECT);

If, for example, we wished to have a list of customers; all that would be required would be to make class CUSTOMER inherit from LINK_OBJECT. In addition to its own data and routines, class CUSTOMER would therefore have an inherited attribute, *link*, which pointed to the next element in the list, and *smaller* would be defined as appropriate for CUSTOMER (e.g. possibly by comparing *customer_id*). Such a list of Customers is depicted in figure 10.3.

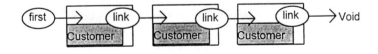

**Figure 10.3**

This method, which has been much used in the past, is laborious, and subject to the same weaknesses as would be the use of class ANY in Eiffel.

Genericity by contrast satisfies the requirements of reliability as well as reuse: it enables us to write general classes, but to derive these with prescribed types; this allows the compiler to guarantee that all the elements in a container conform to the static type with which the class was derived.

## 10.4  Developing generic classes

This section contains two example which illustrate how generic classes may be developed. The first returns to the two-dimensional array which was mapped on to a vector developed in chapter 7. The second develops a new class, with three generic parameters.

Class D2_ARRAY, which is shown in example 10.2, has been altered in a few ways from its original specification in chapter 7: it has been designed to inherit from ARRAY; the creation routine is called *create*, because *make* is used by ARRAY; the names *item* and *put* have been renamed, since these also clash with inherited names; a precondition has been added to each. A preferred technique to resolve the name clashes would have been to use direct repeated inheritance (see chapter 13) which would allow us both to redefine and to keep copies of the original. It would also be wise to use the re-export facilities to restrict the access of clients to inherited features which might prove dangerous. This topic is covered in chapter 11.

```
class D2_ARRAY[G]
    -- implemented using a one-dimensional array
    inherit
        ARRAY[G]
    creation
        create
    feature
        columns: INTEGER;
        rows:INTEGER;
        valid_coordinates(r,c:INTEGER):BOOLEAN is
        do
            Result := r <= rows and c<= cols
                        and  r > 0 and c > 0;
        end -- valid_coordinates
        put_at(element :G; row,col:INTEGER) is
            require
```

```
                            valid_coordinates(row,col);
            do
                    put(element, (row-1)* columns+col-1)
            end -- put_at
            item_at(row,col:INTEGER) :G  is
                    require
                            valid_coordinates(row,col);
            do
                    Result := item((row-1)*columns + col -1)
            end -- item_at
            create(n_row,n_col:INTEGER) is
            do
                    make(0, n_row*n_col -1);
                    columns := n_col;
                    rows := n_row;
            end -- create
    end --D2_ARRAY
```

*Example 10.2 Generic two dimensional array*

We have in example 10.2 developed a routine, *valid_coordinates*, to aid the user to check that preconditions are valid. This allows us to avoid duplicating the code in the *item_at* routine. The reader should again note the use of the formal generic parameter, G in this case, as the argument to a routine, and as the result-type of a routine. Formal generic parameters may be used in the class text wherever a type identifier would be used.

The reader who wishes to use class D2_ARRAY may declare attributes as follows:

```
feature
    names:D2_ARRAY[STRING]
    numbers:D2_ARRAY[REAL]
```

and may create the arrays as shown below:

```
!!names.create(10,10);
!!numbers.create(50,1000);
```

The second case study illustrates how a generic class may have more than one formal generic parameter. It will build a table which is capable of storing information such as that depicted in figure 10.4, in which the information in each of the three columns is of a different type.

Row

| | | | |
|---|---|---|---|
| 1 | Kramer | 20 | 1.5 |
| 2 | Ojukwe | 15 | 3.5 |
| 3 | Smart | 10 | 2.4 |

**Figure 10.4**

To do this we could write a generic class with the following formal parameters:

THREE_COL_TABLE[ C1, C2, C3 ]

and could derive a type from this as follows:

*my_table*: THREE_COL_TABLE[ STRING, INTEGER, REAL ];

The number of actual parameters must be the same as the number of formal parameters.

There are a number of possible alternatives for implementing the generic class THREE_COL_TABLE, including three discrete arrays - one for each column.

To add a row to the table, the heading for the routine *add_row* would be written as follows:

*add_row( lft*:C1, *mid*:C2, *rt:* C3, *row:*INTEGER )

As already indicated in the previous example, formal generic parameters, *C1*, *C2* and *C3* in this case, may be used wherever a type would be used. At this point it is worth reiterating what has already been said about reliability and type checking. The compiler can check the actual generic parameters to find the types of C1, C2 and C3, and so can ensure that only a STRING, or an object of a type that conforms to STRING, can be put into column 1; likewise, only an INTEGER can be put into the middle column, and only a REAL into the right-hand column.

The following accessors could be added to class THREE_COL_TABLE:

    *left(row*:INTEGER*)*: C1
    *middle(row:*INTEGER*)*: C2
    *right(row:*INTEGER*)*: C3

Again the use the formal generic parameters as the result types of the accessor routines should be noted. This gives both the flexibility of deriving classes using different types, as well as the guarantee of compile time checking and reliability. A call to middle(2) would, given the data depicted in figure 10.4, return the value 15. A possible implementation for this class is provided in example 10.4.

```
class THREE_COL_TABLE [C1,C2,C3]
    -- implemented using three arrays
    creation
        make
    feature {NONE}
        lft_col:ARRAY[C1];
        mid_col:ARRAY[C2];
        rt_col:ARRAY[C3];
    feature
        rows:INTEGER;
        valid_row(r:INTEGER) :BOOLEAN is
        do
            Result := r > 0 and  r <= rows
        end -- valid_row
    -- accessor routines
        left(row:INTEGER): C1 is
        do
            Result := lft_col @ row;
        end -- left
        middle(row:INTEGER): C2 is
        do
            Result := mid_col @ row;
        end -- middle
        right(row:INTEGER): C3 is
        do
            Result := rt_col @ row;
        end --right
    -- transformer routines
        insert_left(element :C1; row:INTEGER) is
```

```
                do
                      lft_col.put(element,row)
                end  -- insert_left
                insert_mid(element :C2; row:INTEGER) is
                do
                      mid_col.put(element,row)
                end  -- insert_mid
                insert_right(element :C3; row:INTEGER) is
                do
                      rt_col.put(element,row)
                end  -- insert_right
                add_row(lft:C1;mid:C2; rt:C3;row:INTEGER) is
                do
                      lft_col.put(lft,row)
                      mid_col.put(mid,row)
                      rt_col.put(rt,row)
                end -- add
          -- creation routine
                make(n_row:INTEGER) is
                do
                      !!lft_col.make(1,n_row);
                      !!mid_col.make(1,n_row);
                      !!rt_col.make(1,n_row);
                      rows := n_row;
                end -- make
  end --THREE_COL_TABLE
```

*Example 10.4 Generic THREE_COL_TABLE*

Additionally, a precondition could be written for each accessor and transformer routine :

**require**
> *valid_row(row);*

The reader may notice that three arrays are hidden, so that a client may access their contents only through the routines provided in THREE_COL_TABLE.

An example of the flexibility a generic approach gives may be illustrated as follows: we might at some later stage wish to have a table which had different types of data, e.g those shown in figure 10.5.

Row

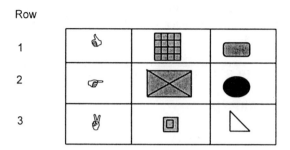

**Figure 10.5**

This could be derived using different types as appropriate:

> *my_table*: THREE_COL_TABLE[ CHARACTER,
>                                          RECTANGLE, FIGURE ];

and it would not be necessary to change any of the code written for THREE_COL_TABLE. Additionally THREE_COL_TABLE could be used to provide a structure with more than 3 columns. For example the number of columns could be increased to five by nesting as follows:

> *my_table*:THREE_COL_TABLE[THREE_COL_TABLE[STRING,
>                                                            INTEGER ,
>                                                            CHARACTER],
>                       RECTANGLE,
>                       FIGURE];

The reader should be able to work out that this would give a five column table with the types from left to right as follows:

STRING   INTEGER   CHARACTER   RECTANGLE   FIGURE

## 10.5 Constrained genericity

Sometimes it is useful to restrict the genericity of a class by specifying that only types with certain properties my be used as actual generic parameters. To illustrate this we can return to an example first introduced in chapter 7, that of sorting an array. Now it would be far better to produce a generic solution for this. To do so it is necessary to ensure that the elements in the array are capable of being ordered. To do this, a generic class would be used, but Eiffel permits us to specify that the actual parameter should conform to COMPARABLE, as shown in example 10.5.

```
class SORTABLE_ARRAY [ S -> COMPARABLE]
    inherit
        ARRAY[S]

end -- SORTABLE_ARRAY
```

*Example 10.5 Constrained genericity*

This means that, when instances of class SORTABLE_ARRAY are declared, only classes which inherit from COMPARABLE may be used as actual arguments. The following would all be valid,

```
feature
    store:SORTABLE_ARRAY[ INTEGER ]
    names:SORTABLE_ARRAY[ STRING ]
    letters:SORTABLE_ARRAY[ CHARACTER ]
```

as would any class that we write that inherits from class COMPARABLE. An implementation for this class is given in example 10.6.

```
class SORTABLE_ARRAY [ S -> COMPARABLE]
    inherit
        ARRAY[S]
    creation
        make
    feature
        sort is
            -- sorts array in ascending order
        local
            sorted:BOOLEAN;
            temp_item: S;
            index, last :INTEGER;
        do
            from
                last := upper ;
                sorted := false;
            until sorted or else last = lower
```

```
        loop
            from
                last := last - 1;
                index := lower -1
                sorted := true
            until index = last
            loop
                index := index + 1;
                if item(index) > item(index+1)
                then
                -- swap with successor element
                    temp_item := item(index+1);
                    put(item(index),index+1);
                    put(temp_item,index);
                    sorted := false;
                end -- if
            end -- loop
        end -- loop
    end -- sort
end -- SORTABLE_ARRAY
```

*Example 10.6 Constrained genericity: SORTABLE_ARRAY*

The use of this class is illustrated in example 10.7.

```
class SORT_TESTER
    creation
        start
    feature
        names: SORTABLE_ARRAY[STRING]
        print_array is
            local
                index :INTEGER
        do
            from index := names.lower - 1
            invariant index < names.upper + 1
            variant names.upper - index
            until index = names.upper
            loop
                index := index + 1;
                io.putstring(names.item(index));
```

```
                    io.new_line;
              end -- loop
         end -- print_array
         start is
              local
                    index:INTEGER
         do
              !!names.make(1,10)
              from index : = names.lower -1
              until index = names.upper
              loop
                    index : = index + 1;
                    io.putstring("enter name => ");
                    io.readword;
                    names.put(clone(io.laststring), index);
              end -- loop
              names.sort;
              print_array;
         end -- start
   end -- TEST_SORTABLE
```

*Example 10.7 Testing Class SORTABLE_ARRAY*

The reader should notice that we are unable to include a routine to print the array in the generic class. To do this is not straightforward. Among the possible solutions are the following:

use a run-time test to establish the type of the elements in the array, and call the appropriate output routine;

define the generic class D2_ARRAY with two parameters, and make the second parameter class PRINTABLE, which would be guaranteed to have a routine called *output* defined in the same way that COMPARABLE is guaranteed to have the < operator.

The first solution would have the disadvantage that class D2_ARRAY would have to be altered to take account of new classes developed, which would defeat the whole idea of a generic class. The second solution, shown in outline in example 10.8, seems better.

```
      class SORTABLE_ARRAY [ S -> COMPARABLE,
                             P -> PRINTABLE]
         ......................
         print (out:P) is
               local
                     index:INTEGER
         do
               from index := names.lower-1
               invariant index < names.upper + 1
               variant names.upper - index
               until index = names.upper
               loop
                     index := index + 1;
                     out.output(item(index))
                     -- code which calls a routine  in class P
                     io.new_line;
               end -- loop
         end -- print_print
      end --SORTABLE_ARRAY
```

*Example 10.8 Generic class with two parameters*

For STRING a class STRING_OUTPUT could then be defined, as a descendant of PRINTABLE. This would make the routine *output* effective as follows:

```
      output (s:STRING) is
      do
            io.putstring(s);
      end;
```

This is far from straightforward. It would mean that a new descendant of class PRINTABLE would have to be written for each CLASS that we wished to use as an actual argument for class SORTABLE_ARRAY. Nevertheless it would mean that class D2_ARRAY would not have to be modified. This example is developed further in chapter 12 when abstract classes are introduced.

## 10.6 Genericity in Eiffel: a summary

This section provides a short summary of the points made in this chapter:

1. Genericity is a mechanism which allows the creation of general reusable classes; it is particularly useful for creating container classes: arrays, lists, trees and so on.

2. Generic classes are class templates from which actual classes may be derived.

3. Actual classes may be derived either as attributes or through inheritance.

4. Generic classes have one or more formal parameters, which are replaced with appropriate class names when an actual class is created from a generic class.

5. A formal parameter name may not be the name of an actual class.

6. Formal generic parameters may be used in the class text wherever a type identifier is allowable.

7. Eiffel supports constrained genericity; this gives added protection by restricting the classes that may be used as actual parameters to those which conform to the type of the formal generic parameter.

### *Exercises*

1. Make notes on genericity and constrained genericity.

2. a) Write the **short** form for a generic class SET which inherits from ARRAY, and which offers the following services:

> Accessors:
> > *empty* -- true if empty
> > *contains* -- true if element passed in as argument is present
>
> Transformer:
> > *insert* -- insert an element
>
> Creators:
> > **infix** "+", *union*
> > **infix** "*", *intersection*
> > **infix** "-", *difference*

b) write the bodies of the routines (note that the creators must not alter any existing sets, and must return new, independent sets with independent elements) (note also that elements in a set may not be duplicated). Hint: clone *Current* and then add/subtract members as necessary, and use *deep_copy*. Test the class from a client class. At least two instances of SET will be needed to test the creators. A print routine for class SET will aid testing.

3. Re-implement THREE_COL_TABLE using linked lists instead of arrays.

4. a) Derive types from THREE_COL_TABLE which would allow the following representation of data:

    i. INTEGER  STRING  REAL  INTEGER  STRING  REAL
CHARACTER
    ii.CHARACTER  STRING  STRING  REAL  REAL  INTEGER
STRING  STRING  REAL

b) Work out how,using the *left, middle and right* accessor routines already defined, the following could be accessed from a structure, *my_table*, with 9 columns as in exercise 4 a) ii:

    row 2  column5;
    row 3  column 7;
    row 2  column 4;

# 11 Adapting Inherited Classes

Frequently, when a class is inherited, the descendant class needs to make alterations to the inherited class. The most common forms of alteration are

- changing the name of an inherited feature to avoid a name clash or to provide a more meaningful name within the context of the new class;

- redefining an inherited feature so that it has a different meaning or behaves differently to the inherited feature;

- changing the visibility of an inherited feature, usually by making it private or restricting its use to a few named classes.

In Eiffel, this is known as feature adaptation, which is included in the inheritance part of an Eiffel class, as shown in the syntax definition below:

```
class <class_name> [ "[" formal generic parameters "] " ]
    [inherit
        <class_type> [ "[" actual generic parameters "] " ]
        [ Rename ]
        [ New-Exports]
        [ Undefine ]
        [ Redefine ]
        [ Select ]
    end ]
    creation
        <routine_name>
    feature
        {routines | attributes }
end
```

It should be noted that order is significant. Rename must come before New-exports, which must come before Undefine, and so on. Whenever one of the feature adaptation subclauses is used, the **end** must be included.

This chapter covers the Rename, New-Exports and Redefine subclauses. The Undefine and Select subclauses are covered in chapters 12 and 13 respectively.

## 11.1 New-exports in Eiffel

It should be emphasised that Eiffel makes a clear distinction between a descendant and a client, and that the declaration of features as private does not affect their visibility in a descendant class. A descendant class has precisely the same access to features as the ancestor class in which they were declared, provided that they have not been renamed or redefined in any intervening class in the inheritance hierarchy.

Sometimes it is desirable that features which have been inherited should not be available to clients of a new class because it would be unsafe for them to be used. We may take as an example the generic class D2_ARRAY, which was introduced in chapter 10, and is reproduced in outline in example 11.1.

```
class D2_ARRAY[G]
-- implemented using a one-dimensional array
    inherit
        ARRAY[G]
    creation
        create
    feature
        columns: INTEGER;
        rows:INTEGER;
        valid_coordinates(r,c:INTEGER):BOOLEAN
        put_at(element :G; row,col:INTEGER)
            require
                valid_coordinates(row,col);
        item_at(row,col:INTEGER) :G
            require
                valid_coordinates(row,col);
        create(n_row,n_col:INTEGER)
    end --D2_ARRAY
```

*Example 11.1 Generic D2_Array*

Class D2_ARRAY inherits from class ARRAY, and is implemented using a one_dimensional array, with mapping functions to access elements of the array. All the features defined for class ARRAY[G] are therefore available for clients of class D2_ARRAY. It is fairly obvious that, for example, it ought not to be possible to access a two-dimensional array using a single subscript. Likewise, there are other inherited features, in addition to *put,* which it would be undesirable for a client to use; these include *force    item    lower    upper    resize*

So, given the declaration of a D2_ARRAY in a client class, as shown in class ARRAY_TESTER in example 11.2, it would be possible for the client to make unsafe calls, some of which are shown.

```
class ARRAY_TESTER
    creation
        start
    feature
        store:D2_ARRAY[REAL];
        start is
        do
            .............
        end -- start
        unsafe_instructions is
        do
                store.force(27.98,110);
                store.resize(20,200);
                store.put(67.76,25)
        end -- unsafe-instructions
end -- ARRAY_TESTER
```

*Example 11.2 Unsafe instructions used by client*

In order to produce a safe class, it is necessary to prohibit access to these features by clients. Eiffel provides a re-export facility for this purpose.

```
class D2_ARRAY[G]
    inherit ARRAY[G]
        export
            {NONE} put, force, item,
                            resize, lower,upper
    end -- inherit ARRAY
```

*Example 11.3 Hiding inherited features*

Example 11.3 indicates that no client of D2_ARRAY may use the facilities listed. Given this alteration, the unsafe_instructions in example 11.2 would not compile. Alternatively, we could decide that clients of D2_ARRAY should be prevented from using all inherited features, as shown in example 11.4.

---

**class** D2_ARRAY[G]
    **inherit** ARRAY[G]
        **export**
            {NONE} **all**
    **end** -- inherit ARRAY

*Example 11.4 Restricting client access to all inherited features*

---

It is possible to be more selective in the restrictions on visibility of inherited features: a named class or classes may each be given different access:

---

**class** D2_ARRAY[G]
    **inherit** ARRAY[G]
        **export**
            {CLASS_A} *put, item* ;
            {CLASS_A, CLASS_B, CLASS_C} *lower, upper*
            {NONE} *force, resize*
    **end** -- inherit ARRAY

*Example 11.5 Restricting access of certain clients to inherited features*

---

Thus in example 11.5 only CLASS_A has access to *put* and *item*, only CLASS_A, CLASS_B and CLASS_C have access to *lower* and *upper*. No class has access to *force* and *resize*.

The syntax rule for the re-export part of feature adapation is given in figure 11.1.

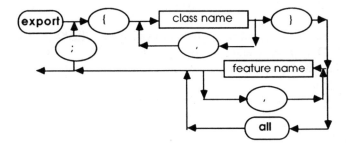

**Figure 11.1**

It should be pointed out in regard to the above rule that NONE is a class which inherits from every class, so that a client list written as {NONE}, (see example 11.5), is syntactically valid. There are additional rules which a compiler should enforce:

(a)   the reserved word **all** may appear only once for each class inherited, so that the following would not be allowed:

> **export**
>> {CLASS_A} **all**
>> {NONE} *feature_a, feature_b, feature_c*
>> {CLASS_C} **all**

the only acceptable form in this case would be

> **export**
>> {CLASS_A, CLASS_C} **all**
>> {NONE} *feature_a, feature_b, feature_c*

(b)   no feature_name may appear twice, so that the following would be invalid:

> **export**
>> {CLASS_A, CLASS_C} *feature_b*
>> {CLASS_D} *feature_a, feature_b, feature_c*

because *feature_b* appears in two different lists; the correct form would be:

> **export**
>> {CLASS_A, CLASS_C, CLASS_D} *feature_b*
>> {CLASS_D} *feature_a, feature_c*

In the last case above, *feature_b* would be available to CLASS_A, CLASS_C, and CLASS_D. *Feature_a* and *feature_c* would be available to CLASS_D only. Any other inherited features would have the same export status that they had in the parent class.

Finally, we need to consider the rules of export and re-export as they affect descendants of clients. The rule is that if a class is listed in a client list as having access to a feature, then its descendants have the same access. This is a sensible rule, not least because when a class is written it is impossible to know which descendants, if any, it will ultimately have.

## 11.2 Renaming features

Sometimes, it is necessary to rename an inherited feature. This occurs in cases of multiple inheritance when a name clashes with another (chapter 13), it also occurs when an inherited name seems unsuitable in the context of a new class. The latter may be illustrated by showing how THREE_COL_TABLE could be altered to allow a bank to hold information on clients. Each entry in a CLIENT_LIST consists of client's name, account no, and current balance. In example 11.6, the new names selected are more appropriate to the application.

```
class CLIENT_LIST
        inherit THREE_COL_TABLE[STRING,INTEGER,REAL]
            rename
                left as name,
                middle as account_no,
                right as current_balance,
                insert_left as insert_name,
                insert_mid as insert_account,
                insert_right as insert_balance
            end
    end -- CLIENT_LIST
```

*Example 11.6 Renaming inherited features*

It should be appreciated that the new names must thereafter be used by all clients and descendants of CLIENT_LIST. The new names must also be used in the text of CLIENT_LIST itself, including any subsequent feature adaptation subclauses. As indicated at the beginning of this chapter, the rename must always be the first in the adaptation clause. The syntax of rename is shown in figure 11.2.

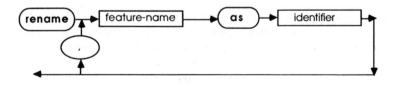

**Figure 11.2**

## 11.3  Redefining features

The ability to redeclare or to over-ride an inherited feature is a fundamental of object-orientation. It allows us to develop new classes by tailoring inherited features to the particular needs of the new class. To do this in Eiffel we simply list the features to be redefined in the redefinition subclause, and then redefine the features in the feature-part of the class.

The constraints of the Eiffel type system and of design by contract put limits on the extent to which a feature can be redefined. The key rules for feature redefinition in Eiffel may be summarised as follows:

1. If the inherited feature being redefined is an attribute, then the new feature must be an attribute;
2. The signature of a new feature must conform to the signature of the inherited feature being redefined;
3. A precondition may not be strengthened, and a postcondition may not be weakened.

Rule 2 needs further elaboration:

- it applies to attributes as well as to routines;
- he type of an attribute must conform to the type of the attribute being redefined;
- he type of a routine which returns a result must conform to the type of the original routine;
- new routine must have the same number of arguments as the routine being redefined;
- he type of the formal arguments must conform to those in the routine being redefined.

That means therefore that if a routine with the following heading:

> *any_routine(x*:CLASS_A;*y*:CLASS_B):CLASS_Z;

is redefined, it must have the same same number of arguments, 2 in this case, the arguments must be of types which conform to CLASS_A and CLASS_B respectively, and the new result-type must also conform to the inherited result-type, CLASS_Z.

Rule 3 is discussed more fully later in the chaper. The syntax of the redefines sub_clause is defined in figure 11.3.

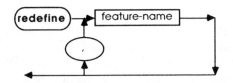

**Figure 11.3**

We can begin with an example by going back to class CLOCK. This class has three attributes for storing hours, minutes and seconds, and is restricted to storing up to 23:59:59. It has routines for incrementing the time by a second, and for setting the time. Now we might wish to inherit from this to create a class which can store almost unlimited elapsed time. To do this one could develop a class TIME_KEEPER, with additional attributes, *days* and *years*, as shown in example 11.7.

```
class TIME_KEEPER
    inherit
        CLOCK
            rename
                set as set_time
            redefine
                display, increment
        end -- inherit CLOCK
    creation
        switch_on
    feature
    -- new attributes
        days, years: INTEGER;
    -- redefined features
        display
        increment
    -- new routine
        set_day_and_year(day, year:INTEGER) is
            require
                non_negative:
                    day >= 0 and year >= 0;
end -- TIME_KEEPER
```

*Example 11.7 Renaming and redefinition*

As shown above, it is necessary to redefine *increment* in order to ensure that the attributes *days* and *years* are incremented at the appropriate time. It would probably be useful to redefine *set*, but Eiffel will not permit a change to the number of parameters, so it is renamed and given a more specific name, *set_time*. A new transformer routine, *set_day_and_year* is introduced, to allow the new attributes to be altered. The routine *display* is redefined to take account of the new attributes, *days* and *years*.

An instance of class TIME_KEEPER is now be able to offer the following services:

> *display*   *set_time*   *increment*   *set_day_and_years*          *switch_on*

The implications of the renaming and the redefinition now need examining. Given the following attribute declarations:

> a_clock:CLOCK;
> a_time_keeper: TIME_KEEPER;

and given the following assignment:
> a_clock := a_time_keeper;

the operations

> *display*        *increment*

would at run-time be bound to the routines defined in class TIME_KEEPER. The following would be rejected by the compiler:

> a_clock.set_time( 10,10,10);
> a_clock.set_day_and_year(10,10);

even though *a_clock* was dynamically attached to an instance of class TIME_KEEPER; the following would be accepted by the compiler, however

> a_clock.set(10,10,10).

The reader is left to complete class TIME_KEEPER as an exercise.


## 11.4 Renaming and redefinition compared

The clear distinction between renaming and redefinition should at this point be emphasised. When a feature is redefined, the new implementation provided has a well defined relationship to the feature it is replacing. The compiler will check to see that any redefinition is valid as indicated in the last section. Renaming a feature, simply provides another name for the original feature. The feature remains exactly the same as before. An error often made is to use renaming simply to free a name for use in the current class. Whilst perfectly allowable, it can lead to difficulties. The danger is that if we rename a feature, and then reuse the original name, this might be confused with a redefinition. In fact if we inherit a feature *f*, rename it as *f2*, and then declare a new feature as *f*, this new *f* has no relationship to the inherited feature *f*. The compiler will *not* check the validity of the new *f* against the old *f*. We can illustrate the significance of this in examples 11.8 and 11.9.

In the first example, class B inherits from class A, and redefines *f*. Class MAIN (example 11.8 c) is a client of both A and B, through the declaration of the attributes *x* and *y*. When y, whose static type is A, is assigned to *x*, the dynamic type of *y* now changes to B. The Eiffel run-time system must at this point ensure that the version of *f* which is called is that redefined in class B. In the case of redefinition, the *f* in class B is simply a different version of the *f* in class A, and the system knows which routine to call if the dynamic type of an entity changes.

```
class A
    feature
        f is
        do
                io.putstring("Class A");
        end -- f
end -- class A
```

*Example 11.8a: Feature redefinition: Class A*

```
class B
    inherit
        A;
            redefine f;
        end
    feature
        f is
        do
                io.putstring("Class B");
        end -- f
end -- class B
```

*Example 11.8b: Feature redefinition: Class B*

```
class MAIN
    creation
        start
    feature
        x:B;
        y:A;
        start is
        do
                !!x;
                !!y;
                y.f -- f as defined in class A is executed
                y := x;
                y.f -- f as defined in class B is executed
        end -- start
end -- MAIN
```

*Example 11.8c Feature redefinition and polymorphism:root class, MAIN*

The example given in 11.8 contrasts with the situation shown in example 11.9, in which class B simply renames *f* as *fb*, and then declares another routine called *f*. The routines *f* in A and *f* in B are totally unrelated: they are different routines, which happen to have the same name. It would be possible therefore to make *f* a function, or to give it some formal arguments - each of which would be prevented if the new *f* were a redefinition.

```
class B
    inherit
        A;
        rename f as fb
    end -- inherit
    feature
        f is
        do
                io.putstring("Class B");
        end -- f
end -- class B
```

*Example 11.9a Renaming to free a name for use*

In this case therefore, the new routine *f* will not be called if an an entity whose static type is class A changes its dynamic type to B. As should be appreciated, this is entirely appropriate given the fact that no guarantees may be made about the relationship between the old *f* and the new *f*.

```
class MAIN
    creation
        start
    feature
        x:B;
        y:A;
        start is
        do
                !!x;
                !!y;
                y := x;
                y.f        -- executes f defined in class A
                           -- dynamic type of y is B
            end -- start
    end -- MAIN
```

*11.9b Renaming and polymorphism*

## 11.5 Feature redeclaration: stacks, ordered lists and queues

This section shows how, using inheritance and feature redeclaration, classes STACK, ORDERED_LIST, and QUEUE may be derived from a generic BASIC_LIST shown in example 11.10. It should be emphasised that this is done purely to illustrate how such data structures could be built. For most purposes the classes available in the Eiffel library provide all the facilities likely to be required.

In class BASIC_LIST constrained genericity has been used to ensure that a search may use the ">" and "<" operators defined in class COMPARABLE.

```
class BASIC_LIST[G -> COMPARABLE]
    feature { BASIC_LIST }
        hd:G
        tail:like Current;
        init(el:G; tl: like Current)
    feature
```

```
head: G is
    require
        not is_empty
size:INTEGER
-- returns number of elements in list
is_empty:BOOLEAN
    ensure
        size > 0 implies  Result = false
is_in(el:G):BOOLEAN is
    -- returns true if el is in list
add (el:G)
    ensure
        old size = size - 1;
        -- head = el
remove
    require
        size > 0
    ensure
        old size = size + 1;
        head = old tail.head
end -- BASIC_LIST
```

*Example 11.10 Outline of a recursive list*

Example 11.10 differs from LINKED_LIST introduced in chapter 10. It has no cursor, and it is a recursive class: BASIC_LIST is either empty (*void*) or it contains a head, and another BASIC_LIST. The representation of a list which currently contains two elements is shown in figure 11.4.

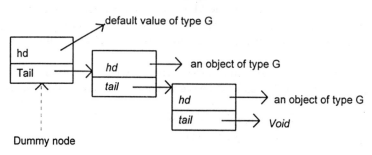

**Figure 11.4**

An empty list consists of a single element with default values, as shown in figure 11.5.

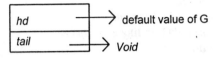

**Figure 11.5**

The implementation of the routines *is_empty* and *size* are given in example 11.11, and should enable the reader to understand how the data in the initial dummy node is always ignored - so that the real beginning of the list is the tail of the dummy node, which is *Void* if the list is empty.

```
is_empty:BOOLEAN is
do
        Result :=  tail = Void;
        ensure
                size > 0 implies Result = false
end -- is_empty
size:INTEGER is
do
        if tail = Void
        then Result := 0
        else Result := 1 + tail.size
        end -- if
end -- size
```

*Example 11.11 Handling of dummy node in BASIC_LIST*

The routine, *size*, routine returns 0 if the tail of the list is *Void*, that is to say if only the dummy node exists; otherwise it makes a recursive call on the tail, and adds one to the result. Likewise, as may be seen in example 11.12, the actual head of the list is referenced by *tail.hd,* and the precondition for the routine *head*, requires that the size of the list is greater than 0, in which case *tail* will not be *void*, and adherence to the precondition will avoid a run-time error.

The reader might also note that in the routine *is_in,* the operators ">" and "<" may be used, because, as mentioned earlier, constrained genericity guarantees that any element will inherit from class COMPARABLE. The remainder of the code for class BASIC_LIST is given in example 11.12.

```
class BASIC_LIST[G -> COMPARABLE]
    feature { BASIC_LIST }
        hd:G
        tail: like Current;
        init(el:G; tl: like Current) is
        do
                hd := el;
                tail := tl;
        end -- init
    feature
    -- routines already supplied: see example 11.11
    -- is_empty:BOOLEAN
    -- size:INTEGER

        head: G is
                require
                        not is_empty
        do
                Result := tail.hd
        end -- head
        is_in(el:G):BOOLEAN is
                -- returns true if el is in list
        do
                if is_empty
                        then Result := false
                elseif el < tail.hd or el > tail.hd
                then Result := tail.is_in(el);
                else Result := true
                end -- if
        end -- is-in
        add (el:G) is
                local
                        new_el:like.Current;
        do
                !!new_el;
                new_el.init(el,tail);
                tail := new_el;
                ensure
                        old size = size - 1;
                        -- head = el
        end -- add
```

*remove* **is**
> **require**
>> *size > 0*
>
> **do**
>> *tail := tail.tail;*
>
> **ensure**
>> **old** *size = size + 1;*
>>
>> *head = **old** tail.head*
>
> **end** -- remove
>
**end** -- BASIC_LIST

*Example 11.12 Class BASIC_LIST[G]*

Readers with some knowledge of data structures may have realised that BASIC_LIST is in fact a stack, a last in first out structure (LIFO), but the normal terminology, *top*, *pop* and *push*, has not been used. The effect of the operations push and pop on a stack *s*, is shown in the figure 11.6. As may be seen items are added and removed at one end only.

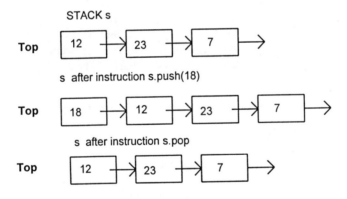

**Figure 11.6**

Should we wish to write class STACK, it becomes a trivial exercise to inherit from BASIC_LIST, and simply to rename the features *head, add* and *remove* as *top, push* and *pop* respectively. This task is left to the reader as an exercise.

We may now discover that we need a list which is always in order, so that the first element in the list will always be the smallest, and the last will always be the largest. This requires us to redefine the *add* routine, since that is the only feature which affects the ordering. This may be done through redefinition as shown in exercise 11.13.

```
class SORT_LIST[G -> COMPARABLE]
    inherit
    BASIC_LIST[G]
        rename add as insert,
        redefine insert
    end -- inherit BASIC_LIST

end -- SORT_LIST
```

*Example 11.13 Renaming and redefining a feature*

The identifier *insert* seems more meaningful in the context of a sorted list than *add*, so it has been renamed prior to redefinition. This means that instances of SORT_LIST no longer have access to *add*.

It should be pointed out that it would not have been possible to redefine *add* as required, had the second postcondition not been commented out. The assertion *head = el,* makes it clear that elements are added at the front of a list, which is not what is required for a sorted list. Were this not commented out, the new routine would not satisfy the postcondition, and an exception would be raised if the postconditions were switched on. The rules regarding the alteration to postconditions will be explained later in the chapter. The redefined routine is given in example 11.14.

```
feature
    insert(el:G) is
        local
            new_el: like Current;
        do
            if is_empty or else el < tail.head
            then
                !!new_el;
                new_el.init(el,tail);
                tail := new_el;
            else tail.insert(el)
            end -- if
    end -- insert;
```

*Example 11.14 Insert routine for SORT_LIST[G]*

The above provides a good example of the use of the semi-strict operators. Without the **or else**, two conditions would have had to be defined to avoid a run-time error:

```
if tail = Void
    then
            !!new_el;
            ..........
elseif  el < tail.hd
    then
            !!new_el;
            .........
else
        tail.insert(el)
end -- if
```

Now the routine *remove* must be considered: as defined in BASIC_LIST it removes the first element. If it were to be redeclared to allow a specific item to be removed, this would require a change to its signature, in a way not allowable in Eiffel. An alternative would be to rename it as *remove_first*, and to define a totally new *remove*. The new *remove* would in this case have no connection with the inherited *remove*. In cases of polymorphic assignment this could lead to undesirable results, as explained earlier in the chapter.

```
class SORT_LIST[G => COMPARABLE]
    inherit
        BASIC_LIST[G]
            rename
                add as insert,
                remove as remove_first
            export
            {NONE}  remove_first
            redefine
                insert
        end -- inherit BASIC_LIST
feature
    insert(el:G)
                -- already given -- example 11.14

    remove(el:G) is
                -- one occurrence of el is removed
```

```
                require
                        is_in (el)
      do
                if el > tail.head
                        then tail.remove(el);
                elseif el  <  tail.head
                then
                        -- should not happen - see precondition
                else   tail := tail.tail
                end -- if
                ensure
                size = old size - 1
        end -- remove
end -- SORT_LIST
```

*Example 11.15 Remove for class SORT_LIST*

It may be noted in example 11.15, that *remove_first* has been hidden: it would probably be undesirable to allow clients to remove elements at the front of a sorted list.

In addition to classes BASIC_LIST, SORT_LIST, and STACK, if the reader has defined this class, as suggested earlier, we shall now construct class QUEUE. A queue is a first in first out structure (FIFO). This means that elements are added to the rear, but as in BASIC_LIST, are still removed from the front. In order to derive a queue, *head* may be renamed as *front*, *remove* as *de_queue*, and *add* as *en_queue*. The routine *en_queue* is then redefined. The code for class QUEUE is given in example 11.16.

```
class QUEUE[G => COMPARABLE]
        inherit
              BASIC_LIST[G]
                    rename
                            head as front,
                            remove as de_queue,
                            add as en_queue
                    redefine
                            en_queue
              end
        feature
              en_queue(el:G) is
                    local
```

```
                              new_el:like Current;
              do
                      if tail = Void
                      then
                              !!new_el;
                              new_el.init(el,tail);
                              tail := new_el
                      else
                              tail.en_queue(el)
                      end -- if
              end -- en_queue
      end -- QUEUE
```

*Example 11.16 Class QUEUE*

The alert reader may have noticed that *en_queue* would be inefficient if there were a very long queue, since it requires the whole list to be traversed to find the last element. If a more efficient QUEUE were needed, then the proper procedure would be to inherit from QUEUE, and to extend the new class by adding a feature,

    *last* : **like** *Current*

initially set to *Void*. The routine *en_queue* would then be redefined to allow it to append an element directly to *last*, without needing to traverse the queue. It would also update *last,* to ensure that it pointed to the latest element added to the queue. The routine *de_queue* would then need to be redefined to take care of the following case:

```
      if tail = Void
        then  last := Void
      end -- if
```

We now have a small data structure library with the inheritance relationships shown in figure 11.7.

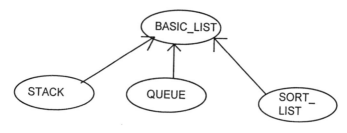

**Figure 11.7**

As stated at the beginning, an OO developer should not reinvent the wheel in the way that we have done, and for most purposes the Eiffel library is sufficient for all data structures likely to be required. For learning purposes, however, it is useful to have some understanding of how such structures may be implemented.

The following two sections of this chapter may be skipped on a first reading.


**11.6  Redeclaring assertions**

When a class is inherited, the rules of Eiffel will not allow us to weaken the original contract. This means that if we wish to make any changes to the assertions, the following rules must be followed:

- Class invariants may only be strengthened
- Preconditions may only be weakened
- Postconditions may only be strengthened

If a programmer wishes to write a new invariant for a class, the new invariant is concatenated to all the inherited invariants, so that the inherited invariants and the new one must all be true to avoid a violation.

The syntax for redefined preconditions and postconditions differs from that used in declarations. For a precondition the form is

    **require else**  Assertion

and for a postcondition,

    **ensure then**  Assertion

In the first case the logic is that of an **or else:** the user must satisfy either the original precondition **or** the new one; in the second case the logic is that of an **and then:** the supplier must satisy the original postcondition **and** the new one.

These rules mean that if a routine to be redefined has no precondition then there is no point in adding one to the redefined routine, because it will have no effect. At run-time the assertion would be evaluated as

**true or else** new precondition

If a routine does not already have a postcondition then this is no problem. At run-time the assertion would be evaluated as

**true and then** new postcondition

Postconditions that are too strong may impede redefinition, and make classes less reusable, as was seen in section 11.4 when *add* was redefined for class SORT_LIST. Our experiences with BASIC_LIST should provide insight into how sensible postconditions can be written. A look again at the original assertions for *add* (example 11.10), indicates that the original postcondition was inappropriate: there was no need to specify where the new element would be placed. It would have been correct for STACK, but for a BASIC_LIST it was over-specified. For *remove,* however, it was necessary that the postcondition should specify the item to be removed. Alternatives, including using a cursor (e.g. LINKED_LIST, chapter 10), might have been considered.

The reader who has followed the case study in the previous section will by now have appreciated that design for reuse is a far from trivial exercise.

## 11.7 Covariance

The concept of covariance is properly covered once the rules of conformance and feature redeclaration are understood. Covariance refers to the conformance rule which allows a formal argument in a routine in a descendant class to be a proper descendant of the formal argument in the parent class.

For example, if CLASS_A has a routine *r*, with CLASS_B as an argument type, *r(arg:*CLASS_B)*,* and the routine is redefined in CLASS_A2, which is a descendant of CLASS_A, then it is allowable for the type of the parameter to be a descendant of class B, say CLASS_B2, *r(arg:*CLASS_B2)*.* At compile time the actual argument may only be of CLASS_B2 or a descendant of CLASS_B2, not of CLASS_B. The more common contravariant rule would not allow this redefinition, and there has been some disagreement in the Eiffel community because of the fact that the redefinition appears to be a strengthening of a precondition. Nevertheless, there are occasions in which covariance is useful, as the following example (11.17) shows.

There are two parallel class hierarchies involved in this example: PERSON and EMPLOYEE; PERSON_VIEW and EMPLOYEE_VIEW.

The feature *print,* which is declared in PERSON_VIEW, is redefined in EMPLOYEE_VIEW using the covariant rule.

```
class PERSON;
    creation
        make
    feature
        year_of_birth:INTEGER;
        name:STRING;
        make(yr:INTEGER;nme:STRING) is
        do
            year_of_birth := yr;
            name := nme;
        end -- make
end -- PERSON
```

*Example 11.17a Class PERSON*

```
class EMPLOYEE
    inherit
        PERSON;
    creation
        make
    feature
    salary:REAL
        set_salary(r:REAL) is
        do
            salary := r;
        end -- set_salary
end -- EMPLOYEE
```

*Example 11.17b Class EMPLOYEE*

It should be noted that class PERSON_VIEW is a client of PERSON through the argument to the print routine, and similarly, EMPLOYEE_VIEW is a client of EMPLOYEE.

```
class PERSON_VIEW
    feature
        print(p:PERSON) is
        do
            io.putint(p.year_of_birth);
            io.putstring(p.name);
        end -- print
end -- PERSON_VIEW
```

*Example 11.17c Class PERSON_VIEW*

```
class EMPLOYEE_VIEW
    inherit
        PERSON_VIEW
            redefine
                print
            end -- inherit PERSON_VIEW
    feature
        print(e:EMPLOYEE) is
        do
            io.putstring(e.name);
            io.putreal(e.salary);
        end -- print
end -- EMPLOYEE_VIEW
```

*Example 11.17d Class EMPLOYEE_VIEW*

The root class, COVAR_TEST, illustrates how covariance is sometimes useful. In this case it allows two views of an employee: that defined in PERSON_VIEW, which outputs *name* and *year_of_birth*, and that defined in EMPLOYEE_VIEW, which outputs *name* and *salary*. It should be apparent that an employee view of a PERSON does not make any sense, and the static type rules will not allow us to attempt this. The instruction

*emp_view.print(a_person);*

would be rejected by the compiler, since PERSON does not conform to EMPLOYEE.

```
class COVAR_TEST
        creation
            start
        feature
            p_view: PERSON_VIEW;
            emp_view:EMPLOYEE_VIEW;
            a_person:PERSON;
            an_employee:EMPLOYEE;

            start is
            do
                !!p_view;
                !!emp_view;
                !!an_employee.make(1967,"Lilian");
                an_employee.set_salary(1900.00);
                p_view.print(an_employee);
                emp_view.print(an_employee);
            end -- start
        end COVAR_TEST
```

*Example 11.17e Using covariance*

The reader should, however, consider the following

```
a_person := an_employee;
p_view.print(a_person);
```

The execution of this causes no problems. At run-time the print routine defined in EMPLOYEE_VIEW would be selected, and it would print out the employee details required since *a_person* is attached to an object of type EMPLOYEE. The following, however, could cause a problem:

```
p_view := emp_view;
!!a_person.make(1908, "Teddy");
p_view.print(a_person);
```

The problem occurs because of the attribute, *salary*. In this case the dynamic type of *p_view* is EMPLOYEE_VIEW, whilst the dynamic type of *a_person* is type PERSON. When the call is made, the system tries to execute the following code:

> *io.putstring(e.name);*
> *io.putreal(e.salary);*

the routine cannot sensibly handle the call to output *salary*, since PERSON has no such attribute. The final call in this sequence is valid at class level, but as a result of previous instructions it is invalid at system level. The reader might wish to try this particular example, to see how it is handled by the Eiffel system being used. Those who wish to read further on the issue of system-level validity should consult Meyer (1992).

### Exercises

1. Explain why it would be unsafe to use *force*, *resize* and *put* in an instance of class D2_ARRAY.

2. The attributes of a class have the following export status:
> $x,y,z$ -- available only to CLASS_A
> $a,b,c$ -- available to all classes

Show how a descendant class could do the following
a) give CLASS_A access to $x$ and $a$, and other classes no access to any;
b) give CLASS_A access to all features, and all other classes no access.

3. a) Implement CLIENT_LIST as a descendant of THREE_COL_TABLE.
b) Write class MENU which offers services: *display_menu, get_selection, hide_menu*. The choices offered by the menu should be as follows: up date customer details, enter new customer, retrieve customer details, display customer details, quit.
c) Write class CLIENT_HANDLER which implements each of the choices offered by the menu.
d) Investigate the file handling facilities available in the class libraries, and provide a further option which allows a table to be filed in and filed out.

4. The postconditions for *add* and *remove* in BASIC_LIST are to be amended as follows:

> -- add
> **ensure**

$$occurs(el) - \textbf{old } (occurs(el)) = 1$$
    -- remove
      **ensure**
$$\textbf{old } occurs(el) - occurs(el) = 1$$

Implement BASIC_LIST, write an *occurs* routine, and test the class with the postconditions switched on.

5. Implement class SORT_LIST; provide a more efficient *is_in* routine than that written in BASIC_LIST. (Hint: since the items are ordered, there is no need to search the whole list.)

# 12 Abstract Classes

An abstract class may be defined as

- a class which has one or more features whose implementation is deferred to a subclass;

- a class which cannot be instantiated.

In Eiffel the word *deferred* tends to be used more than *abstract*. A number of deferred classes may be found in the Eiffel libraries, including classes COMPARABLE and NUMERIC, and in the EiffelBase Library classes such as CHAIN and LIST. If these classes are examined, it should become apparent that these are general classes, at and towards the top of inheritance hierarchies: they describe properties which all descendants must have, but leave the implementation to the descendant classes themselves.

This chapter shows how a deferred class may be written in Eiffel. It also shows how deferred features may be effected, and effected features undefined. It concludes with two case studies to illustrate the use of deferred classes.

## 12.1 Using an Eiffel deferred class: COMPARABLE

We can begin by looking at class COMPARABLE as an example of a deferred or abstract class. Any deferred class in Eiffel begins with the keyword **deferred**:

**deferred** class COMPARABLE
COMPARABLE contains four routines:

```
infix "<" (other:like Current):BOOLEAN;
infix "<=" (other:like Current):BOOLEAN;
infix ">" (other:like Current):BOOLEAN;
infix ">="(other:like Current):BOOLEAN;
```

which may be used to compare objects of any class which inherits from it. The first routine is deferred, that is to say that it has no body, but is written as

```
infix "<" (other:like Current):BOOLEAN is
deferred
    ensure
```

209

> *smaller: Result implies* **not** *(Current >= other)*
> **end** -- infix "<"

The other routines are said to be *effective*. For example the "<=" routine is written using the "<" routine:

> *Result* := **not** *(other < Current).*

In order to be able to use any of the routines a descendant class must make the "<" effective.

As already indicated, it is not possible to have an instance of class COMPARABLE; it is an abstract class designed solely to be inherited. So, for a class, to be able to use the standard operators for comparison, the programmer simply has to inherit COMPARABLE, and make the "<" routine effective:

---

```
class PERSON
    inherit COMPARABLE
    feature
        name: STRING;
        infix "<" (other: like Current):BOOLEAN is
        do
            Result := name < other.name
        end -- infix "<"
    .........
end -- PERSON
```

*Example 12.1 Effecting a deferred feature*

---

This is illustrated in example 12.1, in which class PERSON is made to inherit from COMPARABLE. Instances of class PERSON are ordered by *name*. Since *name* is a STRING, which itself inherits from COMPARABLE, the "<" operator may be used to compare the *name* of *Current* with the *name* of *other*. This example shows how the "<" operator has two meanings in this class's source code: one allows strings to be compared, the other allows the comparison of persons.

Having made class PERSON inherit from COMPARABLE the other routines declared in COMPARABLE may now be used to compare instances of class PERSON. So, for example, given

> *p1,p2*:PERSON;

we can make comparisons such as

$$p1 <= p2$$
$$p1 > p2$$

It should be noted that there is a difference between effecting a feature and redefining it. A redefinition of a deferred feature would only take place if it was necessary to change the signature of the feature. The use of an anchored declaration in COMPARABLE makes this unnecessary. The signature

(*other:* **like** *Current*)

is equivalent in class PERSON to a signature

(*other*: PERSON)

It can be appreciated that anchored declarations are particularly useful in defining deferred classes.

When a feature is made effective, the same rules apply regarding preconditions and postconditions as for redefinition: it is not allowable to strengthen preconditions nor to weaken postconditions. New preconditions and postconditions take the form **require else** and **ensure then,** previously introduced in chapter 11.

The syntax of a class may now be modified to take account of deferred classes

```
[deferred] class <class_name> ["["formal generic parameters"] "]
    [inherit
            <class_type> [  "[" actual generic parameters "] " ]
                    [ Rename ]
                    [ New-Exports ]
                    [ Undefine ]
                    [ Redefine ]
                    [ Select ]
    end]
    creation
            <routine_name>
    feature
            {routines | attributes}
end
```

and the syntax of a routine may also be modified:

```
<routine-name> [argument_part] [result_part] is
        [preconditions]
        [local_part]
deferred | routine - body
        [postconditions]
end
```

## 12.2  Undefining an effective feature

Sometimes it is desirable to make an inherited effective routine deferred. To do
this the undefine mechanism must be used. The undefine sub-clause, which
comes before redefinition, consists of the reserved word, **undefine**, followed by
one or more features. The syntax is shown in figure 12.1; it has the same form as
the redefine sub-clause, except of course that it begins with the keyword
**undefine**.

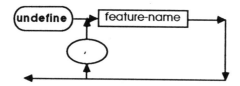

**Figure 12.1**

This is not a greatly used facility, but is useful in cases of multiple inheritance
when a class inherits two or more versions of the same feature, and wishes to use
one version only. The solution is to undefine the version not required, as shown
in the case below in which classes A and B each have an effective routine with
the same name and origin.

```
inherit
    A
            -- assume that a feature f is inherited from A
    end
    B
            undefine f
    end
```

As a result of the undefine, the *f* features inherited from classes A and B are
merged, and the effective *f* feature in the new class is that inherited from A.

## 12.3 Simulating abstract classes

In some hybrid languages there is no facility for developing abstract classes. In such languages they may be simulated by creating bodies of routines which are either empty, have halt instructions, or display messages on the screen such as

'This message should never be displayed'
'Implementation is left to subclasses'

So, for example, class LINK_OBJECT, which was described in section 10.3, would have a dummy routine body for *smaller* with an instruction such as

HALT.

There is of course nothing in such languages to ensure that the routine will not at some time be executed, with undesirable effects. There is no mechanism to ensure that an implementation of the routine is provided in a descendant class, and nothing to prevent the creation of instances of a simulated abstract class.

## 12.4 Case study: deferred class PRINTABLE

We may now return to the example first introduced in chapter 10 where the problem of writing a print routine for the generic class SORTABLE_ARRAY was introduced. It was decided to create a new class, PRINTABLE, which was to be used in the declaration of a formal constrained generic parameter:

**class** SORTABLE_ARRAY [ S -> COMPARABLE, P -> PRINTABLE]

PRINTABLE is a deferred class, which allows an output routine to be defined for any class used as an actual generic argument for SORTABLE_ARRAY.

```
deferred class PRINTABLE
    feature
        output(a:ANY) is
        deferred;
        end -- output
end -- PRINTABLE
```

*Example 12.2 A deferred class*

Class STRING_VIEW, which inherits from PRINTABLE, is illustrated in 12.3. In this case *output* is made effective and redefined, because it is necessary to change the signature.

```
class STRING_VIEW
inherit
        PRINTABLE
    redefine
        output
    end -- inherit PRINTABLE
    feature
        output(s:STRING) is
        do
            io.putstring(s);
        end -- output
end -- STRING_VIEW
```

*Example 12.3 Redefining and effecting a deferred routine*

An actual sorted array would be declared as follows

   *my_list*:SORTABLE_ARRAY[STRING,STRING_VIEW]

and the compiler would be able to check that the first actual parameter conformed to the type of the formal argument in routine *output*. The body of the print routine in class SORTABLE_ARRAY, which has the signature

   *print (out:P)*

where P is a constrained generic parameter, would now contain the single line:

   *out.output(item(index))*

This may seem far from straightforward: a new descendant of class PRINTABLE would be required for each class used as an actual argument for class STORABLE_ARRAY. Nevertheless, it would aid the reusability of class SORTABLE_ARRAY.

## 12.5 Case study: class CHESS_PIECE

This case study shows how abstract classes might be used to help us model chess pieces. We will begin by outlining the essentials of chess:

> there is a chess board consisting of an 8 * 8 matrix, each square has a colour, black or white, and each square may contain a chess piece, or may be unoccupied;

> there are six kinds of chess piece: King, Queen, Rook, Knight, Bishop, Pawn; each has different rules for moving: for example, the King may move one square in any direction, and may not move into a position from which it can be taken; the Queen may move any number of squares vertically, horizontally or diagonally; the Bishop any number of squares diagonally and so on.

If we were producing a chess application, it would be sensible to try to capture this in a hierarchy, such as that shown in figure 12.2.

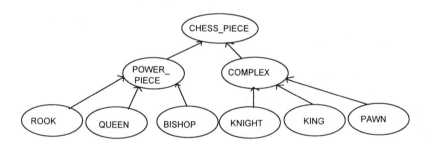

**Figure 12.2**

The pieces are grouped into two: those which may move an unlimited number of squares, and those which are less powerful and more complex. It should be apparent that POWER_PIECE, COMPLEX and CHESS_PIECE are abstract; an instance of any of these classes would never be required.

We may now consider what features each piece would have in common. Each piece has

> a colour
> a position
> an icon, a string or a character that can be displayed

rules to determine what is a legal move
the ability to move

The rules to determine the legality of a move would have to be deferred to the lowest level, since each kind of piece has a different rule.

When considering the abstract class POWER_PIECE, the following features might be included:

is the move diagonal?
is the move vertical?
is the move horizontal?

It is not clear whether COMPLEX_PIECE would actually be required, since the only thing that a King, a Knight and a Pawn seem to have in common, apart from their complexity, is their ability to move only a limited number of spaces at a time. This case study will consider only power pieces.

The abstract class CHESS_PIECE is shown in example 12.4. It has one deferred routine, *is_legal_move*. Routines have been included to initialise the attributes, and to display the chess piece (but not the position) on the screen. There is also a routine, *null_move*, which returns true if the destination and source are the same. All chess pieces need this, so it is correctly placed at the root of the hierarchy.

```
deferred class CHESS_PIECE
    inherit
        CHESS_MATHS
    feature
        row:INTEGER;
        column:INTEGER;
        colour:CHARACTER;
        display_char:CHARACTER;
        is_on_board(r:INTEGER; c:INTEGER):BOOLEAN is
        do
            Result := r > 0 and r <= 8 and c > 0 and c <= 8;
        end -- is_on_board
        is_legal_move(r:INTEGER;c:INTEGER):BOOLEAN is
                require
                    is_on_board(r,c)
        deferred;
        end -- is_legal_move
        null_move(r:INTEGER; c:INTEGER) :BOOLEAN is
```

```
              do
                     Result := r = row and c = column
              end -- null_move
              display is
              do
                     io.putchar(' ');
                     io.putchar(display_char);
                     io.putchar(colour);
                     io.putchar(' ');
              end -- display
              make(r :INTEGER; c:INTEGER; clr:CHARACTER;
                              disp:CHARACTER) is
                  require
                         is_on_board(r,c)
              do
                     row := r;
                     column := c;
                     colour := clr;
                     display_char := disp;
              end --make
              move_to(r :INTEGER; c:INTEGER ) is
              require
                     is_legal_move(r,c)
              do
                     row := r;
                     column := c;
              end; -- move_to
          invariant
                 valid_position: is_on_board(row,column)
    end --CHESS_PIECE
```

*Example 12.4 Class CHESS_PIECE*

A few observations should be made about the implementation. The attributes *colour* and *display_char* are both characters, so that a black queen might for example be displayed as

Qb

and a white bishop as

Bw

The routine, *make*, initialises all the attributes, and is intended to be used as the creation routine for all chess pieces. The invariant requires that a chess piece must always be on the board: each coordinate must be in the range 1 to 8.

It should be noted that CHESS_PIECE inherits from CHESS_MATHS; this class has been created to hold a few integer functions needed in this case study and its continuation in chapter 14:

> *abs(i:*INTEGER):INTEGER;
> *smaller(x,y:*INTEGER):INTEGER;
> *larger(x,y:*INTEGER):INTEGER;

Class POWER_PIECE is shown in example 12.5. Although it introduces no new deferred features, POWER_PIECE is deferred because it fails to make *is_legal_move* effective.

```
deferred class POWER_PIECE
    inherit
        CHESS_PIECE
    feature { }
        is_diagonal(r:INTEGER;c:INTEGER):BOOLEAN is
        do
            Result := abs(c - column)  = abs(r - row)
        end -- is_diagonal
        is_vertical(c:INTEGER) :BOOLEAN is
        do
            Result := c = column
        end --is_vertical
        is_horizontal(r:INTEGER) :BOOLEAN is
        do
            Result := r= row
        end --is_horizontal
end -- POWER__PIECE
```

*12.5 A deferred class:POWER_PIECE*

The functionality of class POWER_PIECE is slight, but it should allow us to simplify the code when the actual classes are written.

Finally, one of the actual classes, class QUEEN, is illustrated in example 12.6. The only task here is to make the routine, *is_legal_move,* effective. It may be noted that, as already indicated, the inherited routine *make* has been used as the creator. There is no need to define a different creation routine for most of the classes since there are no additional attributes. This might not be true in every case; class KING for example might need some attribute to indicate whether the castle move was still legal. We shall not however pursue this case study that far.

```
class QUEEN
    inherit
        POWER_PIECE
    creation
        make
    feature
        is_legal_move(r:INTEGER;c:INTEGER):BOOLEAN is
        do
            Result := not null_move(r,c)
            and then
                (is_diagonal(r,c)
                or is_vertical(c)
                or is_horizontal(r))
        end -- is_legal_move
end --QUEEN
```

*12.6 Effecting a deferred routine*

Class QUEEN therefore consists of a single routine inherited originally from CHESS_PIECE and now made effective. The features available to QUEEN are:

| | | | | |
|---|---|---|---|---|
| *row* | *column* | *colour* | *display_char* | *is_on_board* |
| *null_move* | *make* | *move_to* | *display* | |
| *is_legal_move* | *is_diagonal* | *is_horizontal* | *is_vertical* | |

and of course the routines defined in class CHESS_MATHS. The implementation of CHESS_MATHS is left for the reader to do as an exercise.

It is now possible to test the chess piece, using CHESS_GAME as a root class. The routine *start* requires a user to input the position of the Queen, and it then displays the coordinates of each square to which it would be legal for the Queen to move.

```
class CHESS_GAME
creation
       start
feature
       a_queen:QUEEN;
       start is
              -- displays legal moves of a Queen
              local
                     i,j,c,r,count:INTEGER;
       do
              io.putstring("enter start row");
              io.readint;
              r := io.lastint
              io.putstring("enter start column");
              io.readint;
              c := io.lastint
              !!a_queen.make(r,c,'b','Q');
              from i := 0
              until i = 8
              loop
                     i := i + 1;
                     from j := 0
                     until j= 8
                     loop
                            j := j+1
                            if a_queen.is_legal_move(i,j)
                            then
                                   io.putint(i);
                                   io.putint(j);
                                   io.new_line;
                                   count := count + 1;
                            end -- if
                     end  -- loop
              end -- loop
              io.putint (count);
              io.putstring("possible moves ");
       end -- start
end -- CHESS_GAME
```

*Example 12.8 Root Class for testing QUEEN*

## Exercises

1. a) Design, implement and test class CHESS_MATH;
b) Implement class CHESS_PIECE, POWER_PIECE and QUEEN, using CHESS_GAME as the root class;
c) Implement classes BISHOP and ROOK, and test them in turn by modifying CHESS_GAME. (A bishop may move diagonally, and a rook may move horizontally and vertically.)
d) For Chess enthusiasts only: consider how  *is_legal_move* could be made effective for Knight, King and Pawn (in order of difficulty); is there any value in creating an abstract class, COMPLEX_PIECE?

2. An application is required to handle the payroll for a firm. It has two kinds of employee, those who are paid weekly, and those who are paid monthly. Class EMPLOYEE has been identified as an abstract class. It has attributes *annual_salary*, *last_paid*, and *amount_paid*, a transformer routine *set_salary* which requires the employee's salary to be passed in as an argument, a deferred routine *pay_due,* and a transfomer routine, *pay_out*, which adds *pay_due* to *amount_paid.* The routine *pay_out* also has an integer argument which is used to set *last_paid.* So for example the call
    *anEmployee.pay_out(5)*
will alter the state of *last_paid* to 5.
a) Write classes WEEKLY and MONTHLY, each of which inherits from EMPLOYEE and makes *pay_due* effective. (WEEKLY divides annual salary by 52, MONTHLY by 12). To test each class,write a root class which is a client of WEEKLY and MONTHLY.
b) add a new deferred routine, *pay_type*:STRING, to EMPLOYEE, and make this effective for each actual class e.g. "Monthly"; add a *print_pay* routine to EMPLOYEE, which outputs the following on the screen:

```
Payment Details:

Annual Salary: < annual_salary >Previous_pay: < amount_paid>
Payment Type: < monthly/weekly>  Period: < last_paid + 1>
Payment this period:  <pay_due>
Total pay to_date < amount_paid + pay_due>
```

Amend the root class and test the new features added. For example, write a loop which updates an EMPLOYEE, and prints out the pay details, for each month of the year.

# 13 Multiple and Repeated Inheritance

Previous chapters have introduced single inheritance, and have looked at the ways in which the features of inherited classes may be altered by descendant classes. This chapter completes the study of inheritance by introducing multiple and repeated inheritance.

## 13.1 Multiple inheritance

Multiple inheritance is defined as inheriting directly from more than one parent class. Eiffel provides no limit to the number of classes that may be inherited. Whilst this can be useful, it can also increase complexity, and the reader is advised to exercise caution before using it too freely.

A simple use of multiple inheritance is demonstrated in example 13.1, and the syntax of inheritance, updated to account for multiple inheritance, is given in figure 13.1.

```
class INVOICE
    inherit
        CUSTOMER;
        STORABLE
            rename
                store_by_name as file_out,
                retrieve_by_name as file_in
        end -- STORABLE
    feature
        .......
end -- INVOICE
```

*13.1 Multiple inheritance*

Class INVOICE inherits all the features of CUSTOMER and STORABLE. It could also, of course, have a number of its own features.

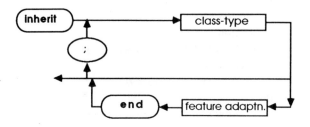

**Figure 13.1**

The syntax of multiple inheritance in Eiffel is relatively straightforward: the key word **inherit** occurs once only, and may be followed by any number of class types, each of which may have its own feature-adaptation part. Each feature-adaptation part is terminated by the keyword **end**.

Whenever a class inherits from one or more classes, problems of name clashes and duplicated routines require attention. Of the two, the name clash is more common: identifiers such as *make, create, add, remove, search, insert, open, close*, and a number of others, occur frequently in Eiffel classes, and rightly so. Software developers should be encouraged to use such words, rather than to think up unique identifiers which mean little or nothing. When clashes occur because of inheritance, the correct solution, as should be apparent, is **not** to go back and alter one of the parent classes, but instead to use the rename facility.

Sometimes, as a result of multiple inheritance, a class obtains multiple copies of a routine, when it only needs one. The solution is to join the features using the undefine facility, as demonstrated in CUSTOMER_SUPPLIER below.

As an example of multiple inheritance, consider the case of a retail firm which is developing an accounting application. This application keeps account of money owing and money owed. Classes CUSTOMER and SUPPLIER have already been developed (examples 13.2 and 13.3). Class CUSTOMER has five attributes, *name, address, ref_number, amount_owing* and *credit_limit*. It also has transformer routines, *add_invoice, credit_payment, change_address, set_limit* and *make,* the last of which is also defined as the creator.

```
class CUSTOMER
    creation
        make
    feature
        name:STRING;
        address:STRING;
        ref_number: INTEGER;
```

```
amount_owing:REAL;
credit_limit:REAL;
-- transfomer routines
add_invoice(invoice_total:REAL) is
        require
                invoice_total > 0
        do
        amount_owing := amount_owing + invoice_total
        end -- add_invoice
credit_payment(payment:REAL) is
        require
                payment > 0
        do
        amount_owing := amount_owing - payment
        end -- credit_payment
change_address(adr:STRING) is
        do
        address := adr;
        end -- change_address
set_limit(limit:REAL) is
        require
                limit > 0
        do
        credit_limit := limit
        end -- set_limit
make(nme,adr:STRING; ref:INTEGER) is
        do
        name := nme;
        address := adr;
        ref_number := ref;
        end -- make
end -- CUSTOMER
```

*Example 13.2 Class CUSTOMER*

Class SUPPLIER is similar to class CUSTOMER, it has attributes *firm,
address, ref_number* and *balance_owed,* and transformers *add_invoice* and
*credit_payment.*

```
class SUPPLIER
creation
    make
feature
    firm:STRING;
    address:STRING;
    ref_number:STRING;
    balance_owed:REAL;
    add_invoice(invoice_total:REAL) is
        require
            invoice_total > 0
    do
        balance_owed := balance_owed + invoice_total
    end -- add_invoice
    credit_payment(payment:REAL) is
        require
            payment > 0
    do
        balance_owed := balance_owed - payment
    end -- credit_payment
    change_address(adr:STRING) is
    do
        address := adr;
    end -- change_address
    make(nme,adr,ref:STRING) is
    do
        name := nme;
        address := adr;
        ref_number := ref;
    end -- make
end -- SUPPLIER
```

*Example 13.3 Class SUPPLIER*

Usually, the sets of customers and suppliers are disjoint, but occasionally a person/firm is both a supplier and a customer. One solution to this is to create a new class: CUSTOMER_SUPPLIER, designed to inherit both CUSTOMER and SUPPLIER, as shown in figure 13.2.

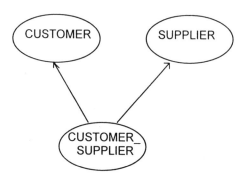

**Figure 13.2**

In order to achieve this the name clashes of each class must first be analysed (see table below). Class CUSTOMER_SUPPLIER is given in example 13.4.

Clearly the new class needs only one *address,* and one *change_address* routine. The latter may be joined simply by undefining one of the two inherited routines. *Address* presents more of a problem: an attribute may not be undefined, so the join in this case may be done by redefining both.

The attribute *ref_number* is a name clash, which can be resolved by renaming as *customer_number* and *supplier_number.*

| Identifier | CUSTOMER | SUPPLIER |
|---|---|---|
| *address* | -- STRING attribute | same |
| *ref_number* | -- INTEGER attribute | STRING attribute |
| *add_invoice* | -- adds to *amount-owing* | adds to *balance-owed* |
| *credit_payment* | -- subtracts from *amount-owing* | subtracts from *balance-owed* |
| *change_address* | -- updates *address* | same |
| *make* | -- sets *name, address, ref_number* | same, but note *ref_number* |

The routines *add_invoice* and *credit_payment* require more thought: in CUSTOMER they alter *amount_owing,* in SUPPLIER they change *balance_owed.* The solution taken is to rename them as *invoice_customer, credit_customer, credit_supplier,* and *pay_supplier* to reflect what they do in each case. Similarly, it is sensible to rename *amount_owing* and *balance_owed* as *customer_balance* and *supplier_balance*. This requires a new routine, *overall_balance*, which subtracts *customer_balance* from *supplier_balance*.

The *make* routines present a difficult problem. The difference in the types of the final argument

> *make*(*nme,adr*:STRING; *ref*:INTEGER) -- CUSTOMER
> *make*(*nme,adr,ref*:STRING) -- SUPPLIER

means that they cannot be merged. It just happens that in our firm customers have an integer reference number, and suppliers have reference numbers such as "NW3400", and we have to live with it! One solution is to rename one, and to use the other. The renamed routine would not be used, but as already indicated, it cannot be undefined. In this case it would be wise to ensure that it was not exported. Another solution would be to rename one and redefine it with an empty body. Whilst not elegant, it would prevent the discarded routine from being used by a descendant, which a re-export clause would not. Since one of the *make* routines is to be discarded, an additional transformer is needed for one of the reference numbers.

Finally, the cases of *name* in CUSTOMER, and *firm* in SUPPLIER must be considered. These are the same real-world entities, so both are not needed. The solution taken is to rename *name* as *firm*, and then to redefine *firm*.

```
class CUSTOMER_SUPPLIER
   inherit
      CUSTOMER
         rename
            ref_number as customer_number,
            add_invoice as invoice_customer,
            credit_payment as credit_customer,
            name as firm,
            amount_owing as customer_balance ,
            make as customer_make
         export
            {NONE} customer_make
         undefine
            change_address
         redefine
            address, firm
         end
      SUPPLIER
         rename
```

```
                              ref_number as supplier_number
                              add_invoice as credit_supplier,
                              credit_payment as pay_supplier,
                              amount_owed as supplier_balance
                      redefine
                              address, firm
                      end
        creation
              make
        feature
              address:STRING;
              firm:STRING;
              set_customer_id(id:STRING) is
              do
                      customer_number := id;
              end -- set_customer_is
              overall_balance:REAL is
                      -- returns current balance
                              -- negative if debit_balance
              do
                      Result := supplier_balance
                                      - customer_balance
              end -- overall_balance
        end -- CUSTOMER_SUPPLIER
```

*Example 13.4 Multiple inheritance: renaming, undefining and redefining*

The facilities available to a client of class CUSTOMER_SUPPLIER may now be summarised:

attributes: *customer_number, firm, customer_balance, address*
            *supplier_number, supplier_balance*
routines:  *change_address, make, invoice_customer,*
            *credit_customer, set_customer_id, credit_supplier,*
            *pay_supplier , overall_balance.*

This class may now be tested as shown in example 13.5

```
class CUST_SUPP_TEST
    creation
        start
    feature
        s_cust:CUSTOMER_SUPPLIER;
        start is
        do
            !!s_cust.make(" The Blagg Corporation",
             " 1319 Main, Topeka, Kansas", "L3409");
            s_cust.set_customer_id(67890);
            s_cust.invoice_customer(1000.45);
            s_cust.credit_customer(500.00);
            s_cust.credit_supplier(3000:97);
            s_cust.pay_supplier(2000:00);
            io.putstring(s_cust.firm);
            io.putstring(s_cust.address);
            io.putint(s_cust.customer_number);
            io.putreal(s_cust.customer_balance);
            io.putstring(s_cust.supplier_number);
            io.putreal(s_cust.supplier_balance);
            io.putreal(s_cust.overall_balance);
        end -- start
end -- CUST_SUPP_TEST
```

*Example 13. 5 Testing CUSTOMER_SUPPLIER*

## 13.2  Repeated inheritance

Any language which supports multiple inheritance must define what happens when the same class is inherited more than once. This may occur, directly or indirectly as shown in figure 13.3. Direct repeated inheritance, as shown in the left-hand section of figure 13.3, is used in the rare cases when a class wishes to have two or more copies of a feature defined in another class. Indirect repeated inheritance occurs as a result of multiple inheritance, when two or more parent classes have a common parent. In the right-hand part of figure 13.3, B and C both inherit from D, therefore A indirectly inherits from D twice.

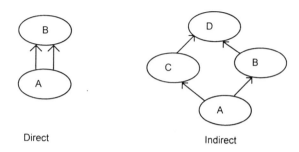

Direct                                                Indirect

**Figure 13.3**

Whenever a class is inherited more than once the same rules apply whether it is a case of direct or indirect repeated inheritance. These may be summarised as shown in the table below.

| **Repeated Inheritance Rules** |
|---|
| • if a feature has been inherited twice or more without any intervening renaming, then the feature is shared - only one copy of the feature is available; |
| • if a feature has been renamed in parent classes or in the current class, then multiple copies of the feature are available; <br>• if the feature is an attribute then a select subclause is needed in one or other of the inheritance clauses to remove potential ambiguity; |
| • if a feature has been redefined in parent classes or in the current class, then more than one version of a feature is available, and a select subclause is needed. |

The next section deals with the case of indirect repeated inheritance.

## 13.3 Indirect repeated inheritance

Usually, indirect repeated inheritance occurs through inheritance for reuse, but sometimes it is useful to design a group of classes to make effective use of this facility. This can be illustrated by reworking the previous example so that CUSTOMER and SUPPLIER are made to inherit from class PERSON, as shown in figure 13.4 and examples 13.6 and 13.7. Class PERSON has for the purposes of this example the features *address*, *change_address*, *name* and *set_name*.

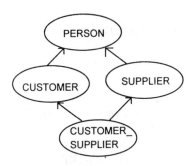

**Figure 13.4**

```
class CUSTOMER
        inherit
                PERSON
        creation
                make
        feature
                ref_number: INTEGER;
                amount_owing:REAL;
                credit_limit:REAL;
                -- transfomer routines
                add_invoice(invoice_total:REAL)
                        require
                                invoice_total > 0
                credit_payment(payment:REAL)
                        require
                                payment > 0
                set_limit(limit:REAL)
                        require
                                limit > 0
                make(nme,adr:STRING; ref:INTEGER)
        end -- CUSTOMER

        Example 13.6 Class CUSTOMER - inheriting from PERSON
```

```
class SUPPLIER
    inherit
        PERSON
    creation
        make
    feature
        ref_number:STRING;
        amount_owed:REAL;
        add_invoice(invoice_total:REAL)
            require
                invoice_total > 0
        credit_payment(payment:REAL)
            require
                payment > 0
        make(nme,adr,ref:STRING)
end -- SUPPLIER
```

*Example 13.7 Class SUPPLIER - inheriting from PERSON*

It will be noticed that the use of inheritance makes CUSTOMER and SUPPLIER shorter and simpler. When class CUSTOMER_SUPPLIER is written (example 13.8), there is a single copy only of the features inherited from PERSON. This removes the need for undefinition and redefinition, and suggests that this is a better solution than that shown in section 13.1.

```
class CUSTOMER_SUPPLIER
    inherit
        CUSTOMER
            rename
                ref_number as customer_number,
                add_invoice as invoice_customer,
                credit_payment as credit_customer,
                amount_owing as customer_balance ,
                make as customer_make
            export
                {NONE} customer_make
        end -- inherit CUSTOMER
        SUPPLIER
            rename
                ref_number as supplier_number,
                add_invoice as credit_supplier,
```

```
                    credit_payment as pay_supplier,
                    amount_owed as supplier_balance
        end -- inherit SUPPLIER
creation
        make
feature
        set_customer_id(id:STRING)
        over_all_balance:REAL
                -- returns current balance
                -- negative if debit_balance
end -- CUSTOMER_SUPPLIER
```

*Example 13.8 Indirect repeated inheritance*

## 13.4 Selecting a feature

This section introduces the final part of feature adaptation, the select subclause. It is used in repeated inheritance when there would be potential ambiguity in cases of polymorphic assignment. This occurs when a class obtains two different versions of the same routine and when a class obtains two copies of an attribute. This section provides an example of the first case. An example of the second case may be found in the next section.

The use of **select** in cases of multiple versions of a routine may be illustrated by returning to the example worked in the previous section. If class PERSON had the following routine,

```
display_name is
do
        io.putstring(name)
end -- display_name
```

which was redefined in class SUPPLIER (and renamed) as

```
display_details is
do
        io.putstring(name);
        io.putstring(address);
end -- display_details
```

class CUSTOMER_SUPPLIER would have two versions of *display_name*: one inherited from PERSON through CUSTOMER, the other inherited through SUPPLIER (and renamed). In this case ambiguity would arise if an entity whose static type was PERSON, was attached to an object whose dynamic type was CUSTOMER_SUPPLIER:

> *p:PERSON;*
> *cs*:CUSTOMER_SUPPLIER;
>
>   ...
>
> *p := cs;*
> *p.display_name;*

To remove this ambiguity, the select subclause would be used to indicate which routine would be called in this case. In example 13.9, the routine selected is that which was redefined and renamed in SUPPLIER.

---

**class** CUSTOMER_SUPPLIER
    **inherit**
        CUSTOMER

        .........
        **end** -- inherit CUSTOMER
        SUPPLIER
        **select**
            *display_details*
        **end** -- inherit SUPPLIER
        ...........

**end** -- CUSTOMER_SUPPLIER

*Example 13.9 Use of **select** to remove ambiguity*

---

It should be appreciated that the compiler would reject the call

> *p.display_details*

although that is the routine that would be selected at run-time. The call

> *cs.display_name*

would of course invoke the routine defined in PERSON.

The syntax of the select part of feature adaptation is similar to the redefine and undefine part. It consists of the reserved word, **select**, and a list of features separated by commas.

## 13.5 Direct repeated inheritance

This section provides an example of the use of direct repeated inheritance to obtain multiple copies of features, and multiple versions of routines. It also discusses the use of direct repeated inheritance in the case when a redefined routine also needs to call its parent routine.

The use of direct repeated inheritance may be illustrated by class RESERVATION (example 13.11), which inherits DATE twice, and also inherits PERSON. It is assumed that PERSON has attributes *name* and *address*, and a creation routine, *make*, which initialises both attributes. Class DATE is given in example 13.10.

```
class DATE
    creation
        set
    feature
        day, month, year :INTEGER;
        display is
        do
            io.putint(day);
            io.putchar(':');
            io.putint(month);
            io.putchar(':');
            io.putint(year);
        end -- display
        set(dd,mm,yy:INTEGER) is
        do
            day := dd;
            month := mm;
            year := yy;
        end -- set
end -- date
```

*Example 13.10 Repeated inheritance-- parent class, DATE*

RESERVATION is designed to be used by a travel agent or a hotel to store the beginning and end of a reservation, and the name and address of the person making the booking. As a result of the repeated inheritance it has two copies of *day, month and year*, two versions of *set* and *display*.

```
class RESERVATION
    inherit
        DATE
            rename
                day as start_day,
                month as start_month,
                year as start_year,
                display as display_start,
                set as set_start
            select
                set_start, start_day, start_month,
                    start_year
        end -- inherit DATE
        DATE
            rename
                set as set_end,
                display as display_booking
            redefine
                set_end, display_booking
            select
                display_booking
        end -- inherit DATE
        PERSON
    creation
        make_booking
    feature
        persons:INTEGER;
        display_booking is
        do
            io.putstring(name);
            io.putstring(address);
            io.new_line;
            io.putstring(" number of persons : ");
            io.putint(persons);
            io.new_line;
            io.putstring("start date: ");
            display_start;
            io.new_line;
            io.putstring("termination date : ");
            io.putint(day);
            io.putchar(':');
```

```
              io.putint(month);
              io.putchar(':');
              io.putint(year);
              io.new_line
          end -- display_booking
          set_end(dd,mm,yy:INTEGER) is
          do
              day := dd;
              month := mm;
              year := yy;
          end -- set_start
          make_booking (p:PERSON; nmbr:INTEGER;
                        start,finish:DATE) is
          do
              set_start(start.day,start.month,start.year);
              set_end(finish.day,finish.month,finish.year);
              make(p.address,p.name);
              persons := nmbr;
          end -- make_booking
      end -- date
```

*Example 13.11 Repeated inheritance of DATE*

A client class with attributes of class PERSON, DATE and RESERVATION, could now create and display a booking.

The most frequent use of direct repeated inheritance in Eiffel is when it is necessary to extend rather than replace the functionality of an inherited routine. To avoid duplicating code, it is useful if the new routine can call the original routine. Smalltalk, for example, allows such calls to be prefixed by *super*, which indicates that the routine required is in the parent class rather than in the current class. Other languages have similar facilities. In Eiffel, however, direct repeated inheritance must be used: one copy of the feature is redefined and one copy is used. Additionally, one or both features must be renamed, and one must be selected. New users of Eiffel are often confused by this, and do not see why the following alternative stategy cannot be taken:

> change the name of the inherited routine, *a*, to *b*
> write a routine, *a*, which calls *b*

Whilst this appears to have the effect required, it is unsafe. The reader who is unconvinced is encouraged to consider again the distinction between renaming and redefinition, Whilst it is possible to achieve the effect of the Smalltalk *super* by using **rename** to free a name for reuse, the effect is to remove any connection between the routine in the parent class and the new routine defined in the descendant: the compiler will not check the conformance of the new routine to that in the parent; in cases when an instance of the descendant class becomes attached to the parent class, the routine defined in the parent class will be invoked. To ensure that the correct routine is called dynamically, that the new routine conforms to the old, and, that the new routine is another version of the old, a programmer must use **redefine** and **select**.

The reader's attention is drawn to *display_booking* in example 13.11, which is a new version of *display* which calls the routine that it has redefined. This version is executed even if an instance of RESERVATION is attached to an entity of type DATE. So for example, in the following situation:

> *d1,d2*:DATE;
> *r*:RESERVATION
>
> *!!d1.set(12,12,95);*
> *!!d2.set(24,12,95);*
> *!!p.make("Arne Kristiansen","1503 Hoiendal, Frederikstad,*
> *       Norway");*
> *!!r.make_booking(p,1,d1,d2);*
> *d1 := r;*
> *d1.display*

the whole booking would be displayed:

> Arne Kristiansen
> 1503 Hoiendal, Frederikstad, Norway
> number of persons: 1
> start date: 12:12:95
> termination date: 24:12:95

### Exercises

1. a) explain the difference between multiple inheritance, indirect repeated inheritance and direct repeated inheritance;
b) explain how two routines may be joined in Eiffel.

2. In chess, a queen may be said to be a combination of a bishop and a rook. Rewrite QUEEN (see chapter 12), so that it inherits its functionality from both those classes.

3. Amend CUSTOMER_SUPPLIER (example 13.9) so that in the case

> *p*: PERSON
> *cs*:CUSTOMER_SUPPLIER;
>
> ...
>
> *p* := *cs*;
> *p.display_name;*

the routine invoked in the call would be that defined in class PERSON.

4. a) Implement classes PERSON, DATE and RESERVATION and develop a root class which allows the user to create and display a reservation.
b) extend the previous application as follows
    i) create a list of bookings using LINKED_LIST;
    ii) write a class MENU, which allows a choice of facilities:
        make reservation; display booking; delete reservation;
        amend reservation;
(Hint: it may be sensible to introduce a new attribute for RESERVATION, booking_number:INTEGER, which may be used to identify a booking uniquely.)
c) Consider whether there is any advantage in using repeated inheritance as opposed to making RESERVATION a client of DATE. (Note the code in *display_booking* which repeats code in DATE.)

5. Explain why the strategy of renaming in order to free a name for reuse, is an unsafe solution to the problem of extending the functionality of an inherited routine.

# 14  Case Studies

This chapter provides two case studies. The first builds on classes developed in the chapters on generic and abstract classes. The second, more complex study, implements a back propagating neural network from scratch. The chapter also illustrates the use of CRC cards in object-oriented design.

## 14.1  Solving the eight queens problem

This is the problem of how eight queens may be positioned on a chess board so that none can be taken by another. There are 92 solutions to this problem, one of which is illustrated in figure 14.1.

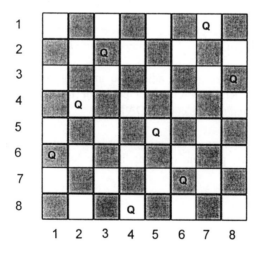

**Figure 14.1**

This case study shows how object-oriented methods may be used to solve it. The solution derived is one which aims at reusability rather than efficiency: at some time we may wish to solve other chess problems.

First, the objects in the system must be identified. We already have class CHESS_PIECE, POWER_PIECE, QUEEN and CHESS_MATHS defined in previous chapters. The other possible objects in the system are

colour (black or white)
square
chess board

Colour may be rejected straight away, it is an attribute both of SQUARE and of CHESS_PIECE. The system should however have a CHESS_BOARD, which may be implemented by reusing D2-ARRAY (chapter 10). Square need not be a class: the only information needed about a square in addition to whether it contains a piece or not, is its colour, but the latter is solely an aid to human players, and plays no part in the rules of chess.

Often it is sensible to separate a view of a class from the actual class: this aids portability, and also allows different views to be built. A text-based view, called CHESS_VIEW, will therefore be constructed.

Finally, CHESS_GAME will be developed, as the root class. The full list of classes to be built/reused are

| | | |
|---|---|---|
| D2-ARRAY | CHESS_PIECE | POWER_PIECE |
| QUEEN | CHESS_MATHS | |
| CHESS_BOARD* | CHESS_VIEW* | CHESS_GAME* |

Those marked with * are still to be constructed.

We will begin by defining the responsibilities and collaborators of class CHESS_BOARD, using the CRC methodology (Class Name, Responsibilities, Collaborators). This is a simple methodology which is easy to follow, and is suitable for relatively small systems. A CRC card is a 6 * 4 card, divided as shown in figure 14.2.

| *Class Name* | |
|---|---|
| *Responsibilities* | *Collaborators* |

**Figure 14.2**

The CRC cards for each of the new classes are given in figures 14.3, 14.4 and 14.5.

| CHESS_BOARD | CHESS_PIECE |
|---|---|
| places piece on board<br>removes piece<br><br>knows whether a square is occupied<br>knows which pieces are on the board<br>knows if a diagnon, vertical or horizontal<br>path is clear<br>knows if any piece can reach a square | |

**Figure 14.3**

| CHESS_VIEW | CHESS_BOARD |
|---|---|
| draws board on screen<br><br>asks chess_pieces to draw themselves<br><br>knows how to access BOARD | CHESS_PIECE |

**Figure 14.4**

| CHESS_GAME | CHESS_BOARD |
|---|---|
| produces solution to 8 Queens problem | CHESS_PIECE<br><br>CHESS_VIEW |

**Figure 14.5**

The new classes are given in short form in examples 14.1, 14.2 and 14.3. As already indicated, CHESS_BOARD (example 14.1) inherits from D2-ARRAY. CHESS_VIEW (14.2) consists of a single routine. CHESS_GAME (14.3) is a client of CHESS_BOARD, CHESS_VIEW, and CHESS_PIECE/QUEEN.

```
class CHESS_BOARD
    inherit
        D2_ARRAY[CHESS_PIECE]
        rename
            valid_coordinates as is_on_board,
            item_at as piece_at,
            put_at as attach
        end
    creation
        make
            -- Must be initialised as 8 * 8 matrix
    feature
        detach(row:INTEGER; col:INTEGER);
            -- removes piece from board
            require
                is_on_board(row,col)
                ensure
                    not is_occupied(row,col)
        is_occupied(row,col:INTEGER):BOOLEAN
            -- true if a piece is attached at position specified
            require
                is_on_board(row,col)
        can_be_reached(row,col:INTEGER;
                            colour:INTEGER):BOOLEAN
            -- checks if a piece can be reached by
            -- another of the opposite colour
            require
                is_on_board(row,col)
        is_clear_path(row,col,dest_row,dest_col:INTEGER)
                            :BOOLEAN
            -- checks path between two squares on board
            require
                is_on_board(row,col);
                is_on_board(dest_row,dest_col);
```

```
    invariant
        rows = 8;
        columns = 8
end -- CHESS_BOARD
```

*Example 14.1 Class CHESS_BOARD :short form*

```
class CHESS_VIEW
    feature
        display (:CHESS_BOARD);
end -- CHESS_VIEW
```

*Example 14.2 Class CHESS_VIEW: short form*

```
class CHESS_GAME
    creation
        start
    feature
        board:CHESS_BOARD;
        view:CHESS_VIEW;
        start
            -- initialises board and view
            -- calls eight queens routine
        eight_queens
            -- displays a solution to eight queens problem
end -- CHESS_GAME
```

*Example 14.3 Class CHESS_GAME: short form*

The implementation of the routines defined in class CHESS_BOARD is shown in examples 14.4, 14.5 and 14.6. Example 14.4 shows *detach*, which puts *Void* in the appropriate cell. Example 14.5 shows the accessor routines, each of which may be traced back to the CRC card. This includes the routines which enable the board to know whether any piece can reach a certain square, and also the routine which checks whether a path is clear. This would be required for every move except that of the Knight, which alone is allowed to jump over pieces. An alert reader may notice that no single accessor has been provided to return a list of the pieces currently on the board, or of the positions currently occupied.

```
detach(row,col:INTEGER) is
        -- removes piece from board
        require
                is_on_board(row,col);
do
        attach(Void,row,col)
end -- detach
```

*Example 14.4 Class CHESS_BOARD: detach routine*

```
is_occupied(row,col:INTEGER):BOOLEAN is
        -- true if a piece is attached at position specified
        require
                is_on_board(row,col);
do
        Result := not (piece_at(row,col) =Void)
end -- is_occupied
is_clear_path(row,col,dest_row,dest_col:INTEGER):
                BOOLEAN is
        -- checks path between two squares on board

        require
                is_legal_move(row,col,dest_row,dest_col);
                source_valid : is_on_board(row,col);
                destination_valid :
                        is_on_board(dest_row,dest_col);
do
        if row = dest_row or col = dest_col
        then Result:= is_clear_row(row,col,dest_row,dest_col)
        elseif is_diagonal(row,col,dest_row,dest_col)
        then Result := is_clear_diagonal(row,col,dest_row,
                dest_col)
        else Result := true -- must be Knight's move
        end -- if
end -- is_clear_path
can_be_reached(r,c:INTEGER; colour:CHARACTER)
                                        :BOOLEAN is
                -- checks if a piece can be reached by
                -- another of the opposite colour
                require
                        is_on_board(r,c)
```

```
            local
                  i,j:INTEGER
      do
            from j:= 0
            until Result or j =8
            loop
                  j := j+1
                  from i := 0
                  until i =8 or Result
                  loop
                        i := i+1;
                        if is_occupied(i,j)
                        then Result :=colour = piece_at(i,j).colour
                        and then piece_at(i,j).is_legal_move(r,c)
                              and then is_clear_path(i,j,r,c)
                        end -- if
                  end -- loop
            end -- loop
      end -- can_be_reached
```

*Example 14.5 Class CHESS_BOARD: accessors*

Example 14.6 provides auxiliary routines: *is_clear_row, is_clear_diagonal* and *is_diagonal*. The latter seems out of place in this class - it requires no knowledge of the state of the board, and it duplicates a routine in POWER_PIECE. This may be an indication of a design flaw: perhaps the classes, or the relationships between them, are not quite correct.

```
      is_clear_row(row,col,d_row,d_col:INTEGER):BOOLEAN is
            require
                  destination : is_on_board(d_row,d_col);
                  source:  is_on_board(row,col);
            local
                  i,j,stop:INTEGER;
      do
            Result := true
            if col = d_col -- is vertical
            then i := smaller(row,d_row) ;
                  j := col
                  stop := larger(row,d_row)
            from i := i + 1
```

```
            invariant i <= stop + 1
            variant stop + 1 - i
      until  i >= stop
      loop
            if is_occupied(i,j)
            then Result := false
            i := i +1
            elseif row = d_row  -- horizontal
            then j := smaller(col,d_col);
                  i: = row;
                  stop := larger(col,d_col)
                  from j := j + 1
                  invariant j <= stop +1
                  variant stop + 1 - j
                  until j > = stop
                  loop
                        if is_occupied(i,j)
                        then Result := false
                        end -- if
                        j := j + 1
                  end -- loop
            end -- if
      end -- loop
end  --is_clear_row
is_diagonal(row,col,d_row,d_col:INTEGER):BOOLEAN is
do
      Result := abs(row-d_row) = abs(col-d_col)
end -- is_diagonal
is_clear_diagonal(row,col,d_row,d_col:INTEGER)
                              :BOOLEAN is
      require
            is_diagonal(row,col,d_row,d_col)
      local
            c,r,stop:INTEGER
do
      Result := true;
      if row < d_row and col < d_col
            or row > d_row and col > d_col
      then from
                  r := smaller(row,d_row) +1;
                  c:= smaller(col,d_col)+1;
```

```
                    stop := larger(row,d_row);
            until not Result or r = stop
            loop
                    if is_occupied(r,c)
                    then Result := false
                    end -- if
                    r := r +1;
                    c := c +1
            end -- loop
        elseif col > d_col and row < d_row
            or col < d_col and row > d_row
        then from
                    r := smaller(row,d_row)+1;
                    c := larger(col,d_col)+1;
                    stop := larger(row,d_row)
            until not Result or r = stop
            loop
                    if is_occupied(r,c)
                            then Result := false
                    end -- if
                    c := c-1;
                    r := r+1
            end --loop
        end -- if
end -- is_clear_diagonal

invariant
        rows = 8;
        columns = 8
```

*Example 14.6 Class CHESS_BOARD: auxiliary accessors*

The main remaining task is to encode the algorithm for solving the eight queens problem. The problem, as previously stated, is to put all eight queens on the board so that each is not in the path of another - this means that only one queen may be on each row, each column, and each diagonal path. The algorithm used (example 14.7) solves the problem the way we would if we were physically to place the queens on the board (see figure 14.6). The first queen is placed on 1,1 the second on 2,1, then on 2,2 then on 3,2 where it cannot be taken; the third rests on 5,3, the fourth on 2,4, the 5th on 4,5 - and then we find there is no place for the 6th queen, because each of the squares in column 6 may be reached. At this point the alogorithm backtracks: the preceding queen is moved to the next safe row - if it exists - and then it tries again with the 6th and succeeding queens - or if a safe row cannot be found for the preceding queen (col 5) the algorithm retraces its steps back to its predecessor(col 4) and so on. When one of the predecessors has successfully been placed, the algorithm then works forward again until, by a process of trial and error, all eight queens are safely positioned on the board. It is much simpler to write in a programming language than to describe in English!

A recursive routine, *queen_in_place*, for insertion in CHESS_GAME, is shown in example 14.7, and the remainder of the class is given in example 14.8. Class CHESS_VIEW may be found in example 14.9. We now have a complete application which should run and produce a solution to the eight queens problem.

Finally, example 14.8 provides an additional routine for CHESS_GAME, which will output all solutions to the eight queens problem.

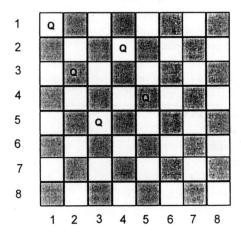

**Figure 14.6**

```
queen_in_place(c:INTEGER) :BOOLEAN is
            local
                    q: QUEEN;
                    r:INTEGER;
        do
```

```
if c> 8
    then Result := true
else
    from
        !!q.make(1,c,'b','Q');
        r := 0
    until Result or r = 8
    loop
        r := r +1
        if not board.can_be_reached(r,c,'b')
            then
            q.move_to(r,c);
                board.attach(q,r,c);
                if not queen_in_place(c+1);
                    then board.detach(r,c)
                else Result := true
                end -- if
        end -- if
    end -- loop
end -- if
end -- queen_in_place
```

*Example 14.7 Routine to solve eight queens problem*

```
class CHESS_GAME
    creation
        start
    feature
        board:CHESS_BOARD;
        view:CHESS_VIEW;
        start is
        do
            board.make(8,8);
            !!view;
            eight_queens
        end -- start
        eight_queens is
        do
            if queen_in_place(1)
            then view.display(board)
            end -- if
```

```
        end -- eight queens
        queen_in_place(c:INTEGER) :BOOLEAN
            -- see example 14.7
end -- CHESS_GAME
```

*Example 14.8 Class CHESS_GAME*

```
class CHESS_VIEW
    feature
        display(board:CHESS_BOARD) is
    do
            from c := 0
            until c = 8
            loop
                c := c +1;
                io.putstring("     ");      -- 5 spaces
                io.putint(c);
            end -- loop
            io.new_line
            io.putstring ("_____")
                    -- 48 underscore characters
            io.new_line;
            from r := 0;
            until r = 8
            loop
                io.putstring("|     |     |     |     |     |     |     |     |");
                    -- 5 spaces between each vertical bar
                io.new_line;
                r := r +1;
                io.putint(r);
                io.putchar('|');
                from c := 0
                until c = 8
                loop
                    c := c+1
                    if board.is_occupied(r,c)
                        then board.piece_at(r,c).display
                    else io.putstring("    ")
                    end -- if
                    io.putstring("  |");
                end -- loop
```

```
            io.new_line;
            io.putstring(" |___|___|___|___|___|___|___|___|");
                        -- vertical bars separated by 5 underscore
                        -- characters
            io.new_line;
        end -- display
end -- CHESS_VIEW
```

*Example 14.9 Class CHESS_VIEW*

```
all_queens(c:INTEGER) is
        local
                r:INTEGER;
                q:Queen
    do
        !!q.make(1,c,'b','Q');
        from r := 0
        invariant r <= 8
        variant 8 - r
        until r = 8
        loop
                r := r+1;
                if not board.can_be_reached(r,c,'b')
                        then
                                q.move_to(r,c)
                                board.attach(q,r,c)
                                if c < 8
                                        then all_queens(c+1)
                                else
                                        view.display(board)
                                end -- if
                                board.detach(r,c)
                end -- if
        end -- loop
end -- all_queens
```

*Example 14.10 All the Eight Queens solutions*

## 14.2 Implementing a back propagating neural network

This section does not attempt to provide a full explanation of neural networks theory or a complete description of the back propagation algorithm. The reader is recommended to look at Hassoun (1995).

Neural networks have been used successfully in a wide range of applications such as image processing, predicting credit-worthiness and pattern matching. Such networks are loosely based on current models of the biological brain. They consist of layers of interconnected neurons, each of which has *n* inputs, where *n* is the number of neurons in the previous layer to which a neuron is connected. Neurons in the first layer receive their inputs from file or keyboard. Each neuron has a collection of *n* weights, corresponding to each input, and each has a single output. This output becomes one of the inputs of the neurons in the next layer, or, if the node is in the output layer, is part of the output from the net.

The neurons in the output layer must have an additional attribute, the *expected* or *desired outcome*, which is used to train the network: each set of inputs has a corresponding expected outcome, which must also be supplied by the user.

An example network is shown in figure 14.7. It has 4 layers: 1 output layer, and three hidden layers. The minimum configuration for a back propagation network would be 1 hidden layer and 1 output layer. The net shown below has 2 inputs and 1 output. For each connection between a neuron and its predecessor there is a weight, set randomly within a specified range, and adjusted as the net is trained. There is also a weight between each input and each node in the first hidden layer.

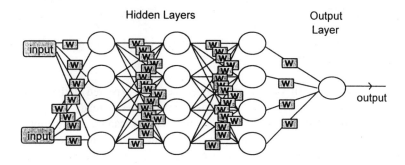

**Figure 14.7 Neural network with 4 layers and 13 neurons**

An additional input and weight at each level, called the *bias,* is not shown in figure 14.7. In practice, therefore, each node in each layer would have an additional weight and connection. Figure 14.8 shows a simpler net, which may be used to implement an exclusive OR function. This net requires two binary digits as input, and will output 1 if true, and 0 if false. In this case the *bias* and its connections to each node are shown.

Before a neural net may be used, it must be trained with a set of input data and *desired* outcomes. So, for example, the XOR function shown in figure 14.7, would be trained with the following set of data and expected outcomes:

| Input 1 | Input 2 | Outcome |
|---------|---------|---------|
| 1       | 1       | 0       |
| 0       | 1       | 1       |
| 1       | 0       | 1       |
| 0       | 0       | 0       |

In training, the following process is followed for each collection of inputs and *desired* outcome:

the controller tells the output layer what output is expected;

the controller passes some data to the first hidden layer and asks it to calculate its output;

the first hidden layer calculates its outputs, and passes these to the next layer and asks it to calculate its output;

each succeeding hidden layer continues this process until the output layer is reached;

the output layer calculates its output, and if it does not fall within the allowed margin of error then it adjusts its own weights and asks its predecessor to adjust its weights;

the process of adjusting weights propagates backwards until the first hidden layer has adjusted its weights.

This is repeated until the difference between the expected and the actual output is within acceptable limits. At this point the net is ready for use. The reader should be warned that training a neural network can take a considerable time. Normally, a trained net is saved on file, so that it can be reloaded and used again without further training. This case study will confine itself to keyboard input. The process of filing and retrieving a trained network, which is library dependent, is left to the reader.

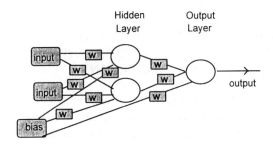

**Figure 14.8 BP network to implement XOR function**

The case study develops a general net which may be configured for any combination of layers, neurons, inputs and outputs. As always, the starting point is to try to identify the classes needed. From the description so far the following candidates may be identified for consideration as classes:

| | | |
|---|---|---|
| Neuron | Input | Desired Outcome |
| Output | Weight | Layer |
| Connection | Bias | |

Clearly, a class NEURON will be needed. *Input* is a numeric data item to which the neurons in the first layer must each have access. *Output* and *weight* are clearly attributes of a NEURON. *Bias* is a global attribute to which all neurons need access. The description of *desired outcome* given earlier, should indicate that this is an attribute only of the neurons in the output layer. This should lead us to identify another class, OUTPUT_NEURON, which is a specialisation of NEURON.

*Layer* and *Connection* need further consideration. A layer is a collection of neurons, each of which, except for the first hidden layer, has connections with all neurons in the preceding and succeeding layers. It would be possible to model each connection as a pointer from each neuron, so that each neuron in the last hidden layer in the first figure shown above would have four input connections and one output connection. Since each neuron in a given layer would have the same pointers this would be unecessary duplication, and it would be more sensible to make connection an attribute of layer, so that each layer knows its predecessor and successor layer. Clearly the first hidden layer has no predecessor, and an output layer has no successor. In addition to LAYER,

OUTPUT_LAYER may be added to the list. From this discussion the following list of classes seems sensible.

|                |                |
|----------------|----------------|
| NEURON         | OUTPUT_NEURON  |
| LAYER          | OUTPUT_LAYER   |
| NEURAL_NETWORK | CONSTANTS      |

A root class, NEURAL_NETWORK, has been added. This is responsible for configuring the network, and for initiating testing and training. Also a class has been specified for the global constants required by the network.

The responsibilities and collaborators of each class (except CONSTANTS) are specified using CRC cards, as shown in figures 14.9 to 14.13.

| NEURON | |
|---|---|
| calculates and stores  weights<br>                for each connection<br>makes adjustments to weights<br>calculates  output | |

**Figure 14.9**

| OUTPUT_NEURON | |
|---|---|
| knows desired outcome<br><br>calculates error signal | |

**Figure 14.10**

| LAYER | NEURON |
|---|---|
| knows predecessor and successor<br>knows how many neurons in layer<br>knows inputs<br>trains its neurons<br>calculate and stores outputs<br>passes outputs to successor<br>makes adjustments to weights of each neurons<br>asks predecessor to adjust weights | |

**Figure 14.11**

| OUTPUT_LAYER | OUTPUT_<br>NEURON |
|---|---|
| calculates network error<br><br>initiates back propagation process<br>of adjusting weights<br><br>receives collection of expected outputs, and<br>informs each output neuron | |

**Figure 14.12**

| NEURAL_NETWORK | LAYER |
|---|---|
| configures network<br><br>trains network<br><br>performs tests on network<br><br>saves/reloads net | OUTPUT_<br>LAYER<br><br>I-O |

**Figure 14.13**

The first class to be built is the basic component of a network, NEURON (example 14.11), whose responsibilities are outlined in figure 14.9. Its attributes consist of an array, to store the weights, and *output* and *delta*. The latter is used as part of the adjustment to the weights during training. It inherits from MATH_CONST, in order to access Euler. OUTPUT_NEURON, which is a specialisation of NEURON, is given in example 14.12. It may be noted that *calc_hidden_delta* has been made private. This is because it would be unsafe to be used. Ideally, it should be redefined, but it is not allowable since the new routine required for this class is different.

```
class NEURON
inherit
      CONSTANTS;
      MATH_CONST
creation
      make
feature {LAYER}
-- attributes
      delta:REAL;
      weights:ARRAY[REAL];
      output:REAL;
-- transfomer routines
      calculate_output(inputs:ARRAY[REAL]) is
            local
                  index:INTEGER;
                  net:REAL;
      do
            from index := 0;
            until inputs.size = index
            loop
                  index := index + 1;
                  net := net + weights.item(index) *
                                          inputs.item(index);
            end -- loop
            output := 1 / (1 + (1/ Euler ^net))
            -- users of Eiffel/S should use
            -- exp(net) instead of Euler ^net
      end -- calculate_output
      adjust_weights(inputs:ARRAY[REAL]) is
            -- used during training to alter weights
            local
```

```
                    index:INTEGER
        do
            from
            until index = weights.size
            loop
                index := index + 1;
                weights.put(weights.item(index) +
                    learning_constant * delta *
                        inputs.item(index), index);
            end -- loop
        end -- adjust_weights
        calc_hidden_delta(adjustment:REAL) is
            -- calculates delta value
            -- must be called before adjust_weights
        do
            delta :=adjustment * output * (1-output);
        end -- calc_hidden_data
        make(size:INTEGER) is
            -- initialises weights using a random number
            local
                    index:INTEGER
        do
            !!weights.make(1,size);
            from index :=0
            until index =size
            loop
                index := index + 1;
                weights.put(rand,index);
                    -- assumes a random number
                    -- in range: -1.0 .. + 1.0
            end -- loop
        end -- make
    end -- NEURON
```

*Example 14.11 Class NEURON*

Class NEURON contains three routines, *calculate_output*, *adjust_weights*, and *calc_hidden_delta*, which are called from class LAYER. The first is passed the inputs, and calculates the output, which consists of a summation of the inputs multiplied by the weights (usually referred to as *net*), which is then passed through a transfer function:

$$\frac{1}{1+e^{-net}}$$

The second adjusts the weights; again it is passed the inputs by layer, and adds, to the existing weight, an increment consisting of the product of the learning constant, delta, and the corresponding input.

$$W(new) = W(old) + \eta * \delta * X$$

The third, *calc_hidden_delta*, is passed a value calculated in the successor layer, *delta_sum*, and uses this to calculate delta as indicated in the code above. For OUTPUT_NEURON all the above are inherited, but *calc_hidden_delta* should not be used. In its place is the routine, *calc_delta*, which uses the attribute, d*esired,* to calculate *delta*. Each OUTPUT_NEURON also returns an error value, which is used by OUTPUT_LAYER to calculate *network_error*.

```
class OUTPUT_NEURON
    inherit
        NEURON
            export
                {NONE} calc_hidden_delta
            end
creation
    make
feature {OUTPUT_LAYER}
    desired: REAL;
    error : REAL is
            -- added to other nodes:gives network error signal
    do
            Result := 0.5 * (desired - output)
                                    * (desired - output)
    end -- error
-- transfomer routines
    set_desired(d:REAL) is
    do
            desired :=d
    end -- set_desired
    calculate_delta is
            -- calculates error signal for the node
    do
            delta := (desired - output) * output *(1- output)
```

```
            end -- delta
    end -- OUTPUT_NEURON
```

*Example 14.12 Class OUTPUT_NEURON*

Class LAYER is given in example 14.13. The reader is encouraged to refer back to figure 14.11 to refresh the memory about the its responsibilities.

```
    class LAYER
        inherit
            CONSTANTS
        creation
            make
        feature
            connections:INTEGER;
            previous, successor: LAYER;
            outputs:ARRAY[REAL]
            size :INTEGER is
            do
                    Result := nodes.size;
            end -- size
            calc_and_train(in:ARRAY[REAL]) is
                    -- used in training: calculates outputs and passes
                    -- them as inputs to next layer
            do
                    inputs := in;
                    calculate_output;
                    successor.calc_and_train(outputs);
            end -- calc_and_train
            display_output is
                    -- does not display the bias
                    local
                            index:INTEGER;
            do
                    from index := 1
                    until index = outputs.size
                    loop
                            io.putreal(outputs.item(index))
                            index := index + 1
                    end -- loop
                    io.new_line
```

```
          end -- display_output
          calc(in:ARRAY[REAL]) is
               -- used with a trained net - calculates outputs
               -- and passes on to successor
          do
               inputs := in;
               calculate_output;
               successor.calc(outputs);
          end -- calc
          set_predecessor(pred:LAYER) is
          do
               previous := pred;
          end -- set_predecessor
          set_successor(succ:LAYER) is
          do
               successor := succ
          end -- set_successor
          make(nmr_weights:INTEGER;nmr_nodes:INTEGER) is
               require
                    nmr_weights > 0;
                    nmr_nodes > 0;
          do
               connections := nmr_weights;
               create_neurons(nmr_nodes);
          end -- make
feature {LAYER}
          adjust_weights is
               local
                    index:INTEGER
          do
               from index := 0
               until index = size
               loop
                    index := index +1;
                    nodes.item(index).calc_hidden_delta
                               (successor.delta_sum(index));
                    nodes.item(index).adjust_weights(inputs)
               end -- loop
               if previous /= void
               then previous.adjust_weights
               end -- if
```

```
     end -- adjust_weights
delta_sum(i:INTEGER):REAL is
     local
               index:INTEGER
do
          from index := 0
          until index = size
          loop
                    index := index +1;
                    Result := Result + nodes.item(index).delta*
                              nodes.item(index).weights.item(i)
          end -- loop
     end -- delta_sum
feature{NONE}
     inputs:ARRAY[REAL]
     nodes:ARRAY[NEURON]
     create_neurons(nmr_nodes:INTEGER) is
          local
                    count:INTEGER;
                    a_neuron:NEURON
do
          from !!nodes.make(1,nmr_nodes);
          until count = size
          loop
                    count := count + 1;
                    !!a_neuron.make(connections);
                    nodes.put(a_neuron,count)
          end -- loop
     end -- create_neurons
     calculate_output is
          -- asks each neuron to calculate its output
          -- stores results in outputs
          local
                    count:INTEGER
do
          !!outputs.make(1,size+1);
          outputs.put(bias,outputs.size);
                    --inserts bias as outputs
          from
          until count = size
          loop
```

```
                         count := count + 1;
                         nodes.item(count).calculate_output(inputs);
                         outputs.put(nodes.item(count).output,count)
                 end -- loop
           end -- calculate_output
     end -- LAYER
```

*Example 14.13 Class LAYER*

The features that require most explanation are, *delta_sum*, and *adjust_weights,* which are used in training. The former requires an integer argument, specifying a weight: it returns the sum of the product of the *delta* of each node and the weight specified. This is illustrated in figure 14.14, which shows a layer with three neurons, each of which has three weights. The result of the call, *delta_sum(1),* to the layer shown in figure 14.14 would return the value $0.021 * 0.02 + 0.010 * 0.01 + 0.011 * 0.03$. This value would then be used by the layer which made the call (the preceding layer of that shown in figure 14.14), as the argument to a call to its first node to calculate *delta*:

> *nodes.item(index).calc_hidden_delta*
> > *(successor.delta_sum(index));*

then, the same node is asked to adjust its weights:

> *nodes.item(index).adjust_weights(inputs)*

This process continues for each neuron in the layer.

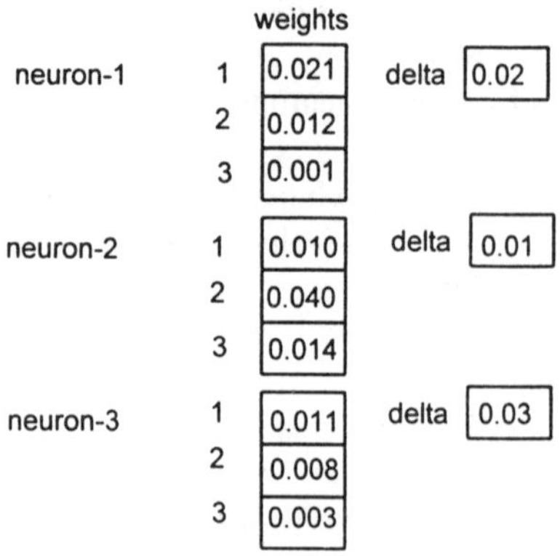

**Figure 14.14**

Example 14.14 shows OUTPUT_LAYER.. It has new features, *set_expected*, and *network_error*, and redefines *create_neurons* and *nodes*, since it must collaborate with output neurons. The routine *calc_and_train* is redefined to allow an instance to decide whether it is necessary to propagate backwards to adjust all the weights in the network. The most significant difference from LAYER is the redefinition of *adjust_weights*. The reader is advised to compare the code for this routine with that of the inherited routine given in example 14.13. The redefined code in *calc_and_train* should also be examined. The attribute, *error_level*, is a global constant obtained by inheriting CONSTANTS indirectly through LAYER.

```
class OUTPUT_LAYER
       inherit
              LAYER
                     redefine
                            nodes,create_neurons ,adjust_weights,
                            calc, calc_and_train
              end
       creation
              make
       feature {NONE}
              nodes:ARRAY[OUTPUT_NEURON]
              adjust_weights is
                     local
                            index :INTEGER;
              do
                     from
                     until index = size
                     loop
                            index := index + 1;
                            nodes.item(index).calculate_delta;
                            nodes.item(index).adjust_weights
                                                         (inputs)
                     end -- loop
                     previous.adjust_weights
              end -- adjust_weights
       feature {LAYER}
              calc_and_train(in:ARRAY[REAL]) is
              do
                     inputs := in;
                     calculate_output;
```

```
            if network_error > error_level
                then adjust_weights;
        end -- if
    end -- calc_and_train
    calc(in:ARRAY[REAL]) is
    do
        inputs := in;
        calculate_output;
    end -- calc
feature
    network_error:REAL is
        local
            index:INTEGER;
    do
        from
        until index = nodes.size
        loop
            index := index +1;
            Result := Result +
                    nodes.item(index).error
        end -- loop
    end -- network_error
    set_expected(out:ARRAY[REAL]) is
        local
            count:INTEGER
    do
        from count := 0
        until count = size
        loop
            count := count+1;
            nodes.item(count).set_desired
                    (out.item(count));
        end --loop
    end -- set_expected
    create_neurons(nmr_nodes:INTEGER) is
        local
            count:INTEGER;
            neuron:OUTPUT_NEURON;
    do
        from !!nodes.make(1,nmr_nodes);
        until count = size
```

```
        loop
                count := count + 1
                !!neuron.make(connections);
                nodes.put(o_neuron,count)
        end -- loop
    end -- set_nodes
end -- OUTPUT_LAYER
```

*Example 14.14 Class OUTPUT_LAYER*

The rest of the chapter consists of relatively trivial, but lengthy code, to implement the root class and the global constants. Most of the I/O responsibilities of NEURAL_NETWORK are in class DATA_HANDLER, which allows the former to be more abstract. The implementation of NEURAL_NETWORK is given in example 14.15, DATA_HANDLER in 14.16, GLOBALS in 14.17 and CONSTANTS 14.18. The reader should note the use made of once routines (see chapter 5) to provide global constants. The code for the case study is complete, apart from the routine *rand,* in class CONSTANTS, which has been left for the reader to implement using the appropriate libary class.

The reader should be reminded that the application allows a neural network with any number of levels and connections to be created. To use it to implement an XOR function, the following inputs may be used to configure the net and prepare for training (input is in bold type):

number of layers => **2**
number of inputs =>**2**
enter bias **-1**
enter learning constant **1**
enter error tolerance **0.001**
input layer: enter number neurons **2**
output layer: enter number neurons **1**
number of sets of training data => **4**

*Bias* is usually -1; *learning_constant* depends on the application, and varies from 0.5 to 10.0; *error level* is kept as small as practicable, the smaller the error level the longer the training time. After the above sequence, the user is then required to enter the appropriate sets of training data and expected outcomes as shown earlier. The data to test the net may then be entered.

```
class NEURAL_NETWORK
    inherit
        DATA_HANDLER
    creation
        start
    feature
        input_layer:LAYER;
        output_layer:OUTPUT_LAYER;
        start is
        do
            get_parameters;
            configure_network;
            train
            test
        end -- make
        test is
            require
                net_is_trained: has_trained
            local
                nmr_tests:INTEGER;
        do
            from
                get_nmr_data_sets("How many tests => ");
                get_inputs;
            until nmr_tests = sets_of_data
            loop
                nmr_tests := nmr_tests + 1;
                input_layer.calc(inputs.item(nmr_tests));
                output_layer.display_output
            end -- loop
        end -- test
        train is
            require
                net_configured: input_layer /= void
                and output_layer /= void
            local
                count:INTEGER;
        do
            get_nmr_data_sets
            ("Number of sets of training data => ");
            get_inputs;
```

```
        get_expected_outcomes(output_layer.size);
from
until
        output_layer.network_error < error_level
                and has_trained
loop
        has_trained := true;
        from count := 0
        until sets_of_data = count
        loop
                count := count + 1;
                output_layer.set_expected.
                                (outputs.item(count));
                input_layer.calc_and_train.
                                (inputs.item(count))
        end -- loop inner
    end -- loop outer
end -- test
configure_network is
        -- configures a network using keyboard as io
        require
                nmbr_layers > 1
local
                prev, temp_layer:LAYER;
                index:INTEGER;
do
        io.putstring(" input layer: ");
        io. putstring("Enter number neurons");
        io.readint;
        !!input_layer.make(nmr_inputs+1,io.lastint);
        prev := input_layer;
        from index := 1
        until index = nmbr_layers - 1
        loop
                index := index + 1;
                io.putstring("layer: ");
                io.putint(index);
                io. putstring("Enter number neurons");
                io.readint;
                !!temp_layer.make(prev.size+1,io.lastint);
                prev.set_successor(temp_layer);
```

```
                    temp_layer.set_predecessor(prev);
                    prev := temp_layer;
            end -- loop
            io.putstring(" output layer: ");
            io. putstring("Enter number neurons");
            io.readint;
            !!output_layer.make(prev.size+1,io.lastint);
            output_layer.set_predecessor(prev);
            prev.set_successor(output_layer);
        end -- configure_network
end -- NEURAL_NETWORK
```

*Example 14.15 Root class for generalised back propagating neural network*

```
class DATA_HANDLER
        -- a collection of data and routines used solely by
        -- NEURAL_NETWORK
    inherit
        CONSTANTS
    feature
        outputs,inputs:ARRAY[ARRAY[REAL]];
        nmr_inputs:INTEGER;
        nmbr_layers:INTEGER;
        has_trained:BOOLEAN;
        sets_of_data:INTEGER;
        get_inputs is
            local
                count,index:INTEGER;
                temp:ARRAY[REAL];
        do
            !!inputs.make(1,sets_of_data);
            from count := 0
            until count = sets_of_data
            loop
                !!temp.make(1,nmr_inputs+1);
                count := count +1;
                from index := 0
                until index = nmr_inputs
                loop
                    io.putstring("input : ");
                    index := index + 1;
```

```
                    io.readreal;
                    temp.put(io.lastreal,index);
                end -- loop
            temp.put(bias,temp.upper);
                -- bias is added to inputs
            inputs.put(temp,count);
        end -- loop
end -- get_inputs
get_expected_outcomes(nmr_outputs:INTEGER) is
        local
            count,index:INTEGER
            temp:ARRAY[REAL]
do
        !!outputs.make(1,sets_of_data);
        from count := 0
        until count = sets_of_data
        loop
            count := count + 1;
            !!temp.make(1,nmr_outputs);
            from index := 0
            until index = nmr_outputs
            loop
                index := index + 1
                io.putstring("expected output : ");
                io.readreal;
                temp.put(io.lastreal,index);
            end -- loop
            outputs.put(temp,count);
        end -- loop
end -- get_expected_outcomes
get_parameters is
        local
            l_const,bs,tolerance:REAL;
do
        io.putstring("Number of layers => ");
        io.readint;
        nmbr_layers := io.lastint;
        io.putstring("Number of inputs => ");
        io.readint;
        nmr_inputs := io.lastint;
        io.putstring("enter bias ");
```

```
                io.readreal;
                bs := io.lastreal
                io.putstring("enter learning constant");
                io.readreal;
                l_const := io.lastreal
                io.putstring("enter error tolerance");
                io.readreal;
                tolerance := io.lastreal;
                set_params(l_const,bs,tolerance)
        end -- get_params
        get_nmr_data_sets(message:STRING) is
        do
                io.putstring(message);
                io.readint;
                sets_of_data := io.lastint;
        end -- get_nmr_data_sets
end -- DATA_HANDLER
```

*Example 14.16 Class DATA_HANDLER*

```
class GLOBALS
    feature {CONSTANTS}
        error_level, learning_constant, bias :REAL;
        set_lc(lc:REAL) is
        do
                learning_constant := lc
        end - set_lc
        set_bias(b:REAL) is
        do
                bias := b;
        end -- set_bias
        set_error_l(el:REAL) is
        do
                error_level := el
        end -- set_bias
end  -- GLOBALS
```

*Example 14.17 Class GLOBALS*

```
class CONSTANTS
    feature {NONE}
        rand:REAL
            -- returns random number: range -1.0 .. + 1.0
        set_params(lc,bs,el:REAL) is
            -- used to set bias and learning_constant
        once
            global.set_lc(lc);
            global.set_bias(bs);
            global.set_error_l(el);
        end -- set_params
        learning_constant:REAL  is
        once
            Result := global.learning_constant
        end --learning_constant
        bias :REAL  is
        once
            Result := global.bias
        end -- bias
        error_level:REAL   is
        once
            Result := global.error_level
        end --error_level
    feature {NONE}
        global: GLOBALS is
        once
            !!Result
        end -- global
end -- CONSTANTS
```

*Example 14.18 Class CONSTANTS*

### Exercises

The reader is recommended to implement and test each of these case studies. In each case the reader is encouraged to reflect about the design, and to try to improve the design and implementation. The following suggestions are offered:

1. There are many loops in both case studies. An abstraction might be used to produce code more elegant than the ubiquitous $i := i+1$ , e.g. an iterator which responds to the messages such as *move, finished, reset, index*.

2. CHESS_BOARD might, for efficiency, sometimes use some of the routines inherited from array, which require a single subscript - particularly since each CHESS_PIECE knows its own position.

3. Consider the inheritance relationships in each case study. In the second in particular, the following alterations might be beneficial:

    NEURON and LAYER -- become deferred classes;
    HIDDEN_NEURON, HIDDEN_LAYER -- new actual classes

4. Consider class DATA_HANDLER which has two arrays of array. Are there any operations on these which can be abstracted to form a new class?

# Appendix 1   Reserved words

These consist of Eiffel keywords, conventionally written in bold in Eiffel texts, and predefined names.

| | | | |
|---|---|---|---|
| **alias** | **all** | **and** | **as** |
| **check** | **class** | **creation** | **debug** |
| **deferred** | **do** | **else** | **elseif** |
| **end** | **ensure** | **expanded** | **export** |
| **external** | **false** | **feature** | **from** |
| **frozen** | **if** | **implies** | **indexing** |
| **infix** | **inherit** | **inspect** | **invariant** |
| **is** | **like** | **local** | **loop** |
| **not** | **obsolete** | **old** | **once** |
| **or** | **prefix** | **redefine** | **rename** |
| **require** | **rescue** | **retry** | **select** |
| **separate** | **strip** | **then** | **true** |
| **undefine** | **unique** | **until** | **variant** |
| **when** | **xor** | | |

Predefined names include the names of special types, which by convention are written in uppercase, as are all class names; other predefined names by convention begin with an upper case letter. The full list is as follows:

| | | |
|---|---|---|
| BIT | BOOLEAN | CHARACTER |
| *Current* | DOUBLE | INTEGER |
| NONE | POINTER | REAL |
| *Result* | STRING | |

# Appendix 2 Special symbols

| | |
|---|---|
| -- | double hyphen - used to precede a comment; the compiler ignores everything that follows on the same line |
| ! !! | single and double exclamation marks, used for object creation |
| = /= | equality/ inequality signs |
| -> | used for constrained genericity |
| { } | used to control visibility of features of a class |
| [ ] | used for declaring parameters of classes |
| ( ) | used to override precedence in expressions and to enclose formal and actual routine arguments |
| .. | used in multiway selection |
| << >> | used for manifest arrays |
| := | assignment operator |
| ?= | reverse assignment |
| ' ' | single quotation mark used for characters |
| " " | double quotation marks used for strings |
| + − | arithmetic signs |
| $ | dollar sign, used for calls to external routines |
| % | used to precede special character codes |
| / | slash, used to precede an ASCII code |
| . | dot, used in calls; also in real numbers |
| : | used in declaring types of attribute, arguments, locals and result types of routines |
| ; , | used as separators |

# Appendix 3 Special characters

| Character | Code | Name |
|---|---|---|
| @ | %A | at sign |
| BS | %B | backspace |
| ^ | %C | circumflex |
| $ | %D | dollar |
| FF | %F | Form Feed |
| \ | %H | back slash |
| ~ | %L | tilda |
| NL(LF) | %N | Newline |
| ` | %Q | back quote |
| CR | %R | carriage return |
| # | %S | sharp |
| HT | %T | horizontal tab |
| NUL | %U | nul character |
| \| | %V | vertical bar |
| % | %% | per cent |
| ' | %' | single quote |
| " | %" | double quote |
| [ | %( | opening bracket |
| ] | %( | closing bracket |
| { | %{ | opening brace |
| } | %} | closing brace |

ASCII characters may be represented as follows:

%/n/

where *n* is an integer representing the code of a character.

# Appendix 4 Using Eiffel/S

There are a number of differences between Eiffel/S and Eiffel as defined by Bertrand Meyer in *Eiffel: The Language*. The most important are:

1. Standard input is provided by class BASIC_IO;
2. PDL (program Design Language Files) replace ACE files;
3. RCL (Run time Control Language) files are used to switch assertions on and off.

The class libraries also differ, but the basic cluster (apart from BASIC_IO) is similar to that defined by Meyer, and in practice causes few problems.

The simplest way to handle basic I-O is to insert the following class in the basic cluster:

```
class STD_FILES
    inherit
        BASIC_IO;
    rename
        last_char as lastchar,
        last_int as lastint,
        last_real as lastreal,
        last_string as laststring,
        put_char as putchar,
        put_string as putstring,
        put_real as putreal,
        put_int as putint,
        put_bool as putbool,
        put_newline as new_line,
        get_int as readint,
        get_real as readreal,
        get_newline as readline,
        get_string as readword,
        get_char as readchar
    end -- inherit BASIC_IO
end -- class STD_FILES
```

and to insert the following once routine in class ANY:

```
   io:STD_FILES
   once
        !!Result
   end -- io
```

To compile an application using Eiffel/S, one of the following commands are entered:

```
ecc < application_name>
ecc -o <application_name> -- for an optimised compile
```

The system looks for a PDL file with the same prefix as the name entered in the command line. If it does not exist, the user is asked to give the names of the root class and creation routine, and the PDL file is generated automatically. It is rare to have to make alterations to a PDL file.

The RCL file, which is used to switch assertions on and off, is compiled by a separate compiler, invoked by the command *ercc*. This compiler produces a default RCL file, compiles it, and produces a .rcb file ('b' stands for binary). This file is monitored by the run time system to check which assertions are switched on. The RCL file may be altered and recompiled independent of the application. An example RCL file is given below:

```
precondition  : all
postcondition : NEURON
invariant  : all
loop_invariant : none
loop_variant  : none
debug  : none
check  : all
debug_key  : training
trace  : none
collect  : on
```

This indicates that postconditions are switched on only for class NEURON, and the only debug key switched on is 'training'. *Collect* refers to the garbage collector, which in this case is turned on.

Users of Eiffel/S are recommended to look at the facilities provided by the following classes

| MATH | -- contains integer and real functions and a random number generator |
| SYSTEM_TIME | -- provides access to the system clock |
| FORMAT | -- provides control over output formats of integers and reals |
| | -- provides functions to covert basic types to and from strings |

More experienced users will need to familiarise themselves with the data structure classes, the file classes and class EXCEPTION, all of which differ from the ISE libraries. No graphics libraries are provided with Eiffel/S, but the EWPL library is available for Windows programming.

# Bibliography

Michael Beaudouin-Lafon, *Object-oriented Languages: Basic principles and programming techniques* (First English Language Edition), Chapman and Hall (1994)

Timothy Budd, *An Introduction to Object-Oriented Programming*, Addison-Wesley, (1991)

B.J. Cox, *Object-Oriented Programming: An Evolutionary Approach*, Addison-Wesley (1986)

N.A.B. Gray, *Programming with Class: A Practical Introduction to Object-Oriented Programming with C++*, Wiley (1994)

M.H. Hassoun, *Fundamentals of Artificial Neural Networks*, MIT Press (1995)

Bertrand Meyer, *Object Oriented Software Construction*, Prentice Hall (1988)

Bertrand Meyer, *Eiffel:The Language*, Prentice Hall (1992)

Bertrand Meyer, *An Object-Oriented environment: Principles and Application*, Prentice Hall (1994)

Bertrand Meyer, *Reusable Software: The Base Object-Oriented Component Libraries*, Prentice Hall (1994)

Robert Rist and Robert Terwillinger, *Object-Oriented Programming in Eiffel*, Prentice Hall (1995)

R. Switzer, *Eiffel:An Introduction, Prentice Hall* (1993)

Pete Thomas and Ray Weedon, *Object-Oriented Programming in Eiffel*, Addison-Wesley (1995)

Richard Wiener, *Software Development with Eiffel: There Can be Life Other Than C++*, Prentice Hall (1995)

# Index

abstract class 209-12
accessor routines 70, 174
ACE files 21-22
anchored declaration 65, 69, 167,
   201, 211
arguments 15, 63-6
ARRAY 102-20
assertions 16, 121-142, 202-3
assignment 15, 25-6, 38, 91-2, 98-9
attributes 14, 24, 25, 26-7, 28, 35,
   66

BOOLEAN 39-44

call 8, 22-3
CHARACTER 44-5
check instruction 133-4
class 8, 14, 82-5
class level validity 206
client 13, 91, 159-162
*clone* 74, 95, 99
comments 20-21
COMPARABLE 39, 97,176, 178-
   9,209-10
compound instruction 50-52
conformance 153-4, 156-7, 203,
   238
constants 27
constrained genericity 175-9
constructor routines 95
container classes 164-5, 168-70
control instructions 48
copy 93, 99, 120
covariance 203-7
CRC cards 241-2, 256-7
creation instructions 29-30,103-4
creation routine 14, 73-4, 98-9,
   149-150

Current 23, 37

**debug** 141-2
*deep-copy* 94, 120
deferred class 209-12
design by contract 16
direct repeated inheritance 235
dynamic type 36, 191, 193,2 34

effecting a feature 209-11
Eiffel/S 22
**ensure** 123, 202-3
equality, tests for 91-5, 97-8, 120
exception handling 137-140
expanded types 28-9
exports 185, 186
external routines 79

feature adaptation 182-207
feature redefinition 188-193
functions 69-73

generic classes 103, 164-80
generic parameters 65, 103, 165,
   167, 171, 172-3, 180

has-a relationship 13

identifiers 32
**if** 52-4
indirect repeated inheritance 230-
   233
**infix** 151, 209, 210
information hiding 10, 14, 88
inheritance 11-13, 15, 144-152,
   158-162
   multiple 222-223